MY DAILY PURSUIT

NEVER BEFORE PUBLISHED

Compiled and Edited by James L. Snyder

My Daily Pursuit

DEVOTIONS FOR EVERY DAY

A.W. TOZER

BETHANYHOUSE
a division of Baker Publishing Group
Minneapolis, Minnesota

© 2013 by James L. Snyder

Published by Bethany House Publishers
11400 Hampshire Avenue South
Bloomington, Minnesota 55438
www.bethanyhouse.com

Bethany House Publishers is a division of
Baker Publishing Group, Grand Rapids, Michigan

Bethany House edition published 2014
ISBN 978-0-7642-1621-3

Previously published by Regal Books

Printed in the United States of America

The Library of Congress has cataloged the original edition as follows:
    Tozer, A. W. (Aiden Wilson), 1897-1963.
        My daily pursuit : devotions for every day / A.W. Tozer ; compiled and edited by James L. Snyder.
            pages cm
        ISBN 978-0-8307-6904-9 (trade paper)
        1. Devotional calendars. I. Title.
    BV4811.T6884 2013
    242'.2—dc23   2013031761

Scripture quotations are from the King James Version of the Bible.

14   15   16   17   18   19   20   7   6   5   4   3   2   1

Contents

Foreword

The struggle in our time is often suggested to be of the intellect, in the assertion that both truth and God are unknowable. But if the questions I've encountered over four decades of speaking in universities as well as churches are any indication, I believe the deeper struggle is more often that of the heart.

I often recall the turning point of my own life: while still in my teens, I found myself lying in a hospital bed after an attempted suicide. The struggle for answers when met by despair led me along that tragic path. But there in my hospital room the Scriptures were brought and read to me. For the first time I engaged the direct answers of God to my seeking heart. The profound realization that God could be known personally drew me, with sincerity and determination, to plumb the depths of that claim.

The words of the Charles Wesley hymn, "And Can It Be that I Should Gain?" come flooding to my mind ever so often:

> Long my imprisoned spirit lay,
> Fast bound in sin and nature's night;
> Thine eye diffused a quickening ray—
> I woke, the dungeon flamed with light;
> My chains fell off, my heart was free,
> I rose, went forth, and followed Thee.

With a simple prayer of trust in that moment, the change from a desperate heart to one that found the fullness of meaning became a reality for me.

A few short years later, I encountered, through his writings, the distinctive pastoral voice of A. W. Tozer, who expounded on the grandest of all themes to which the human mind could ascend and the heart could embrace: the study of God Himself. Tozer's voice was unique in his era, and I read and reread many of his books. Works such as *The Pursuit of God* and *The Knowledge of the Holy* opened up vistas that were life-transforming.

Those truths were timely for me and timeless for anyone hungry to know God. So, his words still speak with power and tenderness today, leaving me with the twin passions of fulfillment and legitimate hunger. One statement of his, from *The Root of the Righteous,* that rang so true in cautioning the Church was that we are often like children skipping through the corridors of the kingdom, looking at everything, while pausing to learn the true value of nothing. Tozer gives us the right kind of pause to learn the value of deep reflection on noble truths.

What a thrill it is, therefore, to be introduced to more of Tozer's writings that have never been released until now. Inside these pages you may recognize a familiar tone on themes like worship—which he referred to as the missing jewel of the church—and the holiness and grandeur of God. Here you will find both practical insight and sobering wisdom such as, "Worship is to feel in the heart. I do not apologize for using the word 'feel.' . . . If you woke up one morning with no feeling in your arm at all, you would call a doctor, because anything without feeling you can be quite sure is dead." Elsewhere Tozer observes, "The God of the evangelical church is so small that we can put Him in our pocket." These are solemn words, and yet we are reminded that a life that has been radically transformed by an encounter with the resurrected Christ will hunger and thirst for God as for no other: "What would today be without living in the conscious presence of God Almighty? I do not want to live any day when that is absent from my life."

It is a great privilege for me to introduce a new generation to A. W. Tozer and to welcome longtime readers to this fresh volume of his daily readings. I am so grateful for the publication of these writings and know that you will treasure them as well. Tozer truly was one of the great explorers of truths that are indispensable if we are to rise above our shallow times. In proportion to the discipline of study, the reader will be rewarded with lifelong treasures.

Ravi Zacharias
Bestselling author
Founder and president of Ravi Zacharias International Ministries

Introduction

The great passion of A. W. Tozer, or maybe I should say obsession, was pursuing God on a daily basis. Nothing, neither family nor friends, was more important than his daily pursuit to be with God. The worship of God was the highest calling of Tozer's life.

During his ministry, Tozer was the keynote speaker at many Bible conferences. At one particular conference, the time came for the service to begin and Tozer had not arrived yet. Thinking he was just running a little late, the leader began the service believing Tozer would soon arrive. As the service progressed without any sign of Tozer, the leader became nervous. Finally, the time came for Tozer to begin his sermon but he was nowhere to be found. At the last moment, someone else filled in, much to the disappointment of the audience.

The next morning the leader found Tozer and asked him very simply where he was last night. "Why did you miss your appointment last night?"

Tozer, with a faraway look in his eyes, simply said, "I had a more important appointment last night." Later, that leader discovered Tozer had spent all night on his knees before God. The most important thing in his life was being in the presence of God.

Living in Chicago for most of his ministry, Tozer had a rather busy schedule with many people wanting his advice or prayer—people like Billy Graham and Senator Mark Hatfield, to name a few. Tozer had a unique way of eluding this disturbance when he needed to be alone with God. When he felt he was becoming a little stale, it was time to leave the world behind and be alone with God.

Early in the morning, he would board a westbound train, get in a Pullman car for privacy and ride for the next four hours. Sequestered in his Pullman car he spent the time on his face before God. No cell phones at the time, thankfully, and Tozer had absolute privacy to spend four hours alone with God without interruption. Once he arrived at his destination, he simply boarded an eastbound train returning to Chicago for another four hours alone with God. With an outspread

Bible on his knees, he quieted his heart before God and waited upon God to speak to him and refresh his spirit.

On a similar trip to Texas, Tozer wrote the first draft of the devotional classic, *The Pursuit of God*, which might explain the impact this book has had on Christianity at large. Pursuing God was not a matter of convenience for Tozer, but rather a matter of passion. Tozer could not start his day without spending quality time alone in the presence of God.

Often during these times, he would take a hymnal and begin his time alone with God by quietly singing a hymn. He simply marinated his soul in those great hymns of the church that he loved so much. Hymns were important in helping him express to God that which was deep in his own heart and soul. It would be a very unusual day for him not to meditate on some great hymn of the church.

Because of his passionate desire for God, Tozer was willing to commit to whatever it took to pursue God daily. This book, *My Daily Pursuit*, is a microcosm of Tozer's daily pursuit. Here you will find the components of his daily pursuit of God.

These devotions are taken from the audio sermons of Dr. Tozer and are not quotations from his published works. These represent what I like to refer to as, "conversational Tozer." His preaching style was very conversational— as if he were talking to one person and baring the passion of his heart to that individual.

The one goal of this devotional is to stir up in the hearts of serious-minded Christians such a passion for God. My prayer is that Tozer will inspire you in your daily pursuit.

James L. Snyder

My Daily Pursuit

January 1

For we have seen his star in the east,
and are come to worship him.
MATTHEW 2:2

For the Christian, everything begins and ends with worship. Whatever interferes with one's personal worship of God needs to be properly dealt with and dismissed. Keep in mind that above all else, worship is an attitude, a state of mind and a sustained act. It is not a physical attitude, but an inward act of the heart toward God. The mighty bestowment of God Almighty upon us who trust in Him is that we might be worshipers. Unfortunately, we have become everything else but worshipers. Sin robs God of this pristine pleasure of worship from those created in His image. Through the miracle of the new birth our alienation with God has been done away with; and through His atonement we have become friends of God and have been brought back again into the sphere of worship.

Each day is a special call for all of us to worship God.

Awake, my soul, to joyful lays,
And sing thy great Redeemer's praise.
SAMUEL MEDLEY (1738–1799)

My heavenly Father, I begin today in joyful worship.
Thou hast called me, and I answer Thee in praise and adoration.
In Jesus' name, amen.

January 2

And my tongue shall speak of thy righteousness
and of right praise all the day long.
PSALM 35:28

Worship embodies a number of spiritual and emotional factors. Worship is to feel in the heart. I do not apologize for using the word "feel." As Christians, we are not to be people without feelings. I certainly do not think we should follow our feelings alone, but I believe that if there is no feeling in our hearts, then we are dead.

Certainly, there is danger in relying only upon feelings.

If you woke up one morning with no feeling in your arm at all, you would call a doctor, because anything without feeling you can be quite sure is dead.

Real worship is, among other things, a feeling in the heart that is appropriately expressed. You can worship God in any manner appropriate to you by feeling in the heart and expressing that humbling but delightful sense of admiring love. Let your heart dictate your worship to the God you love, and who loves you.

Soon, the delightful day will come
When my dear Lord will bring me home,
And I shall see His face.
SAMUEL MEDLEY (1738–1799)

Oh, come, dear Lord, and fill my heart with blessed desire for Thee.
I lift my heart anticipating the shining of Thy blessed face. Amen.

And one cried unto another, and said,
Holy, holy, holy, is the Lord of hosts:
the whole earth is full of his glory.
ISAIAH 6:3

Worship is humbling, but it is also delightful, invoking a sense of admiring awe and astonished wonder. Astonishment and wonder are always found in the presence of the Holy Spirit. The difficulty with this today is that everybody is sure of everything. The proud man cannot worship God any more than the proud devil can worship God.

Without mystery, there can be no worship. If I can understand God, then I cannot worship God. I will never get on my knees and say, "Holy, holy, holy" to that which I can figure out. But the more I know of God, the less I understand about Him.

It is in the presence of the Holy Spirit that I begin to recognize what a sinful man I really am. The apostle Paul said, "Woe is me." Isaiah the prophet cried, "Woe is me!" when he came into the presence of God. They were experiencing the mysterious wonder of that One who is incomprehensible.

'Tis mystery all! The Immortal dies!
Who can explore His strange design?
CHARLES WESLEY (1707-1788)

Our Father which art in heaven, I come to Thee,
adoring the mystery of that which is Thyself. The more I know Thee,
the more I want to know Thee in all the beauty of thy holiness.
In the name of Jesus, I pray, amen.

Princes have persecuted me without a cause:
but my heart standeth in awe of thy word.
I rejoice at thy word, as one that findeth great spoil.
PSALM 119:161-162

As I have tried to figure out what revivals have been down through the years, I have come to this conclusion: Revivals have been a sudden bestowment of the spirit of worship, where people worship God and suddenly the spirit of worship comes on them. It is not something that is worked up, but rather something God bestows; and where His presence is, you will have a revival immediately. Worship always is a result of the presence of God.

What I can explain will never overawe me, will never fill me with astonishment, wonder or admiration. The presence of that most ancient mystery, that unspeakable majesty, which the philosophers have called a *mysterium tremendum*, but we who are God's children call, "Our Father which art in heaven,"—this ought to be present in the church today. Without this, there can be no genuine worship.

Only worship that flows from the awesome manifest presence of God is acceptable to the God and Father of our Lord Jesus Christ.

The Father hears Him pray,
His dear Anointed One;
He cannot turn away,
The presence of His Son.
CHARLES WESLEY (1707-1788)

I long, O Majesty on high, for Thy blessed presence
to overwhelm me to the point of silent worship and awe.
Thy precious Word leaves me speechless. In Jesus' name, amen.

January 5

I will delight myself in thy statutes:
I will not forget thy word.
PSALM 119:16

Many years ago, in France, lived Blaise Pascal—one of the great mathematicians of his time. As a teenager, he wrote advanced books on mathematics that would astonish the most learned mathematicians. He was also a great philosopher and thinker.

On November 23, 1654, between the night hours of 10:30 and 12:30, he met God, and he wrote his experience on a piece of paper. He carefully sewed this document into his coat and always transferred it when he changed clothes. He wore that paper until he died to remind him in some way of that experience.

On that night when Pascal had an intense religious vision and immediately recorded the experience in a brief note to himself, he wrote: "Fire. God of Abraham, God of Isaac, God of Jacob, not of the philosophers and the scholars . . ." and concluded the note by quoting Psalm 119:16: "'I will not forget thy word.' Amen."

This was the ecstatic utterance of a man who had two wonderful, awesome hours in the presence of his God.

God looked past Pascal's greatness and accomplishments and inserted Himself into his life so that for two solid hours Pascal could only characterize what was going on in him as "fire."

Open now the crystal fountain,
Whence the healing stream doth flow;
Let the fire and cloudy pillar
Lead me all my journey through.

WILLIAM WILLIAMS (1717-1791)

Oh God, set my heart on fire from above.
Inflame me with an unquenchable fire to guide me all through my journey.
In Jesus' name I pray. Amen.

Be thou exalted, O God, above the heavens;
let thy glory be above all the earth.
PSALMS 57:5

Perhaps one reason we do not have much confidence in the character of God today is that we do not have a high enough opinion of God. God has been talked down and reduced, modified, edited, changed and amended until He is not the God that Isaiah saw "high and lifted up."

Because God has been reduced in the minds of people, they do not have that boundless confidence in His character that used to be prominent among Christians. Confidence is necessary to respect. You cannot respect a man in whom you have no confidence. Extend that respect upward to God and if you cannot respect God, you cannot worship Him. You cannot have confidence in Him, because where there is no respect there can be no worship. Worship rises and falls in the church depending upon whether the idea of God is low or high; so we must begin with God where everything begins.

God needs no rescuing, but we do, and we must rescue our concepts from their fallen and frightfully inadequate condition so that boundless confidence in Him can reign once again.

Praise the Lord, ye heav'ns, adore Him!
Praise Him, angels in the height;
Sun and moon, rejoice before Him,
Praise Him, all ye stars of light.

EDWARD OSLER (1798–1863)

Dear heavenly Father, the more I meditate upon Thee,
the more my soul rises in worship.
Let me soar into Thy heavens and rejoice in Thee. Amen.

Sing, O heavens; and be joyful, O earth;
and break forth into singing, O mountains:
for the Lord has comforted his people,
and will have mercy upon his afflicted.
ISAIAH 49:13

To worthily worship God as He desires to be worshiped, I must have absolute confidence in Him. I cannot sit down with any person and enjoy fellowship if I have reason to fear he is out to get me or trick me or deceive me or cheat me. My fellowship with Him must be based upon respect and confidence. I have to trust him before I can have fellowship with him; and so when I go to God, I have to raise my affections and confidence to God. In the presence of God, I must come without doubt and nervousness, without worry and fear that God will cheat me, deceive me or let me break down or do something wrong. I need to be so convinced about God to the point that I can go into the presence of God in absolute confidence and say, "Let God be true and every man a liar."

With confidence I now draw nigh,
With confidence I now draw nigh,
And, "Father, Abba, Father," cry.
CHARLES WESLEY (1707–1788)

Dear Father, the very thought of Thee causes my heart to leap in joyful
song in praise. My heart sings of Thee in the night watch. Amen.

To the only wise God our Saviour, be glory and Majesty,
dominion and power, both now and ever. Amen.
JUDE 1:25

It is entirely possible to have respect for a person and not admire him. So, it would be remotely possible to have some kind of theological respect for God and yet not admire what you saw, and not admire Him.

The thing I have reflected on often is that when God made man in His own image, He gave him a capacity to appreciate and admire His Creator.

I often think of it in this way: There are at least two kinds of love—the love of gratitude and the love of excellence. Now, we could love God because we are grateful to Him, or we could go past that and love God because of what He is.

Perhaps love begins with gratitude, but there is a level of love above that called excellence. The first love can love God out of a deep sense of gratitude for what God has done; but above that is the love of excellence. As I begin to focus on God and fellowship in His presence, I begin to share in that quality of His love that simply loves Him for His excellence. He is all that I really need.

Praise Him! Praise Him!
Tell of His excellent greatness.
Praise Him! Praise Him!
Ever in joyful song!
FANNY CROSBY (1820-1915)

Dear God and Father of our Lord Jesus Christ,
the excellence of my nature revealed to me in Jesus Christ
has lifted my soul to the heights of heaven in praise and worship.
May Thy name be glorified in my life today. Amen.

Then shalt thou delight thyself in the Lord;
and I will cause thee to ride upon the high places of the earth,
and feed thee with the heritage of Jacob by father:
for the mouth of the Lord has spoken it.
ISAIAH 58:14

It is a rare Christian who truly knows how to appreciate God, especially in his prayer life.

Yet, the book of Psalms and the Gospels are full of this. Christ did it often in the presence of His disciples, and the apostles modeled it throughout their ministry. Nothing moves the heart more joyously than singing of the excellency of the God we serve.

I wonder if we do not hear this often today because we are strictly Santa Claus Christians. We look to God to put up the Christmas tree and put our gifts under it. We are grateful to God for all the gifts He has given us, and we should be grateful. It is right and proper that we should be; but this is the lower, elementary kind of love.

As a Christian, you need to push beyond this and come into the presence of God, enjoying the infinite excellence of God and admiring Him for who He truly is. This is the love of God's excellence where you want to stay in the presence of God because you are in the presence of utter infinite excellence.

But drops of grief can ne'er repay
The debt of love I owe;
Here, Lord, I give myself away
'Tis all that I can do.

ISAAC WATTS (1674–1748)

In thy precious name, O God, I come to Thee.
My love for Thee draws me deep into Thy heart.
Let me simply revel in Thy presence,
it is all I want to do. Amen.

O satisfy us early with Thy mercy;
that we may rejoice and be glad all our days.
PSALM 90:14

One delightful aspect of reading the Bible is finding people who are utterly fascinated with God. Reading through the book of Psalms stirs the heart as we experience one man's fascination with God.

Wherever God is known by the Spirit's illumination, there exists a fascination and a high degree of moral excitement. That fascination is captured and enhanced by the presence and person of God. It is struck with astonished wonder at the inconceivable elevation and magnitude and splendor of God.

I want to begin with God and end with God. I want to know that I will have an end with God because there is no end in God. This fascination, this sense of worship is where hymns come from. Hymns come out of this sense of admiration and fascination with God.

I want to be charmed and struck with wonder at the inconceivable elevation and magnitude and moral splendor of that One I call "our Father which art in heaven."

Finish, then, Thy new creation;
Pure and spotless let us be;
Let us see Thy great salvation
Perfectly restored in Thee;
Changed from glory into glory,
Till in heaven we take our place,
Till we cast our crowns before Thee,
Lost in wonder, love, and praise.

CHARLES WESLEY (1707–1788

Thy love, O God, fills me with rapturous delight at the very thought of it.
Meditating upon Thy love creates in me the dissatisfaction for this world.
Come, Lord Jesus, come. Amen.

Thou wilt keep him in perfect peace, whose mind is stayed on thee:
because he trusted in thee. Trust ye in the Lord for ever:
for in the Lord Jehovah is everlasting strength.
ISAIAH 26:3-4

Adoration is an important aspect of my personal worship of God. This cannot be worked out by any human effort but rather made incandescent by the fire of the Holy Spirit in my life. My worship of God must be the sense of awful wonder and adoration, to love, yearn and wait on God.

David Brainerd died at the home of Jonathan Edwards when he was 29 years old. During the few years of his life, he had such a passion for God that nothing else could satiate his heart. He would kneel in the snow and be so lost in worship, prayer and intercession that when he was through, the snow would melt around him in a wide circle. We need passion like that today. Oh, for men and women who have such a longing for God that everything else in their life would be pushed away!

I want my worship of God to be just as real. I am not one for imitating the accoutrements associated with worship. I am one for striving to achieve the passion of worship that men like this exhibited in their lives. I want to love God more than any person in my generation.

Beautiful Savior,
Lord of the nations,
Son of God and Son of man!
Glory and honor, praise, adoration
Now and forevermore be Thine!

GERMAN JESUITS, 1677,
TRANS. JOSEPH A. SEISS, (1823–1904)

Dear Lord Jesus, I come to Thee, for Thou has bidden me to come.
With trembling heart, I raise my voice in praise and adoration of Thee.
In Thy precious name I pray, amen.

Hear, O Israel: the Lord our God is one Lord:
and thou shalt love the Lord thy God with all thine heart,
and with all thy soul, and with all thy might.
DEUTERONOMY 6:4-5

John Fletcher, a contemporary of John Wesley, was called the Terrific Fletcher, because of his enthusiastic passion for God. It was a passion that could not be manufactured, but rather was something that came from the very heart of God Himself. Fletcher used to kneel in his little bare room on the floor. When he had lived out his life and gone to be with God, they found that he had made a concave place in the floor where his knees actually wore out the boards. They also found the wall in his room stained with his breath where he had waited on God and worshiped God in the beauty of holiness.

This is what adoration is all about. "Thou shalt love the Lord thy God with all thy heart and with all thy might . . ." It can only mean one thing, and that is to adore God with everything within you.

I rarely use the word "adore." I never say about any person, "I adore him," or "I adore her."

Adoration I keep for the only One who deserves it. In no other presence and before no other being can I kneel in fear, wonder, yearning and awe and feel the same sense of possessiveness that cries, "Mine, mine!"

Holy God, we praise Thy name;
Lord of all, we bow before Thee;
All on earth, Thy scepter claim;
All in heaven above adore Thee.
Infinite Thy vast domain;
Everlasting is Thy reign.
IGNAZ FRANZ (1719–1790)

O God, I worship Thee in the beauty of holiness. Not my holiness,
but Thy Holiness as revealed to me in the Lord Jesus Christ. Amen.

And it shall be to me a name of joy, a praise and an honour before all the nations of the earth, which shall hear all the good that I do unto them: and they shall fear and tremble for all the goodness and for all the prosperity that I procure unto it.

JEREMIAH 33:9

Some people are so theologically suited that they feel it is not right to say, "Mine." When I have gone through hymnbooks, I have seen in a few where the cold, chilly editors, who got out of their deep-freeze and dipped their pen in blue ice water, had the audacity to edit the hymns of Wesley and Watts.

They took away the "I's" and the "me's" and the "mine's" and replaced these words with the word "ours." They were so modest they could not imagine saying, "I love the Lord."

Here is how they would translate a familiar passage of Scripture.

"The Lord is our shepherd, we shall not want. He maketh us to lie down in green pastures . . ." That is togetherness, all right.

When you have met God in the loneliness of your soul, and you and God come to the point where there is nobody else in the world, that is the passion for God we need today. That is the kind of love I need to have for God. I will never be able to love other people in the world until I have mastered my love for God—a passion for God that nothing can diminish.

My Shepherd will supply my need:
Jehovah is His name;
In pastures fresh He makes me feed,
Beside the living stream.

ISAAC WATTS (1674–1748)

My Shepherd and my God, I trust Thee for all things necessary for my life. Thy presence has dispelled all want on my part. Truly, I rest in Thee. In the name of Jesus, I pray, amen.

January 14

As the hart panteth after the water brooks,
so panteth my soul after thee, O God.
PSALM 42:1

My aim each day is to adore God more than anything else. This adoration needs to be poured out at God's feet. David felt this when he was running from King Saul.

While hiding in a cave somewhere, David got a touch of homesickness and happened to say in the hearing of some of his soldiers, "Oh, that I might have a drink out of the good old well of Bethlehem."

Several of the soldiers who overheard this started for that well, and at the risk of their lives, they got the water out of that well. They brought the water back and presented it to David. I am sure they were not expecting what followed.

David looked at the water, and then he looked at the men who brought the water, and finally he said, "I can't drink this. This water cost you your life." Then in an act of reverence such as only David could do, he poured out the water before the Lord his God.

Like David, we admire God; we love Him for His excellence and desire to pour ourselves out at His feet in an active, adoring, wondering love.

Praise my soul, the King of heaven;
To His feet thy tribute bring.
Ransomed, healed, restored, forgiven,
Evermore His praises sing.
HENRY F. LYTE (1793-1847)

Dear God, I live my life at Thy feet in reverence to Thee.
Accept my life as I pour it out before Thee. All I need is in Thee;
all I want is Thee. In Jesus' name I pray. Amen.

Give unto the Lord, O ye mighty, give unto the Lord glory and strength.
Give unto the Lord the glory due unto his name;
worship the Lord in the beauty of holiness.
PSALM 29:1-2

We were born to worship. If we are not worshiping God in the beauty of holiness, we have missed our reason for being born. I embrace the idea that worship is the delightful, awesome, humbling, wonderful experience that we can have in varying degrees. It does not take a building to create worship.

If you burn down the church building and drive away all the people, you have not disturbed Christian worship at all. Keep a Christian from entering the church sanctuary and you have not in the least bit hindered his worship. We carry our sanctuary with us. We never leave it.

We do not enter into a building and then commence to worship. If you are not worshiping God on Monday morning, as you worshiped him the day before, perhaps you are not worshiping Him at all.

When Christians lose their love for God, they become sick. The lack of worship as a natural, spontaneous and continual thing is a sure sign of spiritual sickness. One generation lets this slip a little; it affects the next generation and the next until there is no real, overwhelming desire to worship God. Then worship has to be created from the outside; but that is never true worship.

Let all mortal flesh keep silence,
And with fear and trembling stand;
Ponder nothing earthly minded,
For with blessing in His hand,
Christ our God to earth descendeth,
Our full homage to demand.

FOURTH CENTURY GREEK, ENGLISH TRANS. BY GERARD MOULTRIE

Dear God, I come before you in fear and trembling
and experience You as You long to share Yourself.
Let me know you in the beauty of Thy blessed holiness. Amen.

Arise, shine; for thy light is come,
and the glory of the Lord is risen upon thee.
ISAIAH 60:1

When it comes to worship. if some Christians did not have a calendar filled out for them, they would not know what they were supposed to do. True worship cannot be choreographed by a calendar. Our Lord Himself said these things are not important.

No worship affected by external pressure is worship that truly pleases God; and if it does not please God, it really does not benefit us.

Much that passes for worship today is simply people getting together and having a grand old time, not realizing that the purpose of worship is to honor Christ and lift Him up. This is the work of the Holy Spirit within us. Must I point out that an unsaved person cannot worship God? Must I point out that only those who have within them the Spirit of the living God can worship God in a way that will please and honor Him?

Looking around me, I cannot help but sigh deeply, watching people go through the motions by observing days and referencing objects, thinking they are worshiping God.

Can I hear God saying, "Depart from me, ye workers of iniquity, I never knew you"?

Glory be to Him who loved us,
Washed us from each sinful stain;
Glory be to Him who made us
Priests and kings with Him to reign;
Glory, worship, laud and blessing
To the Lamb who once was slain.

HORATIUS BONAR (1808-1889)

Forgive me, O God, for carelessly coming into Your presence not thinking
of the One I am worshiping. Cleanse my heart from all things that deem
my worship unworthy worship. In the name of Jesus, amen.

A Psalm of David. Give unto the Lord, O ye mighty,
give unto the Lord glory and strength.
Give unto the Lord the glory due unto his name;
worship the Lord in the beauty of holiness.
PSALM 29:2

Worship that is pleasing to God always accords with the nature of God. This is taught throughout the Scriptures and seems so logical and right that we cannot mistake it. We worship God according to what God is, not according to what God is not.

The basic error of idolatry is worshiping God according to what He is not. Jesus said about the Samaritans, "You don't know what you worship."

The Old Testament prophets were quite faithful in pointing out aspects of life in conflict with the nature of God. It was their job to call the people back into alignment with the nature of God. Worship that is out of harmony with the nature of God is not acceptable worship to God.

This is why it is extremely important that we get to know God; because the more we get to know God, the more we begin to understand who we are and what about us can please God. Aren't you overwhelmed with the thought that there is something in you that corresponds to something in God that, in effect, pleasures Him? Don't you want to find what that is and build your life around it?

We come, O Christ, to Thee,
True Son of God and man,
By whom all things consist,
In whom all life began.
In Thee alone we live and move,
And have our being in Thy love.

E. MARGARET CLARKSON (1915–2008)

I seek Thee O God, and long to know Thee;
for in knowing Thee, I begin to understand myself. Let my worship
today pleasure Thee as Thou deserve to be pleasured. Amen.

I will praise thee, O Lord my God, with all my heart:
and I will glorify thy name for evermore.
PSALMS 86:12

One thing difficult to comprehend is that God is unaffected by the attributes of matter. Weight, size and space do not affect Him. All of these things affect us in varying degrees, and our error is in assuming that whatever affects us must affect God. We have a natural tendency to try to bring God down to our level.

The more one gets to know God and understand His nature, the more one begins to wonder at the immensity of God. He is bigger than anything we could ever comprehend. A well-taught Christian will know that the God he worships is not affected by any of the things affecting us.

This is good to know. If God was influenced by what influences me, how could I worship Him? How could I confidently trust Him if He was affected by the same things that affect me?

As I wallow in my mortality, I look up in wondrous joy at Him who is immortal, invisible, God only wise, knowing that He has invited me to share in His nature.

Oh, how I love Jesus!

Immortal, invisible, God only wise,
In light inaccessible hid from our eyes,
Most blessed, most glorious, the Ancient of Days,
Almighty, victorious, Thy great name we praise.
WALTER C. SMITH (1824–1908)

Dear Father in heaven, I love Thee with a love rooted deeply in the
heart of Thy dear Son, even the Lord Jesus Christ, our Savior.
The more I love Thee, the more I rest in peace with myself. Amen.

And God said, Let us make man in our image, after our likeness: and let them have
dominion over the fish of the sea, and over the fowl of the air, and over the cattle,
and over all the earth, and over every creeping thing that creepeth upon the earth.

Genesis 1:26

God made us in His image; and because He made us in His image, there
is a part of me that is like God. I wish all Christians might see this. The
human soul is the most like God of anything that has ever been created.

How can this be since there is so much sin in the world and so much
that seems ungodly? The answer is sin. Man has fallen, but not so far that
God can't restore and redeem us. It's easy for God to do that because God
has material to work with that was once made in His image.

If man were not made in the image of God, redemption would not be
possible. Those who have tried to think of man as coming into this world
without a Creator are, in fact, denying man's redemption. Only what was
created in the image of God can be restored by God.

Part of my worship each day is to celebrate this marvelous truth. I am
redeemed because I have been created in the image of God. Although sin
has all but destroyed that image, God's grace is greater than all of man's
sin put together.

The cross, it standeth fast,
Hallelujah! Hallelujah!
Defying every blast,
Hallelujah! Hallelujah!
The winds of hell have blown,
The world its hate hath shown,
Yet it is not overthrown,
Hallelujah for the cross!

Horatius Bonar (1808–1889)

Our Father which art in heaven, Thy name is hallowed within this heart of mine
as I praise Thee. I rejoice in my salvation through Jesus Christ my Lord. Amen.

I am the Lord thy God, which brought thee out of the land of Egypt:
open thy mouth wide, and I will fill it.
PSALM 81:10

A potter sets about to make a beautiful teapot; and while it is spinning on the wheel, he runs into some problem, and it falls apart. It is broken and not useful anymore, and it does not look like a teapot. It has no artistry, and the soul of the artist is not in it, and cannot be in it, because it has broken. For the potter, however, it is a simple matter to take up that material again, take out the offending parts and fashion it into another vessel.

He could not do that if he was working with iron or a rock. But he can do it with the clay, because clay is the material with which he works. It was broken the first time, but he can restore it using the same material.

God made us in His image; and while we are not altogether clear about what that image of God is, I know that the human soul is like God. In succumbing to the temptation that took place in the Garden, man fell apart; he lost the artistry, the beauty and the holiness of God. He did not lose the potential to become godlike again if he got into the hands of the Divine Artist.

Redemption is taking on the material of fallen man by the mystery of regeneration and sanctification and restoring it again so that he is like God and like Christ. Redemption is not just saving us from hell, although it does that; it is making us so that we can be like God again.

Have Thine own way, Lord! Have Thine own way!
Thou art the Potter, I am the clay.
Mold me and make me after Thy will,
While I am waiting, yielded and still.

ADELAIDE A. POLLARD (1862-1934)

Dear heavenly Father, I yield to the pressure of Thy touch as you make me into that vessel most pleasing in Your sight. In Jesus' name, amen.

God is a Spirit: and they that worship him
must worship him in spirit and in truth.
JOHN 4:24

If we are going to worship God, it must be done correctly. Worship must be spiritual. Along this line, I might say that you cannot worship God without the Holy Spirit. The Holy Spirit is the only One who can properly lead the heart to worship God acceptably. The natural human mind does not know how to worship God acceptably and go in a certain direction so that it is worshiping God.

This is why it is so vastly important that we should know the Holy Spirit. More than once, I have gotten on my knees and apologized to the Holy Spirit for the way the church has treated Him. We have treated Him shoddily. We have treated Him in such a manner that if you were to treat a guest that way, the guest would go away grief-stricken and never return.

Many churches acknowledge Him at the opening and the close of the service. Apart from that, they do not count on His presence. How many people go to church on a Sunday morning counting upon the Holy Spirit to speak to them?

Spirit of God, descend upon my heart;
Wean it from earth, through all its pulses move.
Stoop to my weakness, mighty as Thou art,
And make me love Thee as I ought to love.

GEORGE CROLY (1780–1860)

Holy Spirit, blessed third person of the Trinity,
I honor Thee as the indispensable One in my worship of God.
Teach me to know Thee as Thou art wont to be known. Amen.

Likewise the Spirit also helpeth our infirmities: for we know not what we should pray for as we ought: but the Spirit itself maketh intercession for us with groanings which cannot be uttered.
ROMANS 8:26

The notion that anyone can worship without the Holy Spirit is not only wrong, but dangerous. The notion that we can crowd the Holy Spirit into a corner and ignore Him, quench Him, resist Him and yet worship God acceptably is a great heresy, which we need to correct. Only the Holy Spirit knows how to worship God acceptably.

We have worship leaders trying to replace the Holy Spirit. I think this is reprehensible. The one who stands before an assembly and leads the worship should be the one who has submitted himself to a fresh work of the Holy Spirit. The best preparation for worship is not rehearsal, but surrender.

Some of our best hymns came from men and women so utterly broken before God that only God mattered.

The apostle Paul says that it is impossible to pray without the Spirit, and the most powerful prayers are those in the Spirit. Likewise, we cannot worship without the Holy Spirit. I think it is time that the church of Christ should rethink this whole matter of the place of the Holy Spirit in the church of our Lord Jesus Christ.

Come, blessed, holy, heavenly Dove,
Spirit of light and life and love,
Revive our souls we pray!
Come with the power of Pentecost,
Come as the sevenfold Holy Ghost,
And fill our hearts today.

A. B. SIMPSON (1843–1919)

Heavenly Father, whatever it takes, I pray Thee, bring me to the place where only Thou matter. I pray this in Jesus' name. Amen.

*Then the angel of the Lord put forth the end of the staff
that was in his hand, and touched the flesh and the unleavened cakes;
and there rose up fire out of the rock, and consumed the flesh and the
unleavened cakes. Then the angel of the Lord departed out of his sight.*
JUDGES 6:21

It is my studied opinion that it takes a broken man to worthily worship God.

Israel is an example of this. Israel continued trying to worship God after the fire had left the holy place with no Shekinah glory there—no fire, no light and no presence. Israel continued to worship vainly and futilely, forgetting that the Holy Spirit of worship had left her long ago. She was so practiced in the accoutrements of worship that she failed to realize she was not really worshiping Jehovah.

The sons of the fathers may be worshiping the God of the fathers, but for the most part, they are only going through the motions they saw their fathers do a thousand times before. Where is the glory? Where is the fire? Where is the brokenness before the possible presence of God?

I believe it is time the church rethinks this whole matter of worship. Spirituality is one of the ingredients of worship, and without spirituality, we cannot worship God in a way that is acceptable to Him. And no matter how much we worship, if it is not acceptable worship, then it is vain worship and better not attempted.

Breathe on me, Breath of God,
Till I am wholly Thine,
Until this earthly part of me
Glows with Thy fire divine.
EDWIN HATCH (1835-1889)

*Holy Spirit, fire divine, melt the hardness within my heart
that keeps me from experiencing the fullness of Thy presence.
In Jesus' name, amen.*

January 24

And the glory of the Lord shall be revealed,
and all flesh shall see it together:
for the mouth of the Lord has spoken it.
ISAIAH 40:5

The way to deal with formality and duplicity in our worship is sincerity. It is quite easy to get caught up with formality and duplicity in worship. If my worship is not sincere, and I am just going through the motions, then I should not even be worshiping.

Much that passes for worship today is not sincere. In fact, to be honest about it, much is built upon superstition. If you mumble the right words at the right time it will bring you good luck. If you make motions with your fingers it will bring you good luck.

Good luck has nothing whatsoever to do with worship but has everything to do with carnality and sensuality. These have no place in the worship of God.

My worship of God must be based upon my sincerity in worshiping—not looking for anything added to my life, but rather coming into the presence of God. This is what worship is all about. People talk about blessings, and their definition is about as carnal as you could get.

The blessing of worship is sincerely coming into the presence of God, knowing that you are as welcomed in His presence as He is in your presence.

Jesus, our only joy be Thou,
As Thou our prize wilt be;
Jesus, be Thou our glory now,
And through eternity.

BERNARD OF CLAIRVAUX (1090–1153),
ENGLISH TRANS. EDWARD CASWALL (1814–1878)

Dear God and Father of our Lord Jesus Christ,
I honor Thee as the true God and worship Thee in the simplicity of my sincerity.
May you be glorified in my life today. In Jesus' name, amen.

*Whosoever therefore shall humble himself as this little child,
the same is greatest in the kingdom of heaven.*
MATTHEW 18:4

Jesus desires that we be as sincere as little children, especially when it comes to our worship.

This sincerity must be cultivated in our life, and we must cultivate it prayerfully if our worship is to be accepted by Almighty God. Our preparation and coming into His presence has to do with cultivating the simplicity of our lives. That is, getting rid of everything in our lives that hinders our sincere devotion to the Lord Jesus Christ.

If we would just stop and begin to believe that anything that hinders this is sin, and then deal with it as sincerely as is called for at the time, we would be on our way into the presence of God.

What a terrible thing to spend a lifetime making offerings to the Almighty and find out all of them have been rejected! How many people will come to the end of life and realize nothing they have ever done is acceptable to God?

Each day, we must strip ourselves of anything hindering our coming acceptably into the presence of God.

I hear the Savior say,
"Thy strength indeed is small;
Child of weakness, watch and pray,
Find in Me thine all in all."
ELVINA M. HALL (1822–1889)

*Oh, God, I come before Thee as simply as a child, knowing that,
before Thee, I am as nothing. Be Thou my all in all today, I pray.
In Jesus' name, amen.*

And the Lord went before them by day in a pillar of a cloud,
to lead them the way; and by night in a pillar of fire, to give them light;
to go by day and night: he took not away the pillar of the cloud by day,
nor the pillar of fire by night, from before the people.
EXODUS 13:21-22

One great truth from the Bible is that God made everything for a purpose. God's purpose in making man was to have somebody capable—properly and sufficiently equipped—to worship Him. Man's purpose was to satisfy God's heart and to pleasure Him, but man was felled by sin and is now failing to carry out His created purpose.

Man is like a cloud without water—it has no rain. He is like the sun that gives no heat or the stars that give no light, or a tree that no longer gives any fruit; a bird that no longer sings, a harp silenced that no longer gives off music.

The truth is that God wants us to worship Him, and we are doing what we were created to do when we are worshiping God. When Adam sinned, he broke his fellowship with God; his heart became unstrung, and the voice of Adam died in his throat. In the cool of the day, God came searching, and cried, "Adam, where art thou?" God was seeking worship from Adam, who had sinned.

I need Thy presence every passing hour;
What but Thy grace can foil the tempter's power?
Who, like Thyself, my guide and stay can be?
Through cloud and sunshine, Lord, abide with me!
HENRY F. LYTE (1793–1847)

In thy presence, O Lord God, I bow in reverential worship and
adoration. In my worship I discover Thee, but I also discover myself
and my purpose. In the name of Jesus, amen.

Thou art worthy, O Lord, to receive glory and honour and power:
for thou hast created all things, and for thy pleasure
they are and were created.
REVELATION 4:11

Two aspects of faith in the Christian's life are crucial.

One is that we are as bad as God says we are. If I do not have faith in God's Word concerning my badness I am never going to repent. If I do not repent, I have no chance of changing and if I do not change, I will never come to that place of fellowship with God that He desires. I need to accept what God says about me as unchanging truth. Then, I am on the road to change.

The next aspect is that we are as dear to God as He says we are. If we do not believe He desires us as much as He says He does, we will never come into His presence and give Him the worship He yearns for.

If everybody could suddenly have a baptism of pure cheerful belief that God wanted us and wanted us to worship and admire Him and praise Him, we would be transformed into the most radiantly happy people on the North American continent.

God made us to worship Him and when we are not worshiping Him, we are failing in the purpose for which we were created.

All praise to Him who reigns above
In Majesty's supreme,
Who gave His Son for man to die,
That He might man redeem!
WILLIAM H. CLARK

My Father which art in heaven, my sin is ever before me and if it was
not for the amazing grace that You spread in my direction I would not
be able to come into Thy presence. Hallelujah for the cross! Amen.

There is none holy as the Lord: for there is none beside thee:
neither is there any rock like our God.
1 SAMUEL 2:2

In pursuing God in holy worship, I need to be very clear about something. You cannot worship Him as you will. The One who made you to worship also has decreed how you shall worship Him. God does not accept just any kind of worship.

God has rejected all the worship of mankind in our present condition. Although God wants us to worship Him, and He commands us to and invites us to come, He condemns and rejects all the worship of mankind.

At least four kinds of worship are prevalent on the earth today, and God rejects them all: Cain's worship, Samaritan worship, pagan worship and nature worship.

Abel offered unto God the sacrifice of blood, while Cain came with a bloodless sacrifice and offered to the Lord flowers and the fruit and the growth of the earth. This worship rested upon a mistaken impression of the kind of God He is. Cain came to worship a God of his own imagination. God accepts worship only when it is pure and acceptable by the Holy Ghost.

Praise the Savior, ye who know Him!
Who can tell how much we owe Him?
Gladly let us render to Him
All we are and have.

THOMAS KELLY (1769–1855)

I praise Thee, O God and Father of the Lord Jesus Christ,
for Thou alone art worthy of my praise and worship.
I give it sacrificially unto Thee today. In Jesus' name, amen.

For by grace are ye saved through faith; and that not of yourselves:
it is the gift of God: not of works, lest any man should boast.
EPHESIANS 2:8-9

A horrendous error is infecting the church today: humans occupy a relationship to God that they really do not occupy. Some put their hope in a relationship with God that actually does not exist.

The curse of religion is that it propagates ideas like this.

The belief is that we all are God's children and when we talk about "O God and Father of mankind," this includes everybody. The Bible simply does not teach that God is the Father of mankind.

On one occasion, Jesus accused the Pharisees of being the children of the devil. "Ye are of your father, the devil." That does not quite fit the religious tone of many today. We are all one family, so we are told.

This overlooks the work of redemption. If man is in such a harmonious relationship with God, why did Jesus have to die on the cross? What was the purpose of redemption?

Another error propagated with this kind of thinking is that man is okay as he is. If man is in such harmony with God, why is mankind in such disharmony with one another?

What religion teaches is not borne out by the facts of history.

My hope is built on nothing less
Than Jesus' blood and righteousness;
I dare not trust the sweetest frame,
But wholly lean on Jesus' name.
EDWARD MOTE (1797–1874)

My heavenly Father, I thank Thee for the amazing grace of the Lord
Jesus Christ that has brought me into fellowship with Thee.
I know no other joy than Thy fellowship. Amen.

I made a covenant with mine eyes; why then should I think upon a maid?
JOB 31:1

An idea that seems to be gaining strength these days is that sin is not quite as serious as some of us have imagined it to be. There are all kinds of ways to excuse sin. Perhaps the best way is to call it by some other name.

For some, sin is just a mistake. They actually meant well, but something happened, and they made a mistake. After all, nobody is perfect.

The problem is that being perfect has nothing at all to do with not sinning.

When we lessen the seriousness of sin, we are in dispute with the entire Bible. No matter if you go to the Old Testament or the New Testament, sin is always presented as a terrible thing. The Old Testament sacrifices emphasize God's thoughts about sin. To read through the sacrifices laid out in the Old Testament is to become very weary. God takes a dim view about sin.

I must look at sin and think about sin as God does. As I pursue the Word of God, the Holy Spirit will impress upon me how terrible sin is in God's mind.

God rejects worship not founded on the redeeming blood of the Lord Jesus Christ.

Lord Jesus, for this I must humbly entreat;
I wait, blessed Lord, at Thy crucified feet.
By faith, for my cleansing I see Thy blood flow.
Now wash me and I shall be Whiter than snow.

JAMES L. NICHOLSON (1828–1896)

*Dear Lord Jesus, I praise Thee today for the cleansing power of
Thy blood. I come to Thee, not in my own strength,
but in the purified strength of Thy redeeming grace. Amen.*

So then faith cometh by hearing, and hearing by the word of God.
ROMANS 10:17

Heretics do not necessarily want to teach that there is no Trinity, or that God did not create the universe, and that there is no judgment. The very word "heretic" means one who picks and chooses.

The Samaritans were heretical in that they chose certain parts of the Bible. They had a Pentateuch and accepted it, but they rejected David, Isaiah, Jeremiah, Ezekiel, Daniel, 1 and 2 Kings and the Song of Solomon. They rejected all of Scripture except the Pentateuch.

The Samaritans went one step further: they translated the Pentateuch.

You can translate anything to prove what you are out to prove. All you have to do is say you know Greek or Hebrew, and after that, you are on your own. The Samaritans translated the old Pentateuch in a manner that proved Samaria was a place of worship. Because of that, they were very hostile to the Jews who claimed that Jerusalem was the place to worship.

The Samaritans accepted the Bible, but they just accepted as much of it as they wanted. When you pick and choose, you can believe just about anything.

Remember, it takes all of the Bible to make it the Word of God.

Oh, send Thy Spirit, Lord,
Now unto me,
That He may touch my eyes,
And make me see;
Show me the truth concealed
Within Thy Word,
And in Thy Book revealed,
I see Thee, Lord.

ALEXANDER GROVES (1842–1909)

O Holy Spirit, open my eyes today that I may see
that which You have for me. Blind me to those ways that
lead me away from Thee. In Jesus' name, amen.

*I remember thy judgments of old, O Lord;
and have comforted myself.*
PSALM 119:52

Heresy abounds today, with people believing only what they want to believe. Heretics emphasize certain words or phrases so they can follow along and accept one while rejecting another; doing one thing but refusing another. Heretics are pickers and choosers among the Word of God.

The most dangerous aspect about heresy is that in many regards what they believe is right. It is not what one believes, but rather, it is what one refuses to believe that makes heretics very dangerous. If they were all bad, they would not have much influence in the evangelical church today.

What makes it worse is what they say you can accept and believe, and by doing that they suck you down a certain pathway and eventually lead you away from all the truth. It takes all the truth to make it God's Word. You cannot take only one slice of truth and disassociate it from the rest of the Bible.

Evangelicals need to be careful not to ride their favorite hobbyhorse while ignoring other things and compromising the power of God's Word.

O make Thy Church, dear Saviour,
A lamp of purest gold,
To bear before the nations
Thy true light, as of old,
O teach Thy wandering pilgrims
By this their path to trace,
Till, clouds and darkness ended,
They see Thee face to face. Amen.

WILLIAM W. HOW (1823–1897)

*Thy truth, O God, is my meat and drink each day.
My soul is ravished with hunger that only Thy Word can satiate.
In the blessed name of Jesus I pray, amen.*

Stablish thy word unto thy servant, who is devoted to thy fear.
PSALM 119:38

Ralph Waldo Emerson once walked across a field after a rain with the sun shining on the little puddles of water out over the meadow. Suddenly, his mind had been elevated to a place of such happiness that he was full of fear. He said he was so happy, he was afraid.

Emerson was simply a pagan poet; and a whole lot of worship going on these days is nothing but pagan poetry and nature worship.

Religion has a lot of poetry in it. I enjoy poetry if it is good poetry, but the problem is finding good poetry. Religion brings poetry out more than any other occupation the mind can be engaged in. And there is much that is very beautiful about religion. There is a high enjoyment in the contemplation of the divine and the sublime. The concentration of the mind upon truth always brings a high sense of enjoyment.

This is nature worship. Certainly, nature carries with it a sense of beauty and exhilaration. I enjoy getting out in nature and just having some quiet time. There's nothing wrong with that. The problem comes when people confuse nature worship with true worship.

Thy nature, gracious Lord, impart;
Come quickly from above,
Write Thy new name upon my heart,
Thy new, best name of Love.
CHARLES WESLEY (1707–1788)

I come to Thee O Father, knowing that my true joy comes from Thee.
Thy presence is the great delight of my daily experience.
I pray this in Jesus' name. Amen.

And the priest waited on their offices: the Levites also with instruments
of musick of the Lord, which David the king had made to praise the Lord,
because his mercy endureth for ever, when David praised by their ministry;
and the priests sounded trumpets before them, and all Israel stood.
2 CHRONICLES 7:6

Like many people, I enjoy the music of religion. Some mistake the music of religion as true worship, because music has a way to raise the heart to near rapture. Music can lift our feelings to moments of ecstasy. Music has a purging effect upon us so that it is possible to fall into a happy and elevated state of mind with a vague notion about God and imagine that we are worshiping God when we are doing nothing of the sort.

We are simply enjoying the music. It is that which God has put in us, which even sin has not yet been able to kill.

I do not think there is any poetry in hell. I cannot believe that among the terrible sewage of the moral world, there is going to be anybody breaking into similes and metaphors. I cannot conceive of anyone breaking into song in that terrible place we call hell.

There is no poetry or music in hell, but there is plenty here on earth, even in the unsaved person, because he or she was once made in the image of God. Music is the residue of that image that breaks forth into song.

I can sing now the song of the blood ransomed throng;
In my soul there is peace, rest and calm;
I am free from all doubt and I join in the shout
I'm redeemed by the blood of the Lamb.
RUSSELL K. CARTER (1840-1928)

Praise belongeth unto Thee, O God, and I kneel before
Thee and lift my heart up in worship and praise.
May Thy Name be praised in my life today. In Jesus' name, amen.

February 4

Make a joyful noise unto God, all ye lands:
sing forth the honour of his name: make his praise glorious.
PSALM 66:1-2

Even though people have lost God from their conscious thought, they still have the ability to appreciate the sublime. Certain men out in the world have written books that lift a person to heights of sublimity, and I enjoy reading them.

I have read books on poetry that have just lifted me up into what people refer to as the third heaven. I admit there is not much of that anymore. So much bad poetry is published today, but there is also that which is good, some of it even great poetry. I could spend a whole day meditating on some of the great poets and their work.

Of course, with poetry comes music. Much that is sublime and beautiful in the world is set to music. Music is beauty the ear recognizes. It is wonderful to just sit back, close your eyes and listen to the music of some great orchestra.

The problem with the sublimity of the world, although quite beautiful, is that it does not lift us up high enough. I contend that one hour on your knees, meditating on some of David's psalms will lift you up into the very realm of God Himself.

Praise Him! Praise Him!
Jesus, our blessed Redeemer!
Heavenly portals loud with hosannas ring.
Jesus, Saviour, reigneth forever and ever.
FANNY J. CROSBY (1820–1915)

Dear Lord Jesus, I love Thee and pray that Thy will be
accomplished in my life today. Lift me up into that realm
of absolute adoration and praise. Amen.

O sing unto the Lord a new song: sing unto the Lord, all the earth.
Sing unto the Lord, bless his name; shew forth his salvation from day to day.
PSALM 96:1-2

Sublimity is not just for the ear, it is also for the eye. Along with great poets and musicians are the great artists of the world. The eye can recognize things that are beautiful; and when the heart hears nothing and sees nothing, but only feels, then it is the music of the heart.

Whenever visiting a large city and I have an afternoon to myself, I enjoy going to some museum in the city. I enjoy admiring the great masterpieces of artists who were given a gift from God. Some of those paintings have a degree of sublimity about them that lifts me up. I could spend a lot of time looking at those paintings.

Even so, we can have all of this, enjoy it to the fullest, and still not worship God or be accepted of Him. Even the pagan who rejects Christ can enjoy the sublimity of the poets and musicians and artists. But they can never worship God as He desires to be worshiped.

The sublimity of a great painting can lift me only so far. God's Word can lift me beyond that kind of sublimity into the very presence of God.

Oh, for a thousand tongues to sing
My great Redeemer's praise,
The glories of my God and King,
The triumphs of His grace!
CHARLES WESLEY (1707–1788)

Our heavenly Father, I dedicate my tongue to only sing
Thy praise each day. Let me lift up Thy name before the congregation.
In the precious name of Jesus, amen.

O God, my heart is fixed; I will sing and give praise,
even with my glory. Awake, psaltery and harp:
I myself will awake early.
PSALM 108:1-2

Something in man wants to worship God. The problem is, man wants to worship God the way he wants to worship Him. This is the reason God rejects all such worshipers. Our Lord Jesus said, God is spirit, and they that worship Him must worship in spirit and truth. That little word "must" clears the deck for everything else. Nothing else is acceptable as far as God is concerned. If we are worshiping God, we need to worship Him as He desires to be worshiped.

There is no tolerance here, no broad-minded spirit. But there is the sharp pinpointing of fact so that every man worshiping in his own way is completely rejected.

If our worship is going to be authentic, it must start with God, never with man. Worship is not something man has developed or created. Worship has come exclusively from God. Nothing that does not come from God is genuine or authentic. Worship starts with God, pierces the heart of man and then returns to the God who started it all. True worship maintains this divine cycle.

Christ, whose glory fills the skies,
Christ, the true, the only Light,
Sun of Righteousness, arise,
Triumph o'er the shades of night;
Dayspring from on high, be near;
Day-star, in my heart appear.

CHARLES WESLEY (1707–1788)

O God, my Father, Thy presence fills my heart with such glory
that I can hardly stand it. Fill me with Thyself until all myself
has been pushed out. In Jesus' name, amen.

My soul thirsteth for God, for the living God:
when shall I come and appear before God?
PSALM 42:2

One thing I will not accept or even tolerate is someone who does not really know God telling me how to worship God. My worship of God begins on my knees with an open Bible and my heart panting after God.

I refuse to follow the nature poet who instructs me on how to worship God. I know they are coming from the human standpoint. I am sure there is a lot to be gained from the meditation and propping up of the self-image, and all that goes with that, but I will have none of it.

My worship begins with God. It is the God of Abraham, Isaac and Jacob, not the God of the philosophers or scientists or poets or musicians.

I am not against feelings, but feelings alone can be rather dangerous. Feelings can be wrong. But the end product, if I can call it that, is an overwhelming sense of the presence of God. Call these feelings, if you like, but the feeling focuses on God's presence. Feelings will never bring me into God's presence, and that is where we make a mistake. Whoever can manipulate our feelings controls our worship. I want God alone in that capacity in my life.

As pants the hart for cooling streams
When heated in the chase,
So longs my soul, O God, for Thee
And Thy refreshing grace.
NAHUM TATE (1652–1715) AND NICHOLAS BRADY (1659–1726)

Dear Father, I turn my back on everything and long for Thee and the fullness of Thy presence in my life today. Lead me; oh lead me by the cool streams of Thy grace. In Jesus' name, amen.

Jesus saith unto him, I am the way, the truth, and the life:
no man cometh unto the Father, but by me.
JOHN 14:6

Jesus made it very clear that there is only one way to worship God. If I am going to worship God, I can only do it through the Lord Jesus Christ.

That being the case, I need to know who this Jesus is, not who people say He is. They may be wrong and have wrong information. I hear some people talk about a Jesus I do not recognize. They certainly are not getting their information from the New Testament.

To really come into God's presence, I cannot do it apart from the Lord Jesus Christ. Hence, I need to have a relationship with this One called Christ. I need to know who He is, and I need a personal rapport with Him. Too many people are trying to worship God apart from Jesus Christ.

I will not back down on this, in any degree. There is only one way to come into God's presence, and that is through Jesus Christ. Yes, you can worship without Jesus, but you're not worshiping the God of the Bible.

We worship Thee, Lord Christ, Our Saviour and our King,
To Thee our youth and strength adoringly we bring:
So fill our hearts, that men may see
Thy life in us, and turn to Thee. Amen.
E. MARGARET CLARKSON (1915–2008)

In praise of Thee, O Christ, I lift up my heart.
I long to know Thee other than by hearsay.
Strengthen my heart to know Thee
in all of Thy fullness. Amen.

Brethren, my heart's desire and prayer to God for Israel is,
that they might be saved. For I bear them record that they have a zeal of God,
but not according to knowledge.
ROMANS 10:1-2

I often hear preachers praying, and I confess that in my heart I curl up in scorn when I hear them. They are so afraid they are going to insult some other religion or hurt somebody's feelings when they mention Jesus in their prayers. After all, we cannot offend an atheist who does not believe in God. Really?

I do not think I would ever make a politician, who has to try to please everybody. That is not my bowl of soup. I am determined to stand on truth regardless of who may object to it or be offended by it.

Many think they are worshiping God because they feel good on the inside and are patted on the back and told they are okay. I would be violating my commission as a child of God, and as a preacher of the Word, if I ever did anything of that nature. I could never stand and deliver a whole speech trying to please everybody in the crowd.

Wherever I am, whatever I am doing, I hope and pray to God that I will have the courage to stand up for the real Jesus of the New Testament, regardless of whom I offend.

Stand up, stand up for Jesus, ye soldiers of the cross;
Lift high His royal banner, it must not suffer loss.
From victory unto victory His army shall He lead,
Till every foe is vanquished and Christ is Lord indeed.
GEORGE DUFFIELD, JR. (1818–1888)

O Father of our Lord and Savior Jesus Christ,
I look not for man's approval, but in obedience to Thy command,
I press forward in the duty Thou has placed before me.
Thy command is my delight.
In Jesus' name, amen.

Trust in the Lord with all thine heart; and lean not unto thine own understanding.
In all thy ways acknowledge him, and he shall direct thy paths.
PROVERBS 3:5-6

Every worshiper must submit to truth or he cannot worship God. He can write poems and get elevations of thought when he sees a sunrise. He can do all sorts of things, but he cannot worship God except by faith.

In order to worship God, one needs to admit who God is and that He is who He says He is and what He says He is. Then, one must admit that Christ is who He says He is and what He says He is.

Taking this a step further, one has to admit the truth about oneself—that he is as bad a sinner as God says he is.

I fear that, for the most part, most people are worshiping worship and do not really know it.

Only the spiritually renewed man can worship God acceptably. This means that he has had an infusion of the spirit of the truth and that is the work of the Holy Spirit in his life.

I do not know how you feel about it, but I could commune with God walking out on the street with no other attractions. My worship is communion with the Christ who is within me, and who is also seated on the throne on high.

O blest communion, fellowship divine!
We feebly struggle; they in glory shine.
Yet all are one in Thee, for all are Thine.
Alleluia! Alleluia!

WILLIAM W. HOW (1823-1897)

Dear Lord Jesus, Thy fellowship gets sweeter each day.
I long to know Thee and commune with Thee each day.
I lift up my heart in adoration and praise. Amen.

Blessed is he whose transgression is forgiven, whose sin is covered.
Blessed is the man unto whom the Lord imputeth not iniquity,
and in whose spirit there is no guile.
PSALM 32:1-2

Sin made it impossible for me to know how to worship God, except that the truth enlightened, and does enlighten, me. I have in my hand the Book, the only book that enlightens me. Here is the light that lighteth every man that reads it.

Jesus Christ is the light that lighteth every man that cometh into the world, and the light of the human heart and the light of this Book harmonize. When the eyes of the soul look to the Book of God and come into the Living Word of God, then we know the truth and can worship God in truth and in spirit.

In the Old Testament, a priest could not offer a sacrifice until first anointed with oil, symbolic of the Spirit of God. No man can worship out of his own heart. But still we search among the flowers, the bird nests and tombs and whatever we choose. I cannot worship out of my own heart.

Only the Holy Spirit can worship God acceptably, and He reflects back the glory of God. The Spirit comes down to us and reflects back to God. If it does not reach our heart, there is no reflecting back and, consequently, no worship. Oh how big and broad and comprehensive and wonderful is the work of Christ!

There for me the Saviour stands,
Shows His wounds and spreads His hands;
God is love! I know, I feel;
Jesus weep: and loves me still.

CHARLES WESLEY (1707-1788)

Precious Lord Jesus, I have sought for Thee out in the world and among the things of the world in nature, but I have found Thee in Thy Word, and I rejoice in finding Thee. Amen.

Therefore if any man be in Christ, he is a new creature:
old things are passed away; behold, all things are become new.
2 CORINTHIANS 5:17

Frankly, I am quite tired of those who tout Christianity as a way to stop smoking or drinking or break wild habits of the world. Is that all Christianity is, to keep us from some bad habit? Of course, regeneration will clean us up, and the new birth will make a man right. If that is what Christianity is all about, what about the person whose life is not that bad?

The purpose of God in redemption is to restore us again to the divine imperative of worship. We were created to worship, but sin destroyed that ability. Jesus Christ, on the cross, redeemed us and brought us back to the place where we now can worship and have fellowship with God Almighty.

My clean life is a by-product of my conversion. My life may have pointed out to me that I needed a drastic change, but that is not the purpose for which I was converted. The essence of conversion is to bring me into a right relationship with God and have fellowship with Him.

I rejoice not in my clean life, but in the fellowship I have with Christ. That makes Christianity worth it.

> Once far from God and dead in sin,
> No light my heart could see;
> But in God's Word the light I found,
> Now Christ liveth in me.
>
> DANIEL W. WHITTLE (1840–1901)

Dear heavenly Father, I thank Thee for the wonderful changes in my
life that redemption has made possible. But far more than that,
I praise Thee for Christ living within me day by day.
In Jesus' precious name I pray, amen.

And the Lord God formed man of the dust of the ground,
and breathed into his nostrils the breath of life;
and man became a living soul.
GENESIS 2:7

It is my daily, moment-by-moment fellowship with God that makes me different from all the other things God has created. Some people are intent upon comparing man with animals. As much as they try, they cannot get over man being the only creature that worships God. It is our worship that brings us into fellowship with God.

The Methodists conquered the world with their joyous religion because they were first and foremost worshipers. When they ceased to be worshipers, their religion ceased to have the same effect and power they used to have.

Looking at it this way, Christianity is vague, broad and comprehensive. It takes in the whole nature of God. God desires me to be regenerated in order that I might be capable of worship that is acceptable to Him.

Yes, redemption has cleansed me from my sin. The purpose of that cleansing, however, is to bring me into fellowship with God. Nothing is more important than this. Nothing takes precedence over this. Redemption brought me into favor with God, and that favor has established an intimate communion with God.

O measureless Might, ineffable Love,
While angels delight to hymn Thee above,
The humbler creation, though feeble their lays,
With true adoration shall sing to Thy praise.

ROBERT GRANT (1779–1838)

Eternal God, I come to Thee in the precious name of the Lord Jesus
Christ. My heart is filled with an eternal longing for Thy presence.
Honor me today with Your presence. Amen.

And they thirsted not when he led them through the deserts: he caused the waters to flow out of the rock for them: he clave the rock also, and the waters gushed out.
ISAIAH 48:21

God created you to worship Him, and when Fundamentalism lost her power to worship, she invented religious claptrap to make her happy. That is why I have hated it, preached against it and condemned it all down these years. Some are coming around to my position, who used to be afraid to say anything or stand up against this claptrap. Ventriloquists with dummies on their knees are supposedly worshiping God. Claiming to serve the Lord, but their only joy is of the flesh.

The well of the Holy Ghost is an effervescent artisan well, and you do not have to prime the pump. They that worship Him must worship Him in spirit and in truth. The silver waters of the Holy Ghost flooding up out of the redeemed and cleansed heart of the worshiping man is as sweet and beautiful to God as the loveliest diamond you can find.

This generation needs to rediscover how to worship. I, for my part, am committed to do everything I can to turn people, young people in particular, away from all niceties and come to the place of worshiping the living God as He desires and expects to be worshiped.

> All my life long I had panted
> For a drink from some cool spring
> That I hoped would quench the burning
> Of the thirst I felt within.
> Hallelujah! I have found Him
> Whom my soul so long has craved!
> Jesus satisfies my longings;
> Through His blood I now am saved.
> CLARA T. WILLIAMS (1858–1937)

Dear Lord Jesus, let me never fail Thee in the area of worship. May worship be the high priority of my life, and may I bring it into complete conformity to the truth of Thyself. Amen.

And every creature which is in heaven, and on the earth,
and under the earth, and such as are in the sea, and all that are in them,
heard I saying, Blessing, and honour, and glory, and power, be unto him that sitteth
upon the throne, and unto the Lamb for ever and ever.
REVELATION 5:13

I have a passion to know God. What I have discovered is that God never does anything without purpose. The great central purpose of God, in all His rich, golden glory, was that He might make worshipers out of those who were at one time His enemies.

That He might take those whose backs were turned away and turn their faces toward Him again. That He might persuade those moral beings who had forgotten how to worship and turn them around again in ecstatic and rapturous adoration before the presence of the triune God.

The purpose of Christ in redemption was not primarily to save us from hell, but to save us unto worship that we might be worshipers of the living God. Worship is the normal employment of moral beings. Moral beings worship God as naturally and normally as the birds sing.

Look in the Bible and you will find that every glimpse of heaven shows people worshiping God. Sin destroyed that natural passion, but Jesus Christ, through His redemptive work on the cross, restored to us that wonderful passion we like to call worship. The whole atmosphere of heaven when we get there will be worship, and only the redeemed heart will be able to join in.

"Worthy is the Lamb," the hosts of heaven sing,
As before the throne they make His praises ring;
"Worthy is the Lamb the book to open wide;
Worthy is the Lamb who once was crucified."

JOHNSON OATMAN, JR. (1856–1922)

O God in heaven above, I worship Thee on earth below with a passion
inspired by Thy holy book. Thy face I long to see, and I wait patiently
before Thee. In the name of Jesus I pray, amen.

February 16

Saying, Blessed be the King that cometh in the name of the Lord:
peace in heaven, and glory in the highest.
LUKE 19:38

If we could just get a little peek into heaven, just cup our ear to listen and hear what is going on now, we would see and hear all of heaven and the inhabitants thereof worshiping God. Some people expect to go to heaven and live in a wonderful mansion. I suspect some of those people will be greatly disappointed when they realize that the whole atmosphere of heaven and the whole purpose of heaven will be to worship, adore and admire the Lord God Almighty.

In the Gospels, we have an incident of Jesus approaching Jerusalem and the whole multitude of the disciples began to rejoice and praise God with a loud voice for all the mighty works they had seen.

Some of the Pharisees from among the multitude told Jesus to rebuke His disciples. But Jesus told them that if these should hold their peace, the stones would cry out to God.

It is a moral imperative, my brother and sister, that God will have somebody worshiping Him if He has to raise up a talking, shouting, singing stone.

> "Worthy is the Lamb," let men and angels sing,
> "Worthy is the Lamb," let hallelujahs ring;
> And when life is past, upon the golden shore,
> "Worthy is the Lamb," we'll shout forevermore.
>
> JOHNSON OATMAN, JR. (1856–1922)

Our heavenly Father, what joy comes to my heart in
realizing that all of heaven joins together with us to
sing of Thy praises. Praise ye the Lord! Amen.

And they rose up early on the morrow, and offered burnt offerings,
and brought peace offerings; and the people sat down
to eat and to drink, and rose up to play.
EXODUS 32:6

Worship belongs to heaven and to all beings that are moral beings. It belongs not to the bees, to the birds that fly or the worms that crawl, but to all beings with moral perception and intelligence. It is the business of our tongues to be worshiping God, and when we do not, we are guilty of offending God.

Worship is the missing jewel in evangelicalism today. The church today has decked herself with everything to amuse and entertain. Entertainment, I contend, is the curse of the church. It is the devil's replacement for worship. If only Christians would understand that you cannot come into the presence of God with entertainment on your mind. All of that must be pushed aside in a very disciplined and deliberate manner. It is either entertainment or it is worship. Just as you cannot mix oil and water, so you cannot mix the oil of the Holy Spirit with the watered-down religion passing for Christianity today.

Whatever the cost, everything that competes with and contradicts the spirit of worship must be eliminated from the church. Where are those courageous enough to stand against the tide and raise once again the banner of the Lord?

Stand up and bless the Lord
Ye people of His choice;
Stand up and bless the Lord your God
With heart and soul and voice.

JAMES MONTGOMERY (1771–1854)

Heavenly Father, with so much to distract us from Thee,
I yield myself to the directing power of the Holy Spirit as He guides me
toward You. May my heart this day rest in Thy presence.
In the name of Jesus, I pray, amen.

Give unto the Lord, ye kindreds of the people, give unto the Lord glory and strength.
Give unto the Lord the glory due unto his name: bring an offering,
and come before him, worship the Lord in the beauty of holiness.
1 CHRONICLES 16:28-29

As I look around the country, I see a tremendous church-building boom. Now, do not get me wrong, I am glad for every church building that goes up.

These new church buildings have the latest technology and gadgets that money can buy. No expense has been spared in these buildings. Not only the technology, but also the architecture and the decorations are such as to take a person's breath away. I am one of the first to appreciate the beauty of anything. I have visited some of the most beautiful cathedrals in this country and have stood amazed at the beauty.

One thought grips my heart: At what cost are these buildings being erected and decked with all this beauty?

We have everything; but one shining gem has been lost to the church.

I believe this gem has been lost to the evangelical church of our day. Worship is the missing jewel in evangelicalism, and the awesome, wonderful jewel with its mysterious luster has been all but lost to us. We meet together and go through the rituals and forms of worshiping God, but I am afraid we have forgotten to worship God.

Sing to the Lord of harvest, sing songs of love and praise;
With joyful hearts and voices your alleluias raise:
By Him the rolling seasons in fruitful order move;
Sing to the Lord of harvest, a joyful song of love.

JOHN S. B. MONSELL (1811-1875)

O God and Father of our Lord and Savior Jesus Christ, forgive me for becoming so enthralled with my surroundings that I forget to look up and gaze into Thy face. The radiance of Thy face is all I really need. Amen.

Then flew one of the Seraphims unto me, having a live coal in his hand, which he had taken with the tongs from off the altar: and he laid it upon my mouth, and said, Lo, this hath touched thy lips; and thine iniquity is taken away, and thy sin purged.
ISAIAH 6:6-7

Trying to understand God and His nature, we often refer to fire. Physical fire is not God, and God warned about worshiping fire. We are not fire worshipers, but we recognize that God dwells in fire.

In the Old Testament, the symbolism of fire abounds. In the New Testament, it begins on the day of Pentecost when the Holy Spirit came and sat upon them in cloven tongues of fire. Then in the book of Revelation, we have the candlesticks and the fire resting upon them.

As fire, the Holy Spirit burns deep into our nature, purifying us of everything that contradicts the holiness of God. The fire of the Holy Spirit enables us to be the witness in our generation that He desires us to be. The fire only burns that which is contrary to the holy nature of God.

The fire did not hurt the three Hebrew children in the fiery furnace. Even though they were immersed in the fire, when they came out, they did not even smell of smoke. Oh, we need fire today! We need Christians who are so endued with the fire of the Holy Spirit that people fall prostrate on their knees crying, "Holy, holy, holy!"

God sent His mighty power to this poor, sinful heart,
To keep me ev'ry hour, and needful grace impart;
And since His Spirit came, to take supreme control,
The love enkindled flame is burning in my soul.

DELIA T. WHITE (N.D.)

I beseech thee, O Holy Spirit, fall upon this barren heart of mine and set it all aglow with passion for God. In Jesus' name, amen.

Be not afraid of sudden fear, neither of the desolation of the wicked,
when it cometh. For the Lord shall be thy confidence,
and shall keep thy foot from being taken.
PROVERBS 3:25-26

One key factor to our personal worship is boundless confidence in the character of God. I believe this is the foundation of much of our worship today. We must have respect in God's character, in the being of God, and our worship rises or falls dependent upon the idea that the church has of God.

It seems that from one generation to the next our idea of God changes. God does not change, but somehow our ideas of God and our confidence in God changes to the effect that the God we worship today is less than the God our fathers worshiped.

The evangelical concept of God is very low today. The God of the evangelical church is so small that we can put Him in our pocket or put Him up on the dashboard of our cars to keep from having accidents. So our God today is not much bigger than St. Christopher. The God of popular Christianity cannot be worshipped because He can't be respected. He cannot be respected because He is not big enough.

I refuse to worship any God but the God of the Bible.

Precious secret, I have found it,
Precious Jesus, Thou art mine;
Prove in me Thy boundless fullness;
Live in me Thy life divine.

A. B. SIMPSON (1843-1919)

Thou, O God, art bigger than my mind could ever comprehend.
The beauty of Thy wondrous fullness fills my heart with gratitude that
is all but inexpressible. This I pray in Jesus' name. Amen.

Great is the Lord, and greatly to be praised;
and his greatness is unsearchable.
One generation shall praise thy works to another,
and shall declare thy mighty acts.
PSALM 145:3-4

The sovereign God of our fathers that we sing about is incomparable to that which we call God today. We have lost the sense of who God really is and have replaced our fathers' God with an artificial God that only soothes our conscience in a temporary fashion.

This new God is the God of convenience and entertainment. All this God is interested in is making one happy and feeling good about oneself. If I am not good, I do not want to feel good about myself. I want to feel about myself as God feels about me.

I am all for getting back to believing that our God is bigger than we will ever need. If I cannot respect someone, I certainly cannot worship him. The God of the Bible is such a God I can respect. With my open Bible before me, and prostrate on the ground before God, I begin to experience this God that is big enough for me, and that settles it.

Faith of our fathers, living still
In spite of dungeon, fire and sword;
O how our hearts beat high with joy
Whene'er we hear that glorious Word!
FREDERICK W. FABER (1814–1863)

Dear God of Abraham, Isaac and Jacob, not the God of the scientist,
philosopher or even psychologist. Thou art the God I worship today
in the beauty of Thy holiness. Amen.

I had fainted, unless I had believed to see the goodness of the Lord in the land of the living. Wait on the Lord: be of good courage, and he shall strengthen thine heart: wait, I say, on the Lord.
PSALM 27:13-14

God has made us with the ability to admire, and then He has given Himself to live as the object of our boundless, unlimited admiration.

If you were to bring a canary into a sanctuary and play the piano, I do not believe the canary would sing with the piano. That canary certainly would not be able to understand the beauty of music, as certainly as the lower creatures have not in them the ability to appreciate nor admire, as we do.

Our ability to admire God is the one thing distinguishing us from all other of God's creations. This ability can grow in knowledge and depth and fill the heart with wonder and delight just to admire God.

I once heard a man pray and say, "O God, save us from people and big shots." We have a tendency to admire people and big shots. Our powers of admiration should be reserved for God, and God alone. He is the object of our admiration, and when we admire Him, we are doing what He created us to do.

> God is my strong salvation,
> What foe have I to fear?
> In darkness and temptation
> My light, my help is near.
> JAMES MONTGOMERY (1771-1854)

O God, we've heard man's voice and are weary.
Speak down to us, Lord, for I want to admire Thee.
In Jesus' name, amen.

I will praise thee; for I am fearfully and wonderfully made:
marvellous are thy works; and that my soul knowest right well.
PSALM 139:14

Certain passages in Milton and Shakespeare are so great that the average rank and file cannot rise to take it in. It is too big and wonderful. When we admire enough, it becomes a delightful pain. It becomes an enjoyable agony within the bosom. Why agony? Because we are not big enough inside.

God's desire is to make us bigger. He is going to make us all call upon Him to enlarge our hearts in order to take Him in, in all His fullness.

He wants to make us big enough to admire Him with wonder and delight. This wonder and delight is followed by sheer fascination. This is to be filled with the moral excitement that only God can bring.

I often wonder why many people who sing hymns are not affected by them; why they hear the Scriptures and are unaffected by them. When they pray, it is in a monstrous drone. Nothing seems to affect them. Nothing seems to excite them. Nothing seems to rise up within them with admiring excitement and wonder.

To be dead on the inside is the curse of sin. But for the man or woman who has been made alive on the inside, hymns, Scripture and prayer take them to heights of delightful admiration of the Godhead.

> So shall it be at last, in that bright morning,
> When the soul waketh and life's shadows flee;
> Oh, in that hour, fairer than daylight dawning,
> Shall rise the glorious thought, I am with Thee.
> HARRIET BEECHER STOWE (1811–1896)

O God of glory, my heart is thrilled to sing of Thee. My heart rises to heights of delightful praise and worship as I meditate upon Thee. Amen.

Praise ye the Lord. O give thanks unto the Lord; for he is good:
for his mercy endureth for ever. Who can utter the mighty acts of the Lord?
Who can shew forth all his praise?
PSALM 106:1-2

I firmly believe there is an excitement about love and admiration that captivates and charms the Christian who has ever seen God in holy worship—who has been struck with astonished wonder at the inconceivable elevation and the magnitude and splendor of that being we call God.

This is tragically absent in our present generation. Certainly, there are spots here and there where men and women have found such worship, but it is not common. What is common is a drastic lack of enthusiasm toward God. We are enthusiastic toward everything except God.

I earnestly pray that God will send this to us once again in this generation. I pray that God will send us a man out of the fire—men who walk up and down in the midst of the stones of fire. A person can come back to the world from this fire, not to be a great founder or great promoter or great preacher, but one whose presence with us is as the presence of an angel.

Let's just get excited about God!

Let's talk about Jesus,
The King of kings is He;
The Lord of lords supreme,
Through all eternity;
The great I Am, the Way,
The Truth, the Life, the Door,
Let's talk about Jesus more and more.

HERBERT BUFFUM (1879-1939)

Dear Lord Jesus, I never tire of acknowledging Thy greatness
in my life. Today may I lift Thee up so that all may see
the greatness of Thee. Amen.

And when I saw him, I fell at his feet as dead.
And he laid his right hand upon me, saying unto me, fear not;
I am the first and the last: I am he that liveth, and was dead;
and, behold, I am alive for evermore, Amen;
and have the keys of hell and of death.
REVELATION 1:17-18

When they looked upon Stephen as they were stoning him, they saw his face as the face of an angel shining. He said, I see Jesus lifted up, I see Him standing, And Stephen's face shone. The shining face of Stephen has done more to illuminate the church of the living God than 10,000 theologians and cold teachers of the law.

Certainly, Stephen was the first Christian to endure the full blast of Satan's hatred. Thank God, he came to that fire victoriously.

We need bold, terrible men. We need men and women who have fought their way to endure scorn and may even have been called fanatics—scoffed at and called everything but a Christian. We need men and women today who are willing to push in and beat their way past the flesh, the world and the devil, and cold Christians and deacons and elders. They will have to push themselves until they are fascinated by what they see in Christ.

Those who have truly seen Christ in His glory have eyes for nothing else.

No condemnation now I dread;
Jesus, and all in Him, is mine!
Alive in Him, my living Head,
And clothed in righteousness divine,
Bold I approach th' eternal throne,
And claim the crown. through Christ, my own.

CHARLES WESLEY (1707–1788)

I come to Thee, O God, with praise in my heart
and wonder at Thy splendor. Oh, how I am thrilled by Thy presence
in my heart today! Thank you, Jesus. Amen.

Who shall ascend into the hill of the Lord?
Or who shall stand in his holy place?
He that hath clean hands, and a pure heart;
who has not lifted up his soul unto vanity,
nor sworn deceitfully.
PSALM 24:3-4

Elijah walked off the mountain, girded about his loins with a leather girdle, and into the presence of the king, and said, "I am Elijah. I stand in the presence of God."

That is why Elijah could command fire when the occasion required it. Ezekiel, before God ever allowed him to be a preacher at all, had to have his experience with the fire. Isaiah, before he could ever write his great book, had to see God high and lifted up with his train filling the temple, and had to hear the vibrant voice of the seraphim crying, Holy, Holy, Holy is the Lord God Almighty.

Oh, that God might raise up people like that! I would follow the man with oil on his forehead, and the man with the flame that sits there, and I care not what denomination he calls himself.

The fascination, the inconceivable brightness, the unbelievable elevation, the magnitude of the splendor of God, when it shines in upon the human heart, changes things, and we are not what we used to be.

Refresh Thy people on their toilsome way;
Lead us from night to never ending day;
Fill all our lives with love and grace divine;
And glory, laud, and praise be ever Thine. Amen.

DANIEL C. ROBERTS (1841–1907)

Dear God and Father of our Lord Jesus Christ, blessings from Thy
throne have filled my heart with uncontrollable praise.
Glory, glory, glory to God in the highest! Amen.

For Christ is not entered into the holy places made with hands,
which are the figures of the true; but into heaven itself,
now to appear in the presence of God for us.
HEBREWS 9:24

Adoration is the state of adoring; it means to love with all the power within us. It means to live with fear and wonder and yearning. Our trouble is that we have hearts as big as the world, but the objects of our love are all little peas in the pod. That is what is the matter with people out in the world. God has given them the ability to love, and they cannot find anything worthy of their love.

Out in Hollywood the heart leaps like a drunken bird from one branch to another. It jumps here and there, shrugs it off and often jumps until he or she is married as much as 3 or 4, or 8 or 10 times, because he or she is trying to find something to love and cannot find anything worthy of his or her love.

God made us too big inside. God set eternity in our hearts; and even the fallen man searches for an object worthy of his love.

That is why I grieve when I see people who are made in the image of God off on a little sidetrack doing silly, foolish things—literally spending their lives doing things unworthy of them.

Jesus, our only joy be Thou,
As Thou our prize wilt be;
Jesus, be Thou our glory now,
And through eternity.

ATTR. TO BERNARD OF CLAIRVAUX,
TRANS. EDWARD CASWALL (1814–1878)

My God and Father, my heart yearns for Thee,
and nothing but Thee will fill my heart. I have known such emptiness,
and then I found Thee; and oh, how my heart praises the wonder
and majesty of Thy presence in my heart! Amen.

I am the good shepherd, and know my sheep, and am known of mine.
As the Father knoweth me, even so know I the Father:
and I lay down my life for the sheep.
JOHN 10:14-15

When Jesus walked among men, He affected them in two ways. He affected them with a magnetic yearning and a fear that repulsed. The same heart that yearned for God with a great yearning and awesome fear might have been repulsed by the greatness and elevation and magnitude of the being we call God.

Go through your Bible and see how many times men say "mine." Some tell us we should not use personal pronouns in religion. We can use it about ourselves and about what we have done, where we have been, who we know and what we own; but we should never use it about a relationship to God.

Martin Luther, the great theologian, said that wholehearted religion lies in its personal pronoun. When the human heart cries with the psalmist, a prophet, an apostle or a mystic, it cries out "God is mine." And when the human heart worships God and says "mine," God responds by saying, "Yes, I am. I am yours."

There is nothing as personal as my relationship with God enabling me to worship in a way that pleases and delights Him. Every place and every time and every task is hallowed by His presence.

> The King of my love my Shepherd is,
> Whose goodness faileth never;
> I nothing lack if I am His,
> And He is mine forever.
>
> HENRY W. BAKER (1821–1877)

O God, Thou art mine in ways in which I am just beginning to understand.
As I pursue Thee today, may I rest in Thy presence as one who
truly belongs there. In Jesus' name I pray. Amen.

February 29

Be still, and know that I am God:
I will be exalted among the heathen,
I will be exalted in the earth.
PSALM 46:10

When talking about a burden, Jesus was referring to the burden of the tuneless heart, the burden of the voiceless nightingale. It was the burden of the heart capable of tremendous, infinite love, which could not find an object for that love. It was the burden of the man whose tongue was made to praise God, but has been silent in his mouth for all these years.

I believe in schools and I support them. I believe, however, that you will learn more in a half hour of adoring silence in the presence of God, with your Bible, than you will learn in all the schools you could ever attend. While you spend time adoring God, caught between fear and fascination, between joy and the sharp pangs of repentance, you will learn more about life than you will ever find at any other time.

To know God is not a matter of education, but of illumination. The stairwell to illumination is utter fascination in the presence of God. Push out all other activities and come in silent wonder and admiration in the presence of God. Then God will open up His heart and illuminate Himself to you.

Be still, my soul; the Lord is on thy side;
Bear patiently the cross of grief or pain;
Leave to thy God to order or provide;
In every change He faithful will remain.

KATHARINA A. D. VON SCHLEGEL (1697–1768),
TRANS. JANE L. BORTHWICK (1813–1897)

Dear Lord Jesus, I wait before Thee in the stillness of anticipation.
Teach me that which will draw me closer to Thee.
I rest firmly and joyously in Thy heart. Amen.

The Lord has prepared his throne in the heavens;
and his kingdom rules over all. Bless the Lord, ye his Angels,
that excel in strength, that do his commandments,
hearkening unto the voice of his word.
PSALM 103:19-20

Some argue and give themselves up to science; some give themselves up to technology, some to philosophy, some to the arts and some to music. When we worship the Lord Jesus Christ, we embrace and encompass all possible sciences and philosophies and arts.

He is the Lord of all life, so that He is the Lord of all essential possibilities of life. He is the Lord of all kinds of life. He is the Lord of the intellectual life, the life of imagination and reason. He is Lord over all these things.

We have spiritual life, and He is the Lord of that kind of life. He is the Lord of angels and the Lord of the cherubim and seraphim.

All deep eternal wisdom lies in Jesus Christ as a treasure hidden away, and there is not any kind of wisdom outside of Him. All the deep eternal purposes of God are in Him, because His perfect wisdom enables Him to plan ahead, and all history is the slow development of His purposes.

Though He giveth or He taketh,
God His children ne'er forsaketh,
His the loving purpose solely
To preserve them pure and holy.
CAROLINA V. SANDELL BERG (1832–1903)

Dear heavenly Father, my life rests securely in Thy hand.
Thy provision goes far beyond my ability to comprehend.
I thank Thee for what Thou doest in my life.
In Jesus' name, amen.

For he saith to Moses, I will have mercy on whom I will have mercy,
and I will have compassion on whom I will have compassion.
So then it is not of him that willeth, nor of him that runneth,
but of God that showeth mercy.
ROMANS 9:15-16

There is no book you can read about Christian ethics or any other kind of ethics, which is another way of saying righteousness, that God does not already know and that He is not already Lord of.

In the Old Testament, when the high priest went into the holy of holies to offer sacrifices once a year, he wore a miter on his forehead. On that miter was engraved in Hebrew the words, "Holiness unto the Lord." This Jesus Christ our Lord is Lord of holiness and righteousness in every degree.

He is Lord of all mercy, for He establishes His kingdom upon rebels, of whom He first has to redeem and win, and renew a right spirit within them. He renews these rebels and makes them righteous and gives them the right spirit because He is the Lord of all mercy, and He is the Lord of all power, and He is the Lord of all deity.

Only this kind of Lord can do this kind of thing. Nothing stands in His way of accomplishing His purposes. The devil, in all of his hellish glory, cannot in one measure diminish the purpose of God.

Near the cross, a trembling soul,
Love and mercy found me;
There the bright and Morning Star
Shed its beams around me.

FANNY J. CROSBY (1820–1915)

Dear Lord Jesus, when Thee found me, I was a rebel going in
the wrong direction. Praise Thy name, Thee not only found me,
but Thee turned my life around, and now I face heaven's light. Amen.

Who hath believed our report? And to whom is the arm of the Lord revealed? For he shall grow up before him as a tender plant, and as a root out of a dry ground: he hath no form nor comeliness; and when we shall see him, there is no beauty that we should desire him.

ISAIAH 53:1-2

God put something in the human breast that is capable of understanding and appreciating beauty. God put in us the love of harmonious forms, the love and appreciation of color and beautiful sound. He also put in us the love of moral forms of singing and color. All things that are beautiful to the eye and to the ear are only the external counterparts of that inner beauty which is moral beauty.

It was said of Jesus Christ our Lord, that there was no beauty in Him that we should desire Him, and He was just a man among men. Artists have painted Jesus as a very pretty man, a man with a tender, feminine face and clear beautiful eyes and an open delightful countenance with curly hair streaming down His shoulders.

When the religious leaders sought to crucify Him, they needed to arrange with Judas Iscariot to betray Him. If he had looked as beautiful physically as He is painted, why was it necessary that He had to be betrayed with a kiss?

The beauty of Jesus that has charmed the centuries is His moral beauty.

Hail, Thou once despised Jesus! Hail, Thou Galilean King!
Thou didst suffer to release us, Thou didst free salvation bring.
Hail, Thou universal Saviour, bearer of our sin and shame!
By Thy merit we find favour; life is given through Thy name.

JOHN BAKEWELL (1721–1819)

Blessed Lord Jesus, Thy beauty is far beyond my human mind to grasp. Deep in my redeemed heart, I have discovered the merits of Thy beauty and it has overwhelmed me to the point of adoration. Amen.

He hath made every thing beautiful in his time:
also he has set the world in their heart, so that no man can find out
the work that God maketh from the beginning to the end.

ECCLESIASTES 3:11

Sin has scarred this world and made it inharmonious, unsymmetrical and ugly. When rough men say something is as ugly as hell, they are using the proper and valid comparison, because hell is that against which all ugliness is measured. If you love beautiful things, you had better stay out of hell. Hell will be the epitome of all that is morally ugly; and I believe it will be the ugliest place in the world.

Heaven is a place of harmonious numbers. Heaven is the place of loveliness; heaven is the place of beauty, because the One who is all-beautiful is there. He is the Lord of all beauty, and the earth lies between all that is ugly in hell and all that is beautiful in heaven.

I suppose we will have it like this as long as we are living in this world. Some may wonder why it is like that. Why is it ugliness and beauty? Why is there so much good and so much bad? Why is there that which is pleasant and that which is tragic and hard to live with?

Because the earth lies halfway between heaven and hell. The earth lies halfway between heaven's beauty and hell's ugliness.

For the beauty of the earth,
For the glory of the skies,
For the love which from our birth
Over and around us lies.
Lord of all, to Thee we raise
This our hymn of grateful praise.

FOLLIOTT S. PIERPOINT (1835–1917)

Dear God and Father of our Lord Jesus Christ,
Thy beauty is the beauty of joyous harmony.
Nothing compares to the beauty I have discovered in Thee. Amen.

But whoso hath this world's good, and seeth his brother have need,
and shutteth up his bowels of compassion from him, how dwelleth the love of God
in him? My little children, let us not love in word, neither in tongue;
but in deed and in truth.
1 JOHN 3:17-18

A man once asked me if I thought a Christian could hurt another Christian. I did not have to think very long, and I responded in the positive. Is there anybody in church that has not been hurt by some other Christian, and maybe a dedicated Christian at that?

Why is it that a man will be on his knees praying earnestly one day, and the next day he will hurt another Christian? Why this inconsistency? Should not Christians be immune to this kind of activity?

The sad answer is that we are halfway between heaven and hell.

I like to think these things are not done intentionally and that Christians are looking out for each other. Nevertheless, the tyranny of the world affects us in ways like this.

I need to examine my own heart to make sure that my inner harmony with the Lord Jesus Christ is reflected by my outward harmony with brothers and sisters in the Lord. This does not happen automatically but is a result of my daily discipline and worship of God. That which is on the inside will eventually come out on the outside. This becomes the challenge of my daily walk with my brothers and sisters in the Lord.

Down in the human heart, crushed by the tempter,
Feelings lie buried that grace can restore;
Touched by a loving heart, wakened by kindness,
Chords that were broken will vibrate once more.

FANNY J. CROSBY (1820–1915)

My heavenly Father, Thy touch has awakened within me feelings of
kindness toward my fellow man. O, Holy Spirit, guide me as I
reach out in love and mercy to those around me. Amen.

Thus saith God the Lord, he that created the heavens, and stretched them out;
he that spread forth the earth, and that which cometh out of it; he that giveth breath
unto the people upon it, and spirit to them that walk therein:
I the Lord have called thee in righteousness, and will hold thine hand, and will keep thee,
and give thee for a covenant of the people, for a light of the Gentiles.

ISAIAH 42:5-6

When we go back far enough and trace the cause-and-effect factors, we will discover the One who made them, which is God.

Back of all previous matter—all life, all law and all time—there is God. God gives to human life its only significance. To rule God out is to bring man to a state of utter confusion and an identity crisis. This seems to be where the majority of humanity is today. They have lost their purpose in living and are frantically searching for some reason to exist.

If you take the concept of God, the thought of God, out of the human mind, there is no other reason for being or for living. Men have tried to explore a variety of avenues to justify their existence. Entertainment, for one, comes to mind. Entertainment is the devil's replacement for worship.

A Creator has created us for His purpose. If we do not discover His purpose, we will never understand our purpose in this world. The overwhelming majority of humanity today does not understand what their purpose is in this world.

Praise to the Lord, who with marvelous wisdom hath made Thee!
Decked thee with health, and with loving hand guided and stayed thee;
How oft in grief hath He not brought thee relief,
Spreading His wings for to shade thee.

JOACHIM NEANDER (1650–1680)

Blessed be the God and father of our Lord Jesus Christ, who has brought
into my life purpose designed from before time began. I honor Thee today
with my life in fulfillment of Thy great purpose in me. Amen.

He that hath an ear, let him hear what the Spirit saith unto the churches;
to him that overcometh will I give to eat of the hidden manna,
and will give him a white stone, and in the stone a new name written,
which no man knoweth saving he that receiveth it.
REVELATION 2:17

I am often reminded of what Sam Jones, the famous preacher of another generation, said: "When the average preacher takes a text it reminds me of an insect trying to carry a bale of cotton." That has served to admonish me for many years in my preaching. Some take preaching to be a very casual, entertaining thing. I do not.

I am no more aware of this truth than when it comes to talking about God.

Let me say very simply that without a pure heart and a surrendered mind, no man can preach worthily about God. Quite often this truth has brought me to my knees. I am no more worthy to preach about God than anybody.

Another side of this truth is that without a pure heart and a worthy mind, no person can hear about God worthily. It goes both ways. No man can hear these things unless God touches and illuminates him.

My greatest challenge is twofold. When I come to the pulpit, I must come prepared worthily to speak about God and so prepare the congregation to such an extent that they can worthily hear the truth about God.

Teach me Thy way, O Lord, teach me Thy way!
Thy guiding grace afford, teach me Thy way!
Help me to walk aright, more by faith, less by sight;
Lead me with heav'nly light, teach me Thy way!
BENJAMIN M. RAMSEY (1849–1923)

O Holy Spirit, my heart compels me to preach Thy Word,
but my mind succumbs to the inadequacy of my preaching.
Guide me and empower me to preach in such a way as to glorify
our Father which art in heaven. In the precious name of Jesus, amen.

*And thou, Solomon my son, know thou the God of thy father,
and serve him with a perfect heart and with a willing mind:
for the Lord searcheth all hearts, and understandeth all the imaginations
of the thoughts: if thou seek him, he will be found of thee;
but if thou forsake him, he will cast thee off for ever.*

1 CHRONICLES 28:9

I only have one hope in life—to be used of God. As the poor little donkey rebuked the madness of the prophet, and as the rooster's crow aroused an apostle and brought him to repentance, I pray that God may be willing to use such an unworthy instrument as I.

The more highly we think of ourselves and our abilities and our talents, the less God can use us.

Today we have education and technology and talents, and the thought is that all of these things have to be used by God. I am so glad that is not the case. If that were the case, someone like me would have no use in the Master's hand. But oh, thank God that is not the case! I gladly get in line with the donkey and the rooster as God used them. The beautiful thing about the donkey and the rooster, they had no idea how God was using them.

One of the great delights in heaven, in my opinion, will be learning for the first time exactly how God used us, and that He did in fact use us.

Use me today, O Savior divine!
Cleanse and renew this servant of Thine.
Lord, with thy Spirit fill me, I pray;
Then, in thy service, use me today.

GERTRUDE R. DUGAN (1918–2009)

*I pray, O God, that Thou might humble me and bring me back to earth
so that I understand that I am just an instrument in Thy hands.
Use me as Thou see fit. In the name of Jesus, I pray, amen.*

March 9

Therefore they say unto God, Depart from us;
for we desire not the knowledge of thy ways.
JOB 21:14

It is utterly necessary that we know this God that John the apostle wrote about, that the poets speak about, that theology tries to explain. This One we call our Father which art in heaven. A correct concept of God needs to be restored to the church today.

Man fell when he lost his right concept of God. Satan brought that about. As long as man trusted God, everything was all right. Human beings were healthy and holy, or at least innocent and pure and good, and everything was all right. Then the devil came along and threw a question mark into the mind of Eve.

"Yea, hath God said, . . ." which was equivalent to sneaking behind God's back and casting a reflection on the goodness and character of God. That is where the progressive degeneration began. Some speak of evolution—that man is on his way up; but history shows us that man is on his way down. Degeneration is the plight of mankind today.

When the knowledge of God began to go out of the minds of man, we got into the moral and spiritual fix that we are in now.

Savior, more than life to me,
I am clinging, clinging close to Thee;
Let Thy precious blood applied
Keep me ever, ever near Thy side.
FANNY J. CROSBY (1820-1915)

I know Thee, O God, and I long to know Thee more.
The knowledge of the holy is my pursuit today.
Let me never flag in this pursuit. Amen.

March 10

Yea doubtless, and I count all things but loss for the excellency of the knowledge of Christ Jesus my Lord: for whom I have suffered the loss of all things, and do count them but dung, that I may win Christ.
PHILIPPIANS 3:8

When man loses his confidence in the character of God, he begins his downward plunge. When that happens, you get all mixed up about what God is like, and the only way back is to have a restored confidence in God.

The only way we can have a restored confidence in God is to have a restored knowledge of God. This cannot be overemphasized. We need to get to know God, the God who has revealed Himself in the Word of God.

If we do not know God or what kind of a God He is, we are not going to have confidence in anything He says. If we cannot trust what He says, He no longer has an influence in our life and the development of our years.

It is one thing to read about George Müller and his faith, and it is surely inspiring. But to have George Müller's faith, you would have to become George Müller. If we are going to have God's faith, we are going to have to have Him get into our life and work through us. To know God as He desires and deserves to be known is to have a confidence in Him that expresses itself in a life of faith.

Jesus is all the world to me, my life, my Joy, my all;
He is my strength from day to day, without Him I would fall.
When I am sad, to Him I go, no other one can cheer me so;
When I am sad, He makes me glad, He's my Friend.
WILL L. THOMPSON (1847–1909)

My precious Lord and Savior, Jesus Christ, I have found Thee to be a friend above all other friends. The more I know Thee, the more I long for Thee. The more I long for Thee, the more my heart sings Thy praise. Amen.

For I am not ashamed of the gospel of Christ:
for it is the power of God unto salvation to every one that believeth;
to the Jew first, and also to the Greek. For therein is the righteousness
of God revealed from faith to faith: as it is written,
The just shall live by faith.
ROMANS 1:16-17

If we are not aware of what kind of God our God is, or what He is like, we simply cannot have faith; and so we struggle, wait and hope for faith. Faith does not come, because we do not know the character of God.

Faith, trust and hope are an automatic thing. If we have put our faith and hope and trust in the character of God, it will come naturally. It will flow as naturally as a stream down the mountain. When we know what God is like, that knowledge gets expressed in faith and trust and hope.

The best I could possibly do is simply give you a report on the character of God and tell you what God is like. When I am telling you what God is like, if you are listening with a worthy mind, you will find faith springing up from that knowledge.

Ignorance and unbelief drags faith down, and we can see the results of this all around us, even in the church. A restored knowledge of God will counter this and bring faith up to where it belongs.

O, for a faith that will not shrink,
Though pressed by many a foe,
That will not tremble on the brink
Of any earthly woe.

WILLIAM H. BATHURST (1796-1877)

Dear God, I trust Thee because I know Thee;
and the more I know Thee, the more I trust Thee.
Fill my heart and life with the glory of Thy presence, I pray, amen.

*Many, O Lord my God, are thy wonderful works which thou hast done,
and thy thoughts which are to us-ward: they cannot be reckoned up
in order unto thee: if I would declare and speak of them,
they are more than can be numbered.*

PSALM 40:5

Never has there been a time in the history of the world when we needed more of the knowledge of God. If the average Christian in the average church in America today were to really understand God as He truly is, it would revolutionize American Christianity.

What is needed is revival. A revival is simply gaining an understanding of God and His purpose and desires that we did not know before.

Churches today need to talk more about the core and center and source of all doctrine and theology and truth. This is the greatest need of the hour. We can squabble over all kinds of superficial theological niceties, and that is what we have been doing for at least a generation.

The core of our life is God. Now, what does that mean for the average Christian? What is the difference in the life absolutely focused on God?

If people could see Christians living and acting like Christians whose focus is on God, there would be a tremendous move of God in our country. It is not new technology or new methods or a new message needed, but Christians so focused on God that their life flows in faith.

Revive thy work, O Lord!
And manifest Thy power;
Oh, come upon Thy church and give
A penitential shower!

OSWALD J. SMITH (1889-1986)

*O, Holy Spirit of Pentecost, I need Thee this hour.
Come upon my life and revive me in such a way that those around me
will see the difference and know it is Thee. Amen.*

*And this is life eternal, that they might know thee the only true God,
and Jesus Christ, whom thou hast sent.*
JOHN 17:3

When I started in the ministry, I had to shout through a megaphone in order to be heard. Now we have these little things that look like pens, and you can speak in them and be heard around the world. There is no limit to what we can do in the area of world evangelization.

I cannot keep up with the multiplication of Christian radio and television stations. Christian programming has exploded across this country. Never has there been a time when the gospel has been preached as much as today.

Yet, in spite of all of these good things, most people are just going through the motions, and the reality of Christianity is absent. It is not the good works we do, or the activities we engage in; rather, it is a personal knowledge of God. When we begin to know God, something in our life explodes, and the world begins to notice.

You may be the only tract the world will ever read. Is your life in such accord with God that people can look at you and get to know God?

Not I, but Christ, be honored, loved, exalted;
Not I, but Christ, be seen, be known, be heard;
Not I, but Christ, in every look and action;
Not I, but Christ, in every thought and word.

MRS. ADA A. WHIDDINGTON (1855–1933)

*Dear heavenly Father, although the technology is before us to evangelize
our world, this technology is worthless unless Thou so invade our hearts
and lives that Christ may be seen in us. In Jesus' name, amen.*

I will praise thee with my whole heart: before the gods will I sing praise unto thee.
I will worship toward thy holy temple, and praise thy name for thy lovingkindness
and for thy truth: for thou hast magnified thy word above all thy name.
PSALM 138:1-2

In spite of all the great and wonderful advancements we have seen in the Christian church recently, the losses, although not noticed by many, have been dramatic.

I think I can sum up the loss in the evangelical church by saying this: We have lost our lofty concept of God. Christianity rises like an eagle and flies over the top of all the mountain peaks of all the religions of the world, chiefly because of her lofty concept of God, given to us in divine revelation by the coming of the Son of God who took on human flesh and dwelt among us. In Christianity, the great churches have lived down through the centuries on the character of God. She has preached God, prayed to God, declared God, honored God, elevated God and given witness of God to the world at large.

In recent times, the Church has suffered a loss. We have suffered the loss of that high concept of God. The concept of God held by the average gospel church now is so low as to be unworthy of God and a disgrace to the church.

Change that concept and restore it to its lofty heights, and the church once again will fly above the mountains.

We worship Thee, Lord Christ, our Savior and our King,
To Thee our youth and strength adoringly we bring:
So fill our hearts, that men may see
Thy life in us, and turn to Thee.

E. MARGARET CLARKSON (1915–2008)

My life, O Father, is in Thy hands, and I pray You would
so impact my life that others will begin to know Thee through me.
May my life be the unwritten testimony of Thy grace.
I pray in that name above all names, Jesus. Amen.

He bowed the heavens also, and came down:
and darkness was under his feet.
And he rode upon a cherub, and did fly:
yea, he did fly upon the wings of the wind.
PSALM 18:9-10

I must confess that at times I feel like walking out on a lot that passes for Christianity. When some talk about prayer as going into a huddle with God, you would think God is the coach or the quarterback or something, and they all gather around. God gives the signal, and away they go.

What preposterous abomination! When the old Romans sacrificed the sow on the altar in Jerusalem, they did not commit anything more frightful than when we drag the holy God down and turn Him into a cheap Santa Claus so that we can use Him to get what we want.

At best, God is only the top celebrity. If God were to come to earth now, people would want Him to go on a TV show immediately. If God were to come to earth, they would have a story called "This Is Your Life" and tell God how He got that way. God is only the top celebrity. In the meantime, Christianity has lost its dignity.

Because we have lost our dignity and our concept of Majesty, contemporary religion will never know the dignified, holy God who rides on the wings of the wind and makes the clouds His chariot.

In mansions of glory and endless delight,
I'll ever adore Thee in heaven so bright;
I'll sing with the glittering crown on my brow,
If ever I loved Thee, my Jesus, 'tis now.
WILLIAM R. FEATHERSTONE (1846-1873?)

My Jesus, I love Thee for who Thou art.
Thy beauty is above the cheap religion of our time,
and if ever I needed a glimpse of Thee, O Lord,
it is now. Amen.

Justice and judgment are the habitation of thy throne: mercy and truth shall go before thy face. Blessed is the people that know the joyful sound: they shall walk, O Lord, in the light of thy countenance. In thy name shall they rejoice all the day: and in thy righteousness shall they be exalted.

PSALM 89:14-16

Christianity, if it is anything, is an inward religion, while all other religions are outward. Jesus said that we are to worship in spirit and in truth, and I am wondering if in this generation we have lost the concept of inwardness in our Christianity.

Could it be that we have lost the sense of God's presence?

Nothing is more important to the Christian than living in the presence of God. Living in the conscious presence of God is the delightful occupation of each Christian. Many have lost it and need to regain that magnificent presence of God in their life.

Christians go to church on Sunday and experience the presence of God. But sad to say, when they leave, they leave it behind. Never should we ever leave the sense of God behind. That means we have lost the awe and wonder and holy fear of God. We have lost the sense of delighting in God and His presence.

What would today be without living in the conscious presence of God Almighty? I do not want to live any day when that is absent from my life. Whatever it takes for me to keep in that presence is what I am willing to do.

Jesus, hail! Enthroned in glory, there forever to abide,
All the heav'nly hosts adore Thee, seated at Thy Father's side.
Worship, honor, power and blessing Thou art worthy to receive;
Loudest praises, without ceasing, meet it is for us to give.

JOHN BAKEWELL (1721-1819)

Our Father who art in heaven, Thy presence on earth charms my heart to a wondrous state of gladness. May my day be filled with Thy presence. In Jesus' blessed name, amen.

Until the spirit be poured upon us from on high, and the wilderness be a fruitful field, and the fruitful field be counted for a forest. Then judgment shall dwell in the wilderness, and righteousness remain in the fruitful field. And the work of righteousness shall be peace; and the effect of righteousness quietness and assurance for ever. And my people shall dwell in a peaceable habitation, and in sure dwellings, and in quiet resting places.

ISAIAH 32:15-18

Not long ago, somebody mentioned to me the many gains that have been made in the Christian church. He went through the whole list, and it seemed impressive at the time. Since then, I have given some thought to that. It seems to me that the majority of the gains in the Christian church have been external, while the losses have been internal. They have been the loss of dignity and worship and majesty and awe, along with the inwardness of Christianity and God's presence. Thinking and meditating on this, I am wondering if the losses are worth the gains.

We are in desperate need of a Reformation that will bring the church back to what the old-timers used to call revival. So much of the external claptrap has accumulated over the years that many have not noticed the internal losses.

My prayer is that once again we might become engrossed with the internal aspects of Christianity and less enthusiastic about the external aspects. That we might once again delight in the conscious presence of God. I believe that if this generation of Christians will experience the awesomeness of God's presence in their lives, they never again will be impressed with anything external.

There's a peace in my heart that the world never gave,
A peace it cannot take away;
Though the trials of life may surround like a cloud,
I've a peace that has come here to stay!

ANNE SEBRING MURPHY (1878-1942)

God and Father of our Lord Jesus Christ, I praise Thee
for the peace that is come into my heart through Jesus Christ.
Nothing on the outside compares to Thy presence on my inside. Amen.

And as Moses lifted up the serpent in the wilderness, even so must the Son of man be lifted up: That whosoever believeth in him should not perish, but have eternal life. For God so loved the world, that he gave his only begotten Son, that whosoever believeth in him should not perish, but have everlasting life.

JOHN 3:14-16

I read with a great deal of relish in the Old Testament that when Moses came down off the mountain his face shone with the glory of God. Oh, for that glory once again!

Down through the years, following Pentecost, serious-minded and solemn men, lofty and full of substance and thought and theology typified the preaching of those days. No wonder God moved in His revival splendor among the people of God.

For some reason, the preaching has changed. Some say it has to keep up with the times. I am not so sure that is the reason. Today, much of the preaching is cheap and frivolous and coarse and shallow and entertaining. Many in gospel churches believe that they must entertain the people or they will not come back to church. Men who should know better have lost the seriousness of preaching and have just become silly.

We have lost the loftiness and have become coarse and shallow. We have lost the substance and have become entertainers. Lost, in our preaching, is the sense of lifting up Jesus. We are lifting up everything else but Jesus.

From the cross uplifted high, where the Savior deigns to die,
What melodious songs we hear, bursting on the ravished ear!
Love's redeeming work is done; come and welcome, sinner, come.

THOMAS HAWEIS (1734-1820)

O, Lord Jesus, restore to me a sense of Thy loftiness today. May everything in my life be surrendered to the splendor of Thy exaltation. Amen.

For thus saith the high and lofty One that inhabiteth eternity, whose name is Holy;
I dwell in the high and holy place, with him also that is of a contrite and humble
spirit, to revive the spirit of the humble, and to revive the heart of the contrite ones.
ISAIAH 57:15

I was browsing a used bookstore recently, looking over some of the books that are popular today. I must confess I have never bought a book because it was popular. Sometimes the popular book is the most shallow, at least in my experience.

Looking through these books, I noticed that even in them we have lost substance and have become entertainers. Look at what our Protestant fathers fed on. Many of them were not well educated, but the books they read were the high, holy and devout books written by men enthralled with the presence of God.

They read Taylor's *Holy Living and Dying*; Bunyan's *Pilgrim's Progress* and *Holy War*; Milton's *Paradise Lost*.

I blush today to think about the religious author that is now being handed out to our poor kids.

I pray daily that the spirit of seriousness might fall upon the church once again to such an extent that we will have an insatiable appetite for not only the deep things of God, but for God Himself. When a person nourishes his soul on the high and lofty thoughts of God, he loses his appetite for the watered-down modern-day religion.

Why will ye waste on trifling cares
That life which God's compassion spare;
While, in the various range of thought,
The one thing needful is forgot?
PHILIP DODDRIDGE (1702–1751)

The world, O God, sometimes has me in a nervous twirl.
It is so easy to get caught up with a world opposed to God.
Settle my spirit in Thee today. In Jesus' name, amen.

The words of the wise are as goads, and as nails fastened by
the masters of assemblies, which are given from one shepherd.
And further, by these, my son, be admonished:
of making many books there is no end;
and much study is a weariness of the flesh.
ECCLESIASTES 12:11-12

I would like to be pope for 24 hours, just long enough to get a papal bull going that would read, *I hereby prescribe all religious junk published in the last year to be destroyed.*

As soon as they got rid of all the junk, I would give them some of the great Christian classics to read and say, "Now, you're okay. You have a good start."

I am not sure it is the young people's hope today. They follow what they have been taught. For some reason, the older generation thinks they need to dumb down religion for the young people. I find it otherwise. I believe the young people of today have an appetite for the real thing. When we give them that which is artificial, we do them a great disservice. It is our responsibility as elders in the church to set before these young people the good things of the Lord—to help them establish an appetite for things that will make them strong in the Lord.

Every once in a while, I delight to hear some young man break the ranks and discover for himself one of the great delicacies of the Christian classics.

How long, dear Savior, O how long
Shall this bright hour delay?
Fly swift around, ye wheels of time,
And bring the promised day.

ISAAC WATTS (1674-1748)

I thank Thee, O Father, for the spiritual delights that sharpen my
appetite for Thee. So much today is shallow and unworthy of Thee.
Let me nourish my heart on the delicacies of Thy grace. Amen.

Speaking to yourselves in psalms and hymns and spiritual songs, singing and making melody in your heart to the Lord; Giving thanks always for all things unto God and the Father in the name of our Lord Jesus Christ.
EPHESIANS 5:19-20

I have in my office a well-used old Methodist hymnal that goes back more than a century. In that hymnal, I have found 49 hymns on the attributes of God. I must confess that every day in my office I get on my knees with that hymnal, or one like it, and sing comfortably off-key a great hymn that honors and glorifies God. I think I would have fit in with those old Methodists.

Did you know that mostly uneducated people sang those Methodist hymns? Farmers, sheepherders and cattle raisers; coal miners, blacksmiths, carpenters, cotton raisers, cotton pickers; plain people all over this country sang those lofty hymns.

In my old Methodist hymnbook, there are 1,100 hymns. As I meditate on them, I am amazed at the depth of theology in those old hymns. When those old Methodists congregated on a Sunday morning, they were singing theology.

I would hazard a guess that most of them knew what they were singing, and it was strong doctrinal medicine for the soul. I wonder if many Christians today on a Sunday morning know the theology of what they are singing?

I will sing the wondrous story
Of the Christ who died for me.
How He left His home in glory
For the cross of Calvary.
FRANCIS H. ROWLEY (1854–1952)

O Father in heaven, I delight to sing Thy praise. Although my voice may be comfortably off-key, my heart is in complete harmony with Thy presence. Glory, glory, glory unto Jesus, my Lord. Amen.

Lord, thou hast been our dwelling place in all generations.
Before the mountains were brought forth, or ever thou hadst formed the earth
and the world, even from everlasting to everlasting, thou art God.
PSALM 90:1-2

The tragic and frightening decline in the spiritual state of churches has come about as a result of forgetting what kind of God, God is. This is reflected in our singing.

The great fathers of the church would sing, "O God, our help in ages past, our hope for years to come." How magnificent that old hymn is and what it tells us about God. If we are going to worship God, we need to be worthy of worshiping Him and offer Him worship worthy of Him.

To contrast this hymn, I heard a song recently set to the tune of "It's A Hot Time in the Old Town Tonight." The words went something like this, "One, two, three, the Devil's after me. Four, five, six, he's always throwing bricks. Seven, eight, nine, he misses me every time. Hallelujah, amen."

To compare that gospel jingle to "O God, our help in ages past" is to completely misunderstand the God we are worshiping. Give me a Bible and a hymnal and let me worthily worship God in a way He deserves. Let me have a hymn that reflects the God of the Scriptures, who is worthy of worship. Unless we get to know what God is like, we will never worship Him in a way that pleases Him.

O God, our help in ages past,
Our hope for years to come,
Our shelter from the stormy blast,
And our eternal home!

ISAAC WATTS (1674–1748)

My precious Lord and Savior, Jesus Christ, forgive the flippancy
that is passed off as worship these days. Convict my heart of the least
bit of flippancy so that I may come worthily unto Thee
and worthily worship Thee as it pleases Thee. Amen.

In the year that king Uzziah died I saw also the Lord sitting upon a throne, high and lifted up, and his train filled the temple. Above it stood the seraphims: each one had six wings; with twain he covered his face, and with twain he covered his feet, and with twain he did fly.

ISAIAH 6:1-2

One thing I guard in my spiritual life is that I not lose the vision of the Majesty on high. I need to understand the God I am worshiping; and when I do, there will be restored in my heart an awesome sense of reverence.

I read in Ezekiel that frightening, awful passage where the Shekinah, which is the shining presence of God, lifts up from between the wings of the cherubim and draws to the altar. The Shekinah glory followed Israel all those years and shone over the camp, reminding them of Jehovah's presence.

The time came when God could no longer tolerate the sin in the camp and pulled out His Majesty and removed the Shekinah glory from the camp.

I wonder how many gospel churches, who by their shallowness, coarseness and worldliness, have so grieved the Holy Spirit that He has withdrawn into the shadows of silence?

I never want to come to the place in my life where the Shekinah glory has withdrawn into the shadows of silence. I want to know God in the fullness of His Majesty. I do not want anything in my life to hinder that Majesty in my life.

Hark, the loud celestial hymn
Angel choirs above are raising;
Cherubim and seraphim,
In unceasing chorus praising,
Fill the heavens with sweet accord:
"Holy, holy, holy Lord!"

IGNAZ FRANZ (1719-1790)

Oh Lord, may today be a time of reverence as I approach Thy Majesty. Let me turn my back on all other things and focus on the glorious, ravishing beauty of Thy presence. Amen.

Surely goodness and mercy shall follow me all the days of my life:
and I will dwell in the house of the Lord for ever.
PSALM 23:6

Mercy is one of the attributes of God, not something God has, but something God is. If mercy were something God had, conceivably God might mislead, or He might use it up. But since it is something that God is, we must remember that it is uncreated. The mercy of God did not come into being; it always was, for mercy is what God is, and God is eternal and infinite.

While both the Old Testament and the New Testament declare the mercy of God, the Old Testament says more than four times as much about mercy than the New. Some have the idea that the Old Testament is law and judgment, and the New Testament is all of grace.

What is not factored into this is that God never changes. What He was in the Old Testament, He is in the New Testament, and even t day. He is the same God, and being the same God and not changing, He must therefore be the same in the Old as He is in the New, and the same in the New as He is in the Old. Resting on the mercy of God is resting upon God Himself.

> Surely goodness and mercy shall follow me
> All the days, all the days of my life.
> Surely goodness and mercy shall follow me
> All the days, all the days of my life.
> And I shall dwell in the house of the Lord forever;
> And I shall feast at the table spread for me.
> Surely goodness and mercy shall follow me
> All the days, all the days of my life.

JOHN W. PETERSON (1921–2006) AND ALFRED B. SMITH (1916–2001)

O heavenly Father, as Thou wert, Thou shalt be and art today. I bless Thee
because Thou art unchangeable, and Thy mercies are the same from one gener-
ation to the next. I nourish my soul today on Thy glorious mercy. Amen.

Thou wilt shew me the path of life: in thy presence is fulness of joy;
at thy right hand there are pleasures for evermore.
PSALM 16:11

Goodness is the source of God's mercy, and right here I must apologize for the necessity to use human language to speak of God. Language deals with things that are finite, but God is infinite. When we try to describe God or talk about God, we are always breaking our own rules and falling back into little alluring snares that we do not want to fall into.

God's infinite goodness is taught throughout the entire Bible. God desires the happiness of His creatures, and it is the irresistible urge in God to bestow blessedness on His people. This goodness of God takes pleasure in the pleasure of His people. Unfortunately, we have had drummed into us for so long that if we are happy, God is scared and frightened about us and is never quite pleased with us.

Search the Scriptures and you will find that God takes pleasure in the pleasure of His people, provided His people take pleasure in Him.

> Hark! Ten thousand hearts and voices
> Sound the note of praise above;
> Jesus reigns and heaven rejoices,
> Jesus reigns, the God of love.
> See, He sits on yonder throne;
> Jesus rules the world alone.
>
> THOMAS KELLY (1769–1855)

O God of goodness and mercy, Thy praise echoes in my heart today.
Thy joy is my joy, and my joy is Thy joy, and all of heaven rejoices
together with us. In Jesus' name, amen.

My son, despise not thou the chastening of the Lord, nor faint when thou art rebuked of him: For whom the Lord loveth he chasteneth, and scourgeth every so whom he receiveth. If ye endure chastening, God dealeth with you as with sons; for what son is he whom the father chasteneth not? But if ye be without chastisement, whereof all are partakers, then are ye bastards, and not sons.
HEBREWS 12:5-8

Contrary to some teaching, God never looks down and rejoices to see someone squirm. Yes, God at times must punish, but He is not pleased with Himself for punishing, for God has said He has no pleasure in the death of the wicked.

One of God's amazing attributes is His loving-kindness. Reflecting upon this, we see that God has bestowed upon us the same great goodness as He bestowed upon the house of Israel. He bestowed on them according to His mercies, and according to the multitude of His loving-kindness.

God delights to bless His people, but there are times when He must punish them. The entire history of the nation of Israel is a commentary on this very subject. When God can bless, He blesses to the fullest; and when He punishes, he punishes thoroughly. In punishment, His purpose is to bring His people back to the place where He can bless them. Punishment is not an end in itself; rather it is the path back to blessing and delight in the Lord.

The chastening of the Lord flows out of His great love for His people. He is very careful not to let us get into a place that will bring disgrace upon us or upon Him.

Yea, though I walk through death's dark vale, yet will I fear no ill;
For Thou art with me, and Thy rod and staff me comfort still.
THE SCOTTISH PSALTER

Everlasting God and Father, although my chastening is sometimes difficult, I realize that on the other side of that chastening is a blessing. Lead me in the path of blessing today, I pray. In Jesus' name, amen.

Like as a father pitieth his children, so the Lord pitieth them that fear him.
PSALM 103:13

According to the Old Testament, "mercy" has certain meanings. It means to stoop in kindness to an inferior, to show pity upon and to be actively compassionate. I think the reason some words fall into disuse is because the concept they convey falls into disuse. So it is with the word "compassionate."

The truth is that God is actively compassionate toward suffering man. I like the phrase "actively compassionate." For God to feel compassion at a distance would be one thing; but for God to be actively compassionate toward people is something else altogether.

I am not sure this concept has really taken hold in the heart of many Christians. For many, God is at such a distance in their own minds that they cannot comprehend God as *actively* compassionate toward them.

This active compassion is illustrated for us when Moses was at the burning bush. Moses was to go and deliver Israel from Egypt. God's active compassion was apparent when He did four things for Israel: He heard their groaning; He remembered His covenant; He looked upon their suffering; He pitied them and immediately came down to help them.

My heart rejoices today as I meditate upon the active compassion of God toward me.

> Thy compassions, Lord,
> To endless years endure;
> And children's children ever find
> Thy word of promise sure.
>
> ISAAC WATTS (1674–1748)

*Heavenly Father, I rejoice today in Thine active compassion toward me.
I don't deserve it, but Jesus paid the price so that Thy compassion
can flood my life. Praise the Lord! Amen.*

March 28

*But made his own people to go forth like sheep, and guided them in
the wilderness like a flock. And he led them on safely, so that they feared not:
but the sea overwhelmed their enemies.*
PSALM 78:52-53

Our Lord Jesus, when He saw the multitude, saw them as sheep having no shepherd. He saw their situation and understood it completely and was moved with compassion. He said to His disciples, Give ye them to eat. In other words, He was directing the disciples to do something about a current situation. He was actively compassionate toward people as He saw them as they truly were.

God's compassion reaches into your life as you really are, not as you think you are.

A great many people are merciful in their beds, merciful in their lovely living rooms, merciful in their brand-new cars' but they are not actively compassionate. What they see does not move them to action.

They may read about somebody who is suffering and say, "Isn't that terrible. That poor family is burned out and they're out on the street with no place to go." Then they go about their own business and forget that situation. For a minute and a half, they felt compassion, but they were not actively compassionate. That is, they did not do anything about it.

God's compassion leads Him to activity. God's compassion compels Him to become directly involved in your life. God does not just have pity upon you, but He is actively compassionate toward you and your situation to the point of interjecting Himself into your life.

Goodness and mercy all my life shall surely follow me;
And in God's house forevermore my dwelling place shall be.
THE SCOTTISH PSALTER

*Dear Savior Shepherd, who leadeth me down the straight path of
righteousness, I fear no evil for Thou hast injected Thyself into the affairs
of my life, for which I am eternally grateful. Amen.*

And he said, If now I have found grace in thy sight, O Lord, let my Lord, I pray thee, go among us; for it is a stiffnecked people; and pardon our iniquity and our sin, and take us for thine inheritance.

EXODUS 34:9

This is the day of the common man. We have not only become common, but we have also succeeded in dragging God down to our mediocre level. What is desperately needed today is an elevated concept of God. We need to see the "splendours upon splendours" revealing to us the glory of God.

I fully believe that one hour of meditating on the majesty of God would be worth more than listening to all the preachers in the world. One vision of the majesty of God will do more for you than a lifetime of striving and working.

I want to live like a child who wants to be where he can look up and see his mother's face. I want the gleam of God's majesty and the wonder of His presence to be permanent—the timeless, uncontained, single yet sublimely Three in One. Oh, to know God and to bask in the shine of His face is what life is really all about!

Splendours upon splendours beaming
Change and intertwine!
Glories over glories streaming
All translucent shine!
Blessings, praises, adorations
Greet Thee from the trembling nations
Majesty Divine, Majesty Divine!

FREDERICK W. FABER (1814–1863)

Forgive me, O Lord, for treating Thee less than Thou deserve to be treated. Help me today to see Thee in the splendor of Thy Majesty. Let me never get over it. Amen.

I have been young, and now am old;
yet have I not seen the righteous forsaken, nor his seed begging bread.
He is ever merciful, and lendeth; and his seed is blessed.
PSALM 37:25-26

I have heard of men who were hardhearted and careless, then something happened—they got stirred up and their mercies began to blossom. It never was so of God. God never lay in lethargy, without compassion, because God's mercy is simply what God is. It is uncreated and eternal, with no beginning and no end. It always was and always will be.

When heaven and earth were yet unmade and the stars were yet unformed, and all was only a thought in the mind of God, He was as merciful then as He is now.

Some things in space have burned themselves out. Heavenly bodies have disappeared in an explosion so many light years ago that it will be thousands of earth years before their light stops shining. The light is still coming; the waves are still coming though the source of those waves has long ceased to be.

Nothing that is infinite can be less than it is, and it cannot be any more than it was. It is infinite, which means boundless, unlimited; it has no measurement on any side, because measurements are created things, and God is uncreated. The mercy of God has never been any more then it is now; and it will never be any less than now.

Sing, my soul, adore His name;
Let His glory be thy theme;
Praise Him till He calls thee home;
Trust His love for all to come.

ANONYMOUS (1800)

Thy mercy, O God, is from everlasting to everlasting.
I do not understand it, but I accept it into my life as a precious gift
from the One who loves me as Thou dost. In Jesus' name, amen.

Thou in thy mercy hast led forth the people which thou hast redeemed:
thou hast guided them in thy strength unto thy holy habitation.
EXODUS 15:13

Do not imagine that when the Day of Judgment comes that God will turn off His mercy as the sun goes behind the cloud or as you might turn off a spigot. Do not think for a moment the mercy of God will ever cease to be.

The mercy of God will never be any less than it is now, because the infinite cannot cease to be infinite, the perfect cannot admit any imperfection. Nothing that occurs can increase or diminish the mercy of God nor alter the quality of the mercy of God.

When Jesus died on the cross, the mercy of God did not become any greater, for it was already infinite. We have a mistaken notion that God shows mercy because Jesus died. Jesus died because God is showing mercy. If God had not been merciful, there would not have been an Incarnation, no baby in the manger, no man on the cross and no open tomb.

It was the mercy of God that gave us Calvary, not Calvary that gave us the mercy of God. God has mercy enough to unfold the whole universe in His heart, and nothing anybody ever did could ever, in any way, diminish the mercy of God.

God is love; His mercy brightens
All the path in which we rove;
Bliss He wakes, and woe He lightens;
God is wisdom, God is love.
JOHN BOWRING (1792–1872)

O God, I praise Thee for Thy mercy, which never increases or decreases.
Thy mercy is perfectly sufficient for me today, tomorrow and forever.
I rest upon Thy awesome mercy. In Jesus' name, amen.

I came not to call the righteous, but sinners to repentance.
LUKE 5:32

God's mercy is infinite, but that does not mean a man cannot walk out from under and away from the mercy of God. We can make the mercy of God inoperative toward us by our conduct, since we are free moral agents. That does not change the power of the Word of God or the mercy of God. Man's truancy does not diminish, in the least, nor alter the quality of God's mercy.

The intercession of Jesus Christ at the right hand of God does not increase the mercy of God toward His people. For if God were not already merciful, there would be no intercession of Christ at the right hand of God. And if God is merciful at all, then He is infinitely merciful, and it's impossible for the mediatorship of Jesus at the right hand of the Father to make the mercy of God any more than it is right now.

Keep in mind that no attribute of God is greater than any other attribute of God. It is something we cannot grasp fully, but it does bring me to my knees in adoring worship of this God who changes not.

> The mercy of God is an ocean divine,
> A boundless and fathomless flood;
> Launch out in the deep, cut away the shore line,
> And be lost in the fullness of God.
>
> A. B. SIMPSON (1843–1919)

At Thy right hand, O God, are untold mercies.
Today, may I nourish my soul upon the infinite mercies of Thy grace.
May Jesus be real in me today. Amen.

The Lord is the portion of mine inheritance and of my cup:
thou maintainest my lot.
PSALM 16:5

The love of God is infinite; the mercy of God is infinite; the justice of God is infinite; but one attribute is not greater than the other. All are the same, and yet there are attributes of God that can be needed more at various times.

With man it is different, and so to the fellow lying there, beaten up by robbers, the most needed attribute of that moment was mercy. He needed somebody to have compassion on him, so the Good Samaritan got down off his beast, went over and had compassion for the man beside the road. And that was what he needed at the time.

This is why the mercy of God is wonderful to a prodigal who comes home. There is much more to God than mercy, but the prodigal who needs mercy can see nothing else but the mercy of God. That is the wonderful thing about God. When I am walking with Him, He will be all that I need, all of the time. I do not have to try to figure it out; He has already done that for me.

By faith, I accept the attributes of God and believe that God will bring them to bear upon my life when I need them.

> Ring the bells of heaven! There is joy today
> For a soul returning from the wild!
> See, the Father meets him out upon the way,
> Welcoming His weary, wandering child.
> WILLIAM O. CUSHING (1823-1902)

O Father of the prodigal, how I embrace the infinite mercy that flows
from Thy loving heart. No matter how far down I go, Thy mercy is
more than sufficient, and for this, I thank Thee.
In the blessed name of Jesus, I pray, amen.

As for me, I will call upon God; and the Lord shall save me. . . .
God shall hear, and afflict them, even he that abideth of old. Selah.
Because they have no changes, therefore they fear not God.
PSALM 55:16,19

We can sing hymns about the amazing grace of God, and yet the grace of God is not any greater than the justice of God, or the holiness of God.

The difference is not in God; rather, the difference is in us. It is in what we need the most desperately at any particular time. God is always the same, but we are not. There are times when we need the mercy of God or the love of God to flood our soul and lift us out of the quagmire of depression. The amazing thing about God is that whatever we need at the time, God is.

Theologically speaking, we know that all of the attributes of God are the same. They are eternal and infinite—they change not. But our needs change. When we need the love of God, we are not thinking so much of the holiness of God.

When we are in a jam, we need a certain attribute of God. At times, we do not know which attribute we might need, but God is faithful to reveal Himself in our present situation. God knows us better than we know ourselves, and He knows exactly what we need and when we need it.

Eternal Father, strong to save,
Whose arm hath bound the restless wave,
Who bidd'st the mighty ocean deep
Its own appointed limits keep;
Oh, hear us when we cry to Thee
For those in peril on the sea.

WILLIAM WHITING (1825-1878)

Eternal God, I revel in Thine attributes, and I love to meditate on them one at a time. I cannot embrace them all in one humongous hug, but I have confidence that when I need Thy love, when I need Thy mercy, when I need Thy justice, Thou wilt be there for me. Amen.

And the Lord passed by before him, and proclaimed, The Lord, The Lord God, merciful and gracious, longsuffering, and abundant in goodness and truth, Keeping mercy for thousands, forgiving iniquity and transgression and sin, and that will by no means clear the guilty; visiting the iniquity of the fathers upon the children, and upon the children's children, unto the third and to the fourth generation.

EXODUS 34:6-7

The root of my understanding of the attributes of God is simply that when I come to God, my need will determine which of God's attributes, at that moment, I need to celebrate.

Just as the judgment of God is God's justice confronting moral iniquity, and then judgment falls, so the mercy of God is God's goodness confronting human guilt and suffering.

When the goodness of God confronts human guilt and suffering, God listens, hears and acts accordingly—that is His mercy.

It is hard to separate these attributes, although we do so to study them and understand them. But in reality, they are simply shades of God's nature and character. They blend in, one with another, and it is very difficult to separate them; in fact, it is impossible.

The great news is that you do not have to try to separate them. In your despair, you do not have to try to figure out which of God's attributes you need at the time. You know that if you come to God in your state, He will reveal Himself to you according to your current need.

Sovereign Father, heavenly King,
Thee we now presume to sing;
Glad Thine attributes confess,
Glorious all, and numberless.

CHARLES WESLEY (1707-1788)

Eternal God and Father, I come to Thee, knowing full well that Thou knowest all things and will reveal to me that which will satiate my heart. In the blessed name of Jesus I pray, amen.

He is the Rock, his work is perfect: for all his ways are judgment:
a God of truth and without iniquity, just and right is he. They have corrupted
themselves, their spot is not the spot of his children: they are a perverse and crooked
generation. Do ye thus requite the Lord, O foolish people and unwise? is not he
thy father that hath bought thee? hath he not made thee, and established thee?
DEUTERONOMY 32:4-6

All men are recipients of God's mercy. Do not think for a minute that when you repented and came back from the swine pen to the father's house is when mercy began to operate. Mercy was operating all the time.

If you had not had the mercy of God all the time—stooping in pity, withholding judgment—you would have perished long ago. God holds up His justice because of His mercy. He waits because the Savior died. All of us are recipients of the mercy of God. All the time you were sinning against Him, He was having pity on you, for God is not willing that any should perish.

The vilest criminals you can think of and the blackest hearts that lie in the lowest wallow in the city are the recipients of the mercy of God. It does not mean they are saved. It does not mean they will be converted and finally reach heaven. It does mean that God is staying His justice because He is exercising His mercy. God's mercy does not make us repent; rather God's mercy paves the way for us to come to that point of repentance. Not all will come, but all can.

That awful day will surely come,
Th' appointed hour makes haste,
When I must stand before my Judge,
And pass the solemn test.

ISAAC WATTS (1674-1748)

Dear heavenly Father, Thy mercy amazes me when I think of the
dreadfulness of my own soul. My joy is that when I stand before Thee,
Christ will be at my side all the way. Praise His wonderful name. Amen.

April 6

For in that he died, he died unto sin once:
but in that he liveth, he liveth unto God.
ROMANS 6:10

When God's justice confronts human guilt, it brings the sentence of death; but the mercy of God postpones the execution, because mercy is also an attribute of God and does not contradict the other, but works with it.

When the justice of God sees iniquity, there must be judgment; but the mercy of God, which brought Christ to the cross, offered all men the cancellation of that judgment.

I do not at all claim to understand it, but I am so happy about the things I do know, and delightedly happy about the things I do not. I celebrate what I do not know, because it all falls into the hands of God, who knows all things perfectly.

I know that God, the mighty maker, died for man the creature's sin there on the cross. I know that God turned His back on that holy, holy, holy man; and when He gave up the ghost and died, the penalty was dealt with and full forgiveness made possible.

I do not know how it is possible, but I do know that through Jesus Christ, God's justice and mercy flows into my life in a melody that results in forgiveness.

> Well might the sun in darkness hide
> And shut his glories in,
> When Christ, the mighty Maker, died
> For man the creature's sin.

ISAAC WATTS (1674–1748)

Heavenly Father, I rejoice in both Thy justice and Thy mercy that bring
into my life the joy of forgiveness and reconciliation with Thee.
All I need to know is that Thine attributes meet every need I have. Amen.

Surely his salvation is nigh them that fear him; that glory may dwell in our land. Mercy and truth are met together; righteousness and peace have kissed each other. Truth shall spring out of the earth; and righteousness shall look down from heaven. Yea, the Lord shall give that which is good; and our land shall yield her increase. Righteousness shall go before him; and shall set us in the way of his steps.

PSALM 85:9-13

It is a mystery of the Godhead, but in heaven was registered an atonement for all mankind. I know that, yet I do not know why, and I do not know what happened. I only know that in the infinite goodness and wisdom of God, He worked out a plan whereby the second person of the Trinity, incarnated as a man, could die in order that justice might be satisfied while mercy rescued the man for whom He died. It was not plan B, but rather the plan from eternity.

Whatever your denominational preference, this mercy is what you will need to go to heaven on. You cannot go to heaven on spirituals, choruses and cheap books; but you can go to heaven on the mercy of God in Christ, for that is what the Bible teaches.

So many are trying to get in line with the culture that they miss the fact that in order to go to heaven you need to get in line with God's mercy.

Blessed be the glorious tidings
To a suffering world revealed.
Christ has made a full atonement;
By His stripes we may be healed.

A. B. SIMPSON (1843-1919)

Dear heavenly Father, how marvelous are Thy works toward me; they are past finding out. I cannot understand the mystery behind it all, but I can accept by faith that which You have done for me. In Jesus' name, amen.

For I know the thoughts that I think toward you, saith the Lord, thoughts of peace,
and not of evil, to give you an expected end. Then shall ye call upon me,
and ye shall go and pray unto me, and I will hearken unto you.
And ye shall seek me, and find me, when ye shall search for me with all your heart.
JEREMIAH 29:11-13

God takes pleasure in the pleasure of His people, and suffers along with His friends. How could a perfect God suffer? Suffering means that somewhere there is a disorder. We do not suffer as long as we have a psychological and physical order; but when we get out of order, we suffer. From a human standpoint, it does not make sense.

But then, we do not operate from a human standpoint. We operate by faith, which means we have confidence in what God says, whether we understand it or not. And boy, are there many things I do not understand! If my Christian walk depended upon what I understood, I would not be taking another step, I assure you. In fact, I might be taking a few steps backward.

As long as something is declared in the Bible, you can take it by faith. You believe it, you try to understand it if you can and you thank God and your little intellect that you can have a little fun leaping about rejoicing in God. If you read it in the Bible and your intellect cannot understand it, then there is only one thing to do, and that is to look up and say, "O Lord God, Thou knowest."

O to grace how great a debtor daily I'm constrained to be!
Let Thy goodness, like a fetter, bind my wandering heart to Thee.
Prone to wander, Lord, I feel it, prone to leave the God I love;
Here's my heart, O take and seal it; seal it for Thy courts above.
ROBERT ROBINSON (1735-1790)

Heavenly Father, I believe it although I do not understand it.
My joy is not in what I understand but in what I believe Thou hast done
for me. In the blessed name of Jesus, I pray, amen.

April 9

But we see Jesus, who was made a little lower than the angels
for the suffering of death, crowned with glory and honour;
that he by the grace of God should taste death for every man.
HEBREWS 2:9

One thing I have noticed about evangelicals. We know too much; we are too slick, and we have too many answers. In my mind, it would be refreshing to hear somebody say, "I don't know" and "Oh, Lord God, Thou knowest."

I am thinking about the suffering of God. I do not understand it. In my mind, suffering would seem to indicate some imperfection, and I am confident that God is perfect. Suffering would seem to indicate some loss or lack, and yet we know God can suffer no loss and He cannot lack, because He is infinitely perfect in all His being.

I do not know how to explain this. I only know the Bible declares that God suffers with His children and that in their entire affliction, He was afflicted; and in His love and mercy, He carried them and made their bed in their sickness. I know this, but I do not know how.

A great old theologian once said, "Don't reject the fact because you don't know the method." Don't throw away the fact because you don't know how it isn't so.

The cross He bore is life and health,
Though shame and death to him,
His people's hope, His people's wealth,
Their everlasting theme.
THOMAS KELLY (1769–1864)

Blessed Lord Jesus, I bow before Thee today in deep appreciation of all
Thou hast done on my behalf. It is way beyond my understanding,
but not beyond my acceptance. Amen.

The Lord did not set his love upon you, nor choose you, because ye were more in number than any people; for ye were the fewest of all people: But because the Lord loved you, and because he would keep the oath which he had sworn unto your fathers, hath the Lord brought you out with a mighty hand, and redeemed you out of the house of bondmen, from the hand of Pharaoh king of Egypt.

DEUTERONOMY 7:7-8

The Scriptures indicate there will come a time when we are going to know everything, and we will know things perfectly. I suppose it means that within certain limits we are going to know perfectly and, possibly, we will know everything. I am looking forward to the time, because there is so much I really do not know now.

I love hymns, but I must confess some hymn writers should have been out cutting the grass instead of writing a hymn. One hymn writer wrote, *I wonder why He loved me so?* The entire hymn goes on in this vein. Some people only have questions.

There is only one answer to why God loves you so, and that is because God is love; and there is only one answer to why God has mercy on you, and that is because God's mercy is an attribute of His deity. God will always be true to Himself no matter how much we do not understand it.

Do not ask why. Simply thank Him for the vast, wondrous and mysterious aspects of His attributes.

> How Thou canst think so well of us,
> Yet be the God Thou art,
> Is darkness to my intellect,
> But sunshine to my heart.
>
> FREDERICK W. FABER (1814–1868)

God, my heavenly Father, Thy thoughts toward me are more than I can truly comprehend. I revel in the fact that Thy thoughts are indeed toward me, and I praise Thee for thinking in my direction. Amen.

Like as a father pitieth his children, so the Lord pitieth them that fear him.
For he knoweth our frame; he remembereth that we are dust.
PSALM 103:13-14

When Jesus introduced the disciples to the fact that He would soon die on the cross, everyone to a man opposed the idea. Of course, Peter was the loudest voice in opposition. Not so, Lord, not so, Peter declared. The rest of the disciples nodded in agreement.

In spite of and over all of their objections, Jesus went to the cross and died; if He had not died, they could not have lived. At the time, they did not understand this truth; but later on, after Pentecost, they understood it. When they understood it, for the first time they really began to live.

Mercy was compassionate in the only way it could be at the moment, by dying. So Christ Jesus our Lord died there on that cross, for He loved us and pitied us as a father pities his children.

One of the basic truths coming from this is that we who have received mercy must show mercy; and we must pray that God will help us to show mercy. This mercy can only come by atonement, but the good news is that atonement has been made. Mercy can operate toward us because of the atonement.

Children of the heavenly Father
Safely in His bosom gather;
Nestling bird nor star in heaven
Such a refuge e'er was given.
CAROLINA V. SANDELL BERG (1832–1903)

Dear Lord Jesus, Thy death seems like such a tragedy until I get
on the other side of the cross. I can live for You today because
You died for me yesterday. Praise the Lord! Amen!

Casting all your care upon him; for he careth for you.
1 PETER 5:7

Never be ashamed to go and tell God about all your troubles. He knows all about your troubles anyway.

For some reason, some Christians do not believe this. It is the cause of much discouragement in the Christian life. We carry about ourselves burdens that we really do not have to carry. We are hesitant to go to God and to be honest with Him, as if God does not know everything anyway. We go about with the notion that nobody knows what we are going through, and we have to go through it by ourselves.

Somebody knows all right—a fellow sufferer that retains feelings for our pain and still remembers His tears, agonies and cries. He is now at the right hand of the Father Almighty, sitting, crowned in glory, waiting for that great coronation day that is yet to come.

He has not forgotten the plight of humanity. He still wears in His hands the nails of the cross. He has not forgotten the tears and the agonies and the cries, and He knows everything about you.

When you come to Him, you come to someone who perfectly knows you, your problems and your burdens; but more than that, He has vowed before the Father in heaven to carry those burdens for you.

Nobody knows the trouble I've seen, nobody knows but Jesus.
Nobody knows the trouble I've seen, glory Hallelujah!
Sometimes I'm up, sometimes I'm down, oh, yes, Lord,
Sometimes I'm almost to the groun', oh, yes, Lord.

AFRICAN-AMERICAN SPIRITUAL

O Lord, I sometimes feel so alone, and that nobody really cares.
But one gaze into Thy blessed face, and all my sorrows are gone.
I thank Thee for caring for me and for carrying my burdens. Amen.

We then that are strong ought to bear the infirmities of the weak,
and not to please ourselves. Let every one of us please his neighbour for his good
to edification. For even Christ pleased not himself; but, as it is written,
The reproaches of them that reproached thee fell on me.
ROMANS 15:1-3

Many people express the desire to serve God. I applaud these aspirations and want to do all I can to encourage people to serve God. Where this breaks down is that we cannot serve a God we do not know. The more we know about God, the more we will know how we can serve this God, and know what He expects.

It is tremendously important that we know what God is like. The answer is more valuable to you and of greater importance than any other question you could ask. If you know the answer, it will carry you a long way in serving God.

When I see what some people are doing in the name of serving God, I can only conclude that they have no idea of the God they are trying to serve. Some are doing reprehensible things to the nature of God as revealed in the Holy Scriptures. To do something contrary to God's nature and call it service is sheer ignorance and an affront to God.

Get to know God, and then you can serve Him in a way that is pleasing unto Him. And brother, if it pleases God, it will certainly please you.

O ye that are spending your leisure and powers
In pleasures so foolish and fond,
Awake from your selfishness, folly, and sin
And go to the regions beyond.

A. B. SIMPSON (1843–1919)

O Master and Savior, I yield my heart and life to Thee, not as I please
but as it pleases Thee. May all I do lift Thee up for all to see. Amen.

For the Lord your God is God of gods, and Lord of lords, a great God,
a mighty, and a terrible, which regardeth not persons, nor taketh reward.
DEUTERONOMY 10:17

If you know God, you know that He is absolutely and perfectly just. However, I cannot let it stop there. I am going to have to define justice a little bit so you know what I mean.

What do I mean by justice?

I find justice indistinguishable from righteousness in the Old Testament. The same word and slight variations, but "judgment," "justice," "just" and the like, are all the same root word. It means uprightness, rectitude. Moreover, to say that God is just or that the justice of God is a fact is to say that there is uprightness in God; there is rectitude in God.

Righteousness, justice, right justice and judgment are said to be the habitation of God's throne. So the just and righteous men are indistinguishable one from the other. To say that God is just is to say He is equitable and morally equal in all that He is.

God's justice is never in conflict with His righteousness. This may be something hard for us to grasp—that God in all of His acts toward us is perfectly just and righteous. Whatever God does in my direction I can rest assured that it is exactly what I need it to be and what He wants me to be.

Sweet is the memory of Thy grace,
My God, my heavenly King;
Let age to age Thy righteousness
In songs of glory sing.
ISAAC WATTS (1674-1748)

I rest securely in Thee, O God, for I am confident that Thou hast
my best interests in mind for the longest period of time.
Thou knowest what I need, and I know that I only need Thee.
In the blessed name of Jesus my Lord, amen.

Thou hast a mighty arm: strong is thy hand, and high is thy right hand.
Justice and judgment are the habitation of thy throne:
mercy and truth shall go before thy face.
PSALM 89:13-14

Israel, in her day, charged God with having ways that were unequal. In reality, it was the house of Israel that had unequal ways. Imagine charging God as being unequal in His ways!

That word "unequal" means inequity. The word "inequity" and the word "iniquity" are about the same. Change one letter and you have "iniquity." It means that the iniquitous person is not morally equal; he is not morally symmetrical; he is unequal to himself.

Then the word "judgment," as it relates to justice—righteousness and judgment—is the habitation of Thy throne. And what is the judgment of God? It is the application of justice to a moral situation. It may be favorable or unfavorable. When God judges man, He brings justice to that man's life and applies justice to the moral situation that man's life created.

If the man's ways are equal, then justice favors the man. If, however, the man's ways are unequal, then of course it is on the other side, and God pronounces sentence on that man.

I want my life to be on God's side of the equation.

Safe is my refuge, sweet is my rest,
Ill cannot harm me, nor foes e'er molest;
Jesus my spirit so tenderly calms,
Holding me close in His mighty arms.

WINFIELD MACOMBER (1865-1896)

I love Thy justice, O God, for it always brings me into line with Thy mercy.
I rest safely in the judgment of Thy mercy. I pray this in Jesus' name. Amen.

Now I Nebuchadnezzar praise and extol and honour the King of heaven,
all whose works are truth, and his ways judgment:
and those that walk in pride he is able to abase.
DANIEL 4:37

Justice is not something God has; it is something God is. God is love; and just as God is love, justice is something that God is.

You sometimes hear it said that justice required God to do this or that. I do not doubt that I sometimes use expressions myself that are semantically improper because the human language is tough. When you talk about God, language staggers in an effort to describe Him. God is so much bigger than our language; only the heart can truly express adoration to God.

The Old Testament prophets and the New Testament apostles put such pressure on language in an effort to tell the story. Sometimes it is impossible to describe what God is in human language. Nevertheless, we try. Sometimes in trying to explain God, we use the wrong words. Sometimes we get the wrong emphasis on a word. Only the Holy Spirit can straighten this mess out for us. Thank God for His faithfulness.

Just remember, justice is not something outside of God, to which God must conform. Justice does not require God to do anything.

God moves in a mysterious way
His wonders to perform;
He plants his footsteps in the sea,
And rides upon the storm.
WILLIAM COWPER (1731–1800)

Dear God and Father, I find refuge in Thy justice. Although words fail
me in expressing my gratitude, the Holy Spirit has enabled me
to worship Thee in a worthy manner. In Jesus' name, amen.

Ah Lord God! behold, thou hast made the heaven and the earth by thy great power and stretched out arm, and there is nothing too hard for thee: Thou shewest lovingkindness unto thousands, and recompensest the iniquity of the fathers into the bosom of their children after them: the Great, the Mighty God, the Lord of hosts, is his name.
JEREMIAH 32:17-18

Nothing in God's created world is able to make God—to require God—to do anything. Whatever requires God to do something would then become God. If we have a God that is required to do anything, then we have a weak God who has about His neck some yoke and yields Himself to pressure from the outside.

This is an error in speaking, for it postulates a principle of justice that lies outside of God and to which God has to conform.

To think that is to think wrongly about God. It would mean something is bigger than God and is compelling God to do something He may not want to do. To think this way is to completely misunderstand God. The more we understand God, the more we back away from such erroneous thinking.

If justice requires God to do something, then this principle of justice is above God. Who enforces that principle? Who created that principle? If there is such a principle, then that principle is superior to God, for only a superior can compel obedience. If there is anything that can compel God, that something is bigger and greater than God, and we will have to stop saying, O mighty God.

Great God, how infinite art thou!
What worthless worms are we!
Let the whole race of creatures bow,
And pay their praise to thee.
ISAAC WATTS (1674-1748)

O Mighty God, I come before Thee recognizing the immense nature of Thyself. No one is higher than the Highest, and no one deserves my worship more than Thee. Hallelujah! Amen.

*Know therefore this day, and consider it in thine heart, that the Lord he is God
in heaven above, and upon the earth beneath: there is none else.*

DEUTERONOMY 4:39

Nothing outside of God can make God do anything or compel Him to do
any kind of action contrary to His will. I wish we could keep this in mind.
This was the common doctrine of the Puritans in another generation. It
was the common teaching of the Presbyterians, the Methodists and all
the rest. But this has been lost in the shuffle, and God has been made
into a little God not worthy of being worshiped.

It is important to understand that all God's reasons for doing anything
come from within Him. They do not come from without Him, and there
is no pressure group that can force God to do anything. God is absolutely
complete in Himself and operates in a harmonious unity, especially in
His relationship with mankind.

This is hard for us to grasp, because everything we do is because
somebody is pressuring us to do it. Some outside pressure compels us to
do things sometimes that we would not do on our own. This cannot be
transferred into the area of God. He is not like us and is not susceptible
to outside pressure.

When I come to Him, I know that I am coming to Him, and His love
for me is a genuine love that I can count on.

God the omnipotent! King who ordainest
Thunder Thy clarion, the lightning Thy sword;
Show forth Thy pity on high where Thou reignest:
Give to us peace in our time, O Lord.

HENRY F. CHORLEY (1808-1872)

*O God, I often feel the pressure of the outside world endeavoring
to conform me into its image. How glad I am that nothing pressures
Thee into doing anything. All Thou doest flows from a heart
of infinite love. Glory be to God. Amen.*

But he is in one mind, and who can turn him?
and what his soul desireth, even that he doeth.
JOB 23:13

All God's reasons for doing anything lie inside of God. Nothing lies on the outside to be brought to bear upon Him and force Him to do something contrary to His nature. Everything God does flows from within. That is, they are what God is. God's reasons for doing what He does spring out of what and who He is.

Nothing has been added to God and nothing has been removed from God. Our God is exactly what He was before He created Adam, and He will be exactly what He is when the heavens are no more. He has never changed in any way, because He is the unchanging God.

We have been lied to, cheated, sold down the river, skinned, fleeced, betrayed and deceived so much that we have come to project our cynicism into the very throne of God. Unknown to us, we have within our minds a feeling that God is like that too.

God, being perfect, is incapable of loss or gain, of getting larger or smaller. He is incapable of knowing more or knowing less. God is just God, and God acts from within, not in obedience to some outside law. He is the author of all and acts like Himself all the time.

Unresting, unhasting, and silent as light,
Nor wanting, nor wasting, Thou rulest in might;
Thy justice, like mountains, high soaring above
Thy clouds, which are fountains of goodness and love.
WALTER C. SMITH (1824–1908)

Eternal God and Father, Thou truly art the same yesterday and today and forever. The more I get to know Thee, the more I trust in Thy unchangeable ways. I pray this in Jesus' name. Amen.

*For a thousand years in thy sight are but as yesterday when it is past,
and as a watch in the night.*
PSALM 90:4

One of the great truths of Scripture that encourages my heart so much is that God always acts like Himself. No archangel, no 10,000 angels with swords, no cherubim or seraphim anywhere can persuade God to act otherwise than as Himself.

I am very susceptible to outside pressures. How I feel on any given occasion is a result of the outside pressures around me. If the outside is cold, I am cold. If the outside is sunny and bright, I feel cheerful and happy. However, when it comes to God, that is a different story.

God always acts as becomes Himself, and He always will. He redeemed man within that mighty framework. He could not change. If He could change then He could not be God, for He would have to go from better to worse or from worse to better. Being God, and being perfect, he could not go either direction; He has to remain God.

This is wonderful news to me! When I come to God, I never have to worry if I am meeting Him in the right mood. He is always the same. He never changes. No outside pressure of any kind changes Him. Hallelujah! When I find God, I find God.

O how sweet the glorious message
Simple faith may claim;
Yesterday, today, forever, Jesus is the same.
Still he loves to save the sinful,
Heal the sick and lame,
Cheer the mourner, still the tempest;
Glory to His name!

A. B. SIMPSON (1843–1919)

*When I come to Thee, O God, I ever find Thee as Thou hast been
in the past. Thy heart is always open to me, for which I am eternally glad.
"Always the same"—Thy blessed theme. Amen.*

Therefore hearken unto me, ye men of understanding: far be it from God, that he should do wickedness; and from the Almighty, that he should commit iniquity.
JOB 34:10

Anselm of Canterbury (c. 1033–1109) was one of the great church fathers, a great theologian, a great saint and a great thinker all in one. Often referred to as the second St. Augustine, he once posed a very important question to God.

How dost Thou stare at the wicked if Thou art just and supremely just?

In our day, we have cheapened religion, salvation and our concept of God to such a place where we expect to stumble into heaven whistling, and God will take us in. That is what we expect, and we do not worry much about it. We read a few verses, mumble a little prayer and that is all there is to it. We are in.

We have a marked New Testament and a tract, and we expect to just stumble up to the pearly gates, rap on the gates and say, "Well, God, I'm here." We have reduced God in our thinking. I believe that the old serious theologian asked God the proper question. How can God really look at us, who are so wicked, and He being supremely just?

If we are serious about our relationship to God, we, too, will ask a serious question.

How God can look at the likes of me and you and invite us into His fellowship is the mystery of the justice and mercy of God.

Thy way, not mine, O Lord,
However dark it be;
Lead me by Thine own hand,
Choose out the path for me.

HORATIUS BONAR (1808–1889)

O holy and righteous God, that Thee can look at me as I am and open up Thy heart and invite me in is one mystery I shall never fathom. But Thy way is the perfect way, and that is the way I come. In Jesus' name, amen.

I know that, whatsoever God doeth, it shall be for ever: nothing can be put to it, nor any thing taken from it: and God doeth it, that men should fear before him.
ECCLESIASTES 3:14

The basic questions that need answers are those dealing with God.

One thing we need to get hold of is that the being of God is unitary.

Today we write fiction, sing choruses, and rock 'n' roll our way to glory. Brethren, some solid questions need answering. For one, we need to understand what it means that God is unitary.

First off, it means that God is not composed of parts. We are not unitary beings, but are composed of spirit, soul and body. We have memory and forgetfulness. We have attributes that were given to us. Some of these things can be taken away from us, sections of our brain, yet we still function. Limbs can be cut out by surgery and we could still live on. We can forget, we can learn, and still live on. That is because we are not unitary. When God made us, He made us a composite.

God is not like that at all. He is one unitary being without parts; and what He is, He was yesterday, is today and will be forever.

Arms of Jesus, fold me closer
To Thy strong and loving breast,
Till my spirit on Thy bosom
Finds its everlasting rest;
And when time's last sands are sinking,
Shield my heart from all alarms,
Softly whispering, "Underneath Thee
Are the ever lasting arms."

A. B. SIMPSON (1843-1919)

Our Father Which Art in Heaven, I come to Thee in the simplicity of Thy unity. Let me humble myself in all my parts and worship Thee in the beauty of Thy holiness. I pray this in Jesus' name. Amen.

And the scribe said unto him, Well, Master, thou hast said the truth:
for there is one God; and there is none other but he.
MARK 12:32

In the Old Testament, the Jews believed in the being of God as unitary. They taught the unitary being of God, and the church today teaches that so far as the church teaches anything. Saying that God, the being of God, is unitary—that there is one God, and not only one God, but that God is one. That is the distinction.

We must not think of God as composed of parts working harmoniously together, for there are no parts with God. We must think of God as one; and because God is one, His attributes never conflict with each other.

Because man is not unitary, but composed of parts, man may become frustrated. He may be a schizophrenic, and part of him may war with another part of him; his sense of justice may war with his sense of mercy.

Many times, a judge in the courtroom sits on a bench and is caught between mercy and justice. Listening to the case, he does not know what to do.

God is never caught in such a situation. His mercy and His justice never conflict. What a God we serve!

Glory be to God the Father,
Glory be to God the Son,
Glory be to God the Spirit,
Great Jehovah, Three in One!
Glory, glory, glory, glory,
While eternal ages run!

HORATIUS BONAR (1808-1889)

Eternal God and Father of our Lord and Savior Jesus Christ, I rest comfortably
in Thine arms of mercy and justice. Bless Thy holy name! I praise Thee for
the unity of Thyself in all of its ramifications to me. Amen.

The law of the Lord is perfect, converting the soul: the testimony of the Lord is sure, making wise the simple. The statutes of the Lord are right, rejoicing the heart: the commandment of the Lord is pure, enlightening the eyes. The fear of the Lord is clean, enduring for ever: the judgments of the Lord are true and righteous altogether.

PSALM 19:7-9

We sometimes think of God as presiding over a court of law where the sinner has broken the law of justice and appears before the court. Justice is out there somewhere, outside of God. The sinner has sinned against that external justice, gets arrested and put in handcuffs and is brought before the bar of justice. God's mercy wants to forgive the sinner, but justice says, "No, he's broken my laws; he must die."

If we think that, we might as well be pagans and think about God the way pagans do. We are making a man out of God. That is not good Christian theology; never was and never can be. To think less of God is to think wrongly of God, because everything that God is harmonizes with everything else that God is; and everything that God does is one with everything else that God does. "Harmony" is not really a good word to use here when thinking of God.

Harmony requires that two get together and for a time be one. But there is nothing like that in God. God just is.

Come, ye disconsolate, where'er ye languish,
Come to the mercy seat, fervently kneel;
Here bring your wounded hearts, here tell your anguish;
Earth has no sorrow that heaven cannot heal.

THOMAS MOORE (1779–1852)

I praise Thee, O God, for Thy justice, which is perfect in every regard. I cannot comprehend the depth of Thy mercy and how Thy justice is fulfilled, but in Jesus Christ, my Savior, I accept the fullness of Thy grace. Amen.

But let him that glorieth glory in this, that he understandeth and knoweth me,
that I am the Lord which exercise lovingkindness, judgment, and righteousness,
in the earth: for in these things I delight, saith the Lord.
JEREMIAH 9:24

One question people keep asking is, "How can God be just, yet acquit the wicked?" That question is answered in the fact that God is unitary. God's justice and God's mercy do not quarrel with each other.

Jesus Christ is God, and all that can be said about God can be said about Christ. He, too, is unitary. He took on Himself the nature of man, but that nature of man is man. The God, the eternal God, who was before man was, and who created man, is a unitary being, and there is no dividing of the substance. Therefore, that holy One who suffered in His own blood for us was infinite, almighty and perfect.

Infinite means without bounds, without limits, shoreless, bottomless, topless, forever and ever, without any possible measure or limitation. So, what the suffering of Jesus did in the atonement on that cross, under that darkening sky, was infinite in its power.

Man's wickedness in no way compromises God's justice. All of the wickedness of all the wicked men throughout the ages cannot be compared to one whisper of God's mercy.

The question is not how God can be just and acquit the wicked, but rather it is how God cannot act like Himself when confronted with any situation.

Judge not the Lord by feeble sense,
But trust Him for His grace;
Behind a frowning providence
He hides a smiling face.

WILLIAM COWPER (1731–1800)

Almighty God, Thy ways at first seem so harsh and unrelenting.
But as I pierce the veil of unknowing, I find that joy in Thee that rushes
grace to my heart. In the blessed name of Jesus, I pray, amen.

For it pleased the Father that in him should all fulness dwell;
And, having made peace through the blood of his cross, by him to reconcile
all things unto himself; by him, I say, whether they be things in earth,
or things in heaven.
COLOSSIANS 1:19-20

As a young boy, my father often took me out to hunt rabbits. Once, when we were out looking for rabbits, I let out a yell.

"What's the matter?" my father asked. I had almost seen a rabbit.

To almost see something, to almost do something, to almost be something is a fix people get in because they are people. The good news is that almighty God never is almost anything. God is always exactly what He is: the almighty One. When God the almighty Maker died, all of His power was in that atonement. You can never overstate the efficaciousness of His atonement. You can never exaggerate the power of the cross. The atonement in Jesus Christ's blood is perfect, and nothing can be added to it. It is spotless, impeccable, flawless and perfect as God is perfect.

So the question, "How dost thou spare the wicked if thou art just?" is answered in Jesus. The effective passion of Christ, His holy suffering on the cross and His resurrection from the dead cancel our sins and abrogate our sentence. Not almost, but forever. Within the economy of God's thinking and doing, there is no almost. When we yield ourselves completely to Him, He gives Himself completely to us. What a bargain!

> Was it for crimes that I have done,
> He suffered on the tree?
> Amazing pity, grace unknown,
> And love beyond degree!
>
> ISAAC WATTS (1674–1748)

Dear Father, I cannot comprehend Thy justice, particularly as it applies to my life. I know what I deserve. How I praise Thee that Jesus Christ made it possible for me to experience Thy mercy! Amen.

*For we know him that hath said, Vengeance belongeth unto me,
I will recompense, saith the Lord. And again, The Lord shall judge his people.
It is a fearful thing to fall into the hands of the living God.*
HEBREWS 10:30-31

No matter how nice, refined and lovely you think you are, you are a moral situation; you have been, and you still are. When God confronted you, He found that your ways were not equal; He found inequity in your life and iniquity.

Because he found iniquity there, God's sentence was death. Everybody has been or is under sentence of death. How can people be so jolly under the sentence of death? How can they be so careless? For the soul that sinneth, the Scripture says, it shall die.

When justice confronts a moral situation, it either justifies that person if that person corresponds to the justice of God, or it condemns that person if that person is unequal—if he has inequity and iniquity in him. That is how we got that death sentence.

When God, in His justice, sentences a sinner to die, He does not quarrel with His mercy; He does not quarrel with His kindness; He does not quarrel with His compassion or pity, for they are all attributes of a unitary God, and they cannot quarrel with each other.

O quickly come, dread Judge of all,
For, awful though Thine advent be;
All shadows from the truth will fall,
And falsehood die, in sight of Thee.
O quickly come; for doubt and fear
Like clouds dissolve when Thou art near.

LAWRENCE TUTTIETT (1825-1897)

*My heavenly Father, Thy compassion toward me
has chased away all doubt that I might have of Thee.
I revel in Thy love because of Jesus. Amen.*

And said unto them, Thus it is written, and thus it behooved Christ to suffer,
and to rise from the dead the third day: And that repentance and remission of sins
should be preached in his name among all nations, beginning at Jerusalem.
And ye are witnesses of these things.

LUKE 24:46-48

When God sentences a man to die, mercy concurs, and pity concurs; compassion concurs and wisdom concurs; and everything in God concurs in that sentence. But oh, my brethren, the mystery of the atonement! Through the mystery of the atonement, the soul that avails itself of that atonement—the soul that throws itself out on that atonement—for that soul the moral situation has changed. God has not changed, but the sinner's moral situation has changed.

Jesus Christ did not die on the cross to change God. He died to change a moral situation.

When God's justice confronts an unprotected sinner, that justice sentences him to die; and all of God concurs in that sentence. When Christ, who is God, went onto the tree and died there in infinite agony, He suffered more than they suffer in hell. He suffered all that they could suffer in hell. For everything that God does, He does with all that God is, so that when God suffered for you, God suffered to change your moral situation.

Blessed be the glorious tidings
To a suffering world revealed.
Christ has made a full atonement;
By His stripes we may be healed.

A. B. SIMPSON (1843-1919)

I praise Thee, O God and Father of the Lord Jesus Christ.
Thou hast made full atonement for me and I am able, through Jesus Christ,
to access the fullness of that blessing. Praise be unto God. Amen.

Know therefore that the Lord thy God, he is God, the faithful God, which keepeth covenant and mercy with them that love him and keep his commandments to a thousand generations; And repayeth them that hate him to their face, to destroy them: he will not be slack to him that hateth him, he will repay him to his face.

DEUTERONOMY 7:9-10

When God looks at an atoned sinner, He does not see the same moral situation that He saw when He looked at that sinner who still loved his sin. When God looks at the sinner who still loves his sin and rejects the mystery of atonement, justice condemns him to die. But when God looks at the sinner who has accepted the blood of the everlasting covenant, justice sentences him to live, and God is just in doing both things.

When God justifies a sinner, everything in God is on the sinner's side. All the attributes of God are on the sinner's side. It is not that mercy is pleading for the sinner and justice is trying to be tempted, but all of God does all that God does.

Therefore, when God looks at a sinner and sees him not atoned for, or at least he does not accept the atonement, it does not apply to him. His moral situation is such that justice says he must die. God looks for the atoned sinner who in faith knows he has been atoned for and has accepted it. Justice says he must live. The unjust sinner can no more go to heaven than the justified sinner can go to hell.

> Not all the outward forms on earth,
> Nor rites that God has giv'n,
> Nor will of man, nor blood, nor birth,
> Can raise a soul to heav'n.

ISAAC WATTS (1674-1748)

I stand amazed, O God, of the redeeming grace that has been afforded me. Not my works, praise God, but Thy work has sealed the deal. Hallelujah for the cross! Amen.

Hearken unto me, ye stouthearted, that are far from righteousness:
I bring near my righteousness; it shall not be far off, and my salvation shall not
tarry: and I will place salvation in Zion for Israel my glory.

ISAIAH 46:12-13

Justice is over on our side now, because the mystery of the agony of God on the cross has changed our moral situation. Justice looks and sees equality, not iniquity, and we are justified.

Justification was lost for a while, regulated to the dustbin, and then brought out again to the forefront by the Reformers. We stand on it today, and when we talk about it, it is not just the text we manipulate.

We are justified by faith because the agony of God on the cross changes the moral situation of man. It did not change God at all. The idea that the angry scowl went off the face of God and He began grudgingly to smile is a pagan concept and not Christian at all.

God is one. Not only is there only one God, but God is unitary—one with Himself and indivisible. The mercy of God is simply God being merciful; and the justice of God is simply God being just; the love of God is simply God loving; and the compassion of God is simply God being compassionate. It is not something that runs out of God; it is something that God is—all three persons of the Trinity.

Christ has for sin atonement made,
What a wonderful Saviour!
We are redeemed! The price is paid!
What a wonderful Saviour!

ELISHA A. HOFFMAN (1839-1929)

Dear heavenly Father, to meditate upon Thine agony on the cross is
simply beyond my contemplation. But today I delight in the benefits of Thine
agony and the salvation that comes to me through Jesus Christ. Amen.

God is not a man, that he should lie; neither the son of man, that he should repent:
hath he said, and shall he not do it? or hath he spoken, and shall he not make it good?
NUMBERS 23:19

The age-old question continues to haunt the minds of men: How can God be just, and justify the sinner? Anselm said that compassion flows from goodness, and that goodness without justice is not goodness. You could not be good and not be just.

Furthermore, he adds, when God punishes the wicked it is the just thing to do because it is consistent with the wicked man's deserts. When God pardons the wicked man, it is a just thing to do because it is consistent with God's nature. Therefore, we have God the Father, God the Son and God the Holy Ghost always acting like God.

It is possible for you to get up some morning and be grouchy. Your best friend may turn a cold face on you. Politicians may be for something this election, but next election may be a different story. We can get better, or we can get worse, always changing from one day to the next.

The marvelous and mysterious truth about God is that God is always the same. He is not up one day and down the next, as we are. The only truly stable thing is God. What He is today He always was and ever will be.

O the deep, deep love of Jesus, vast, unmeasured, boundless, free!
Rolling as a mighty ocean in its fullness over me.
Underneath me, all around me, is the current of Thy love;
Leading onward, leading homeward, to my glorious rest above.

SAMUEL T. FRANCIS (1834–1925)

O heavenly Father, how I praise Thee that Thou art always God.
Thy love, unfailing and unchanging, washes my soul anew each day.
In Jesus' name I pray. Amen.

Jesus said unto him, If thou wilt be perfect, go and sell that thou hast, and give to the poor, and thou shalt have treasure in heaven: and come and follow me.
MATTHEW 19:21

We ought to be glad that we cannot sneak into heaven through a cellar window. We need to praise God that we are not going to get into heaven by God's oversight.

Some believe that God is so busy with the world and the upkeep of the world that He will not notice while you just sneak in. You are there for 1,000 years before God sees you and discovers you are in heaven. Or, you were a member of such and such a church, and God says to you, Well, that's a pretty good church, just come on in. So you go in thinking everything is fine.

Remember the story Jesus told? A man got into the banquet but he did not have a robe. Someone noticed him and asked him what he was doing there. He was out of place, so they bound him and threw him out into outer darkness.

There will be nothing like that in God's kingdom, because God, the all Wise One, knows all that can be known, and He knows everybody. He knows you, and God will never permit an unequal man in heaven.

I am so grateful that God is in absolute charge of heaven.

Oh, sweet and blessed country, the home of God's elect!
Oh, sweet and blessed country that eager hearts expect!
In mercy, Jesus brings us to that dear land of rest,
Who art, with God the Father, and Spirit, ever blest.
BERNARD OF CLUNY (TWELFTH CENTURY)

I long, O Father, to reach that blessed country promised to those who trust in Thee. My rightful place is in Thy presence, and I long for Thee. In Jesus' blessed name, amen.

For the word of the Lord is right; and all his works are done in truth. He loveth righteousness and judgment: the earth is full of the goodness of the Lord. By the word of the Lord were the heavens made; and all the host of them by the breath of his mouth.
PSALM 33:4-6

The great God Almighty, who is always one, looks upon a moral situation and sees either death or life. All of God is on the side of death or life. He does not divide Himself between the two. If He sees iniquity and inequity—a sinner uncleansed and unprotected by the atonement, there is only one answer, "God have mercy on me, a sinner."

That is the only answer God responds to. When that sinner beats on his breast and throws himself on the mercy of God, he then receives the benefits of the infinite agony of God on the cross. God looks on that moral situation and says that life and all of hell cannot drag that man down. (Just as none of heaven can pull that man up.)

Oh, the wonder and the mystery and the glory of the being of God!

I am not left to my own devices. I am not left to try to figure out what is right and wrong and how I am going to sneak my way into heaven. God has made a wondrous provision for me; and when I throw myself on the perfect mercy of God, He looks in my direction with mercy.

Oh, let us launch out on this ocean so broad,
Where floods of salvation o'erflow;
Oh, let us be lost in the mercy of God,
Till the depths of His fullness we know.

A. B. SIMPSON (1843–1919)

Dear Lord Jesus, Thy mercy is a mystery to me beyond my ability to fully comprehend. But it is Thy mercy that fills my heart with glorious hope of salvation. Praise Thy name forever. Amen.

For the which cause I also suffer these things: nevertheless I am not ashamed:
for I know whom I have believed, and am persuaded that he is able to keep that
which I have committed unto him against that day.
2 TIMOTHY 1:12

There are two kinds of faith: nominal faith and real faith.

Nominal faith accepts what it is told and can quote text after text to prove it. It is amazing how nominal faith, nominal belief, can weave texts into garments, cloaks and curtains for the church. We have so many of these all around the church, and I must admit that for the most part they are beautiful. But they serve no function in our spiritual walk.

The other kind of faith is what I refer to as real faith. This faith depends upon the character of God and looks nowhere else.

The Scripture does not say of Abraham that he believed the text and it was counted unto him for righteousness. Abraham believed God. It is not what Abraham believed, but who Abraham believed that truly counted.

The man who has real faith, as over against nominal faith, has found the right answer to one important question: What is God like? No question is more important and demands a proper answer.

What is God like? The men of true faith have found an answer to that question, by revelation and illumination. They know in whom they have believed.

I know not why God's wondrous grace to me He hath made known,
Nor why, unworthy, Christ in love redeemed me for His own.
But "I know whom I have believed, and am persuaded that He is able
To keep that which I've committed unto Him against that day.
DANIEL W. WHITTLE (1840–1901)

Dear God of Abraham, Isaac and Jacob, my faith is rooted deep
in whom Thou art. Not the God of the scientists or philosophers or
theologians. My faith is not in what I believe, but in whom I believe, and
I believe in Thee. In the blessed name of Jesus, I pray, amen.

And he said unto them, These are the words which I spake unto you,
while I was yet with you, that all things must be fulfilled, which were written
in the law of Moses, and in the prophets, and in the psalms, concerning me.
LUKE 24:44

I believe the difficulty with the church today is that we have stopped with revelation, and revelation is not enough. Revelation is God's given Word. It is an objective thing, not subjective. It is external, not internal. It is God's revelation of truth; and a man may believe that, and believe it soundly, and hold it to be true yet have only objective revelation of truth that has been objectively revealed.

We must go a step further—to illumination. The man of real faith believes the Word, but he has been illuminated so that he knows what the Word means. That does not mean he is a better Bible teacher, but it means that he has what the old Quakers called an Opening. His heart has been opened to the Word.

As far as I am concerned, you cannot have too many texts. Do not get me wrong and think that I believe the texts are not valuable. They are. However, texts are a means toward an end, and that end is God. The given revelation is a means toward God. The text is never the end; God is the end.

Gather all the text you can gather, but do not stop there. Allow the Holy Spirit to move you on into the area of illumination.

O send Thy Spirit, Lord, now unto me,
That He may touch my eyes and make me see;
Show me the truth concealed within Thy Word,
And in Thy Book revealed I see Thee, Lord.

ALEXANDER GROVES (1842–1909)

O Holy Spirit, Thou breath of God, breathe on me that I might see Thee
truly as Thou desires me to see Thee. Illuminate my heart with
the brilliance of Thy presence. I pray this in Jesus' name. Amen.

How sweet are thy words unto my taste! yea, sweeter than honey to my mouth!
Through thy precepts I get understanding: therefore I hate every false way.
PSALM 119:103-104

If a Bible translation existed somewhere that I do not have, I would not know what it is. My basic thought is, I will never fight over or get all worked up and steamed up over a translation. Some are good, and some are not.

The reason we have such a battle over Bible translations today is that some people have the idea that the text is an end in itself. The text is a means to an end.

The big mistake being made today is in thinking that if we get the Word said in a different way, there will be some magical effect on it. If it is read in the King James Version, that is okay. However, if we get a new version, varying just a little, we have automatically received something new. That thinking does not follow.

Illumination is what matters in the Word of God, as a means toward an end, just as roads are a means to a destination. The road is not anything in itself. Nobody ever built a road and planted flowers along the edge and said, "This is a road." What they say is, "This is the way, a means toward somewhere."

The Bible is a whole series of highways, all leading toward God. When the text has been illuminated in the believer, he or she knows that God is the end toward which he or she is moving, and that believer has real faith.

O may I love Thy precious Word, may I explore the mine,
May I its glorious riches take, may light upon me shine.
O may I find my armor there, thy word my trusty sword;
I'll learn to fight with every foe the battle of the Lord.

EDWIN HODDER (1837-1904)

I love Thy Word, O God, it is my meat and drink every day. May Thy
Holy Spirit reveal to me the beauty of Thyself in this Bible. Amen.

And he said, Draw not nigh hither: put off thy shoes from off thy feet,
for the place whereon thou standest is holy ground.
EXODUS 3:5

When Leonardo da Vinci painted his famous Last Supper, he had little difficulty with it except for the faces. He painted the faces without too much trouble except for one. He did not feel himself worthy to paint the face of Jesus. He held off, unwilling to approach it, but knowing he must. Then in the impulsive carelessness of despair, he painted it quickly and let it go. There was no use, he thought, he couldn't paint it.

In speaking of the holiness of God, I feel very much the same. I sometimes think there is no use for anybody to try. The more I meditate upon God and His attributes, the more I am amazed at the mystery of it all. How can you explain mystery?

Like da Vinci, I press on in faith, hoping and believing that God will illuminate the truth of Himself in such a way that I may know Him better. That is the goal, after all. If I wrestle with Bible truth and do not come into the presence of God, what have I been doing? How does an intellectual understanding reveal to me the heartbeat of the God who created me?

Holy, Holy, Holy, Lord God Almighty!
Early in the morning our song shall rise to Thee;
Holy, Holy, Holy, merciful and mighty!
God in three Persons, blessed Trinity!
REGINALD HEBER (1783–1826)

O heavenly Father, with bowed head I open my Bible and allow
the Holy Spirit to illuminate it to the point that my heart begins to sing
in adoring wonder at the God I love. Amen and amen!

But the natural man receiveth not the things of the Spirit of God:
for they are foolishness unto him: neither can he know them,
because they are spiritually discerned.
1 CORINTHIANS 2:14

A truth sometimes forgotten is that we are fallen human beings—spiritually, morally, mentally and physically. We are fallen in all the ways that men can fall, being what they are, and we are all born into a tainted world. We learn from the cradle on to adjust to this. We nurse it in with our mother's milk; we breathe it in the very air. Our education deepens it and our experience confirms it. Evil impurities everywhere, and everything is dirty.

Even our whitest white is dingy gray and our noblest heroes are soiled heroes. So we learn to excuse, overlook and not expect too much from each other. We do not expect all truth from a teacher; we do not expect all faithfulness from our politicians; and we quickly forgive them when they lie to us, and vote for them again. We do not expect honesty from the merchants, and we do not expect complete trustworthiness from anyone.

We only manage to get along in this kind of world by passing laws to protect ourselves, not only from the criminal element but from the best people there are, who might at the moment of temptation take advantage of us.

How helpless guilty nature lies,
Unconscious of its load!
The heart, unchanged, can never rise
To happiness and God.
ANNE STEELE (1717-1778)

Heavenly Father, the tragedy of our times is that we have lost
the ability to conceive of the holy. Help us to rise above our human
deficiencies and discover the God Thou art. Amen.

The Lord reigneth; let the people tremble: he sitteth between the cherubims; let the earth be moved. . . . Let them praise thy great and terrible name; for it is holy.
PSALM 99:1,3

When we think of the holiness of God, we cannot comprehend it and we certainly cannot define it. Holiness means purity, and purity means that it is unmixed; there is nothing else in it.

We may talk of moral excellency but that is inadequate, for we say to be morally excellent is to excel somebody else in moral character. But about whom are we speaking when we say that God is morally excellent? He excels somebody. Who is it that he excels? The angels? The seraphim?

Still, that is not enough when we come to God.

God is not now any holier than He ever was. Being unchangeable and unchanging, He can never become holier and never was holier than He is now, and He will not be any holier in the future. This holiness He did not get from anyone or from anywhere. He did not go into some infinitely distant realm and absorb His holiness. He is holiness itself beyond the power of thought to grasp and beyond any word to express.

I think I can safely say that if you can express it, it is probably not God. He dwells in the *mysterium tremendum* from eternity past to eternity future.

Holy, Holy, Holy! All the saints adore Thee,
Casting down their golden crowns around the glassy sea;
Cherubim and seraphim falling down before Thee,
Which wert and art and evermore shalt be.

REGINALD HEBER (1783–1826)

*Eternal God and Father of our Lord Jesus Christ,
I bow before Thee in humble expectation of discovering
Thy presence. Thou art so far beyond me, and yet there is
something within me drawing me to Thee. Amen.*

May 10

One thing have I desired of the Lord, that will I seek after;
that I may dwell in the house of the Lord all the days of my life,
to behold the beauty of the Lord, and to inquire in his temple.
PSALM 27:4

All the great masters of the English language have given to us great works of poetry and prose. What a delight it is to read them! But when we come to God and His holiness, no language can express it adequately.

Because this is so, God resorts to association and suggestion. He cannot tell us outright what He is, because He would have to use words we do not know the meaning of. Then we would take the word He used and translate it downward into our terms.

If God were to use a word describing His holiness, we could not understand the word as He uttered it. He would have to translate it down into our unholy mess. If He were to tell us how white He is, he would translate it into terms of dingy gray.

God uses association and suggestion by showing how it affects the unholy.

Moses at the burning bush, standing before the holy fiery presence, knelt down, took off his shoes and hid his face, for he was afraid to look upon God. How do you explain Moses' experience with God? How did Moses understand this experience?

Human language falls short of conveying to us the absoluteness of God in His beauty and holiness.

Praise ye the Father for His loving-kindness,
Tenderly cares He for His erring children;
Praise Him, ye angels, praise Him in the heavens,
Praise ye Jehovah!
ELIZABETH R. CHARLES (1828–1896)

As did Moses of old, O Father, I hide my face from Thee; and yet something
within me longs to see Thy face. Language fails me but my heart rises up
in adoring praise. In the precious name of Jesus, I pray, amen.

The fear of the Lord is the beginning of wisdom;
and the knowledge of the holy is understanding.
PROVERBS 9:10

There are two words for "holy" in the Old Testament—the Hebrew Bible. One is used almost exclusively of God, the Holy One. I find it rarely used of anything or any person except God.

I have been greatly fascinated by this verse in Proverbs, that this word should be the abstract, the holy, rather than the Holy One.

The phrase that really intrigues me is "the knowledge of the holy." The inference here is not just holy, but the Holy One. This is where the focus should be.

Holiness is not based on the things we do or do not do. We have erred tremendously in this area and have caused great harm to Christianity. We are not seeking so much holiness as we are seeking the Holy One. Many have an abstract idea of holy, which has absolutely no bearing upon their relationship with God; their understanding of holy has everything to do with their relationship to the world around them.

However, if I am in harmony with the Holy One, I will have all of the holiness I need to live in this world.

My goal is God Himself, not joy, nor peace,
Nor even blessing, but Himself, my God;
'Tis His to lead me there, not mine, but His—
"At any cost, dear Lord, by any road!"

FREDERICK BROOK (N.D.)

Holy God and Father, I come before Thee in the holy hush that Thou deserves. To know Thee is to know and understand the holiness that is to be my life. I pray this in the name of Jesus, amen.

But as he which hath called you is holy, so be ye holy in all manner
of conversation; because it is written, Be ye holy; for I am holy.
1 PETER 1:15-16

When we think of the word "holy," we are thinking of the Holy One.
However, another word for "holy" flows throughout the Scripture. This
first word is used in reference almost exclusively to God, while this second
word is focused toward created things. It is something, so to speak, that
is holy by contact or association with the Holy One.

We read of holy ground, holy Sabbath, holy city, holy habitation or
holy people. These all get their holiness from their association with the
Holy One.

Focus with me a little on this Holy One and the creatures. This Holy One
only allows in His presence holy creatures, holy beings. Today's Christian
needs to consider and meditate on this truth.

In our humanistic day of watered-down, sentimental Christianity,
we have lost the sense of holy in the church. With all the ruckus, noise
and entertainment in the church, there is little room to cultivate a sense
of holiness unto the Lord.

When will today's Christian learn that gathering together for worship
is not to please ourselves and do what entertains and excites us, but has
everything to do with pleasing God. God is only pleased with holy and
with holiness.

Almighty God, thy grace impart;
Fix deep conviction on each heart,
Nor let us waste, on trifling cares,
That life which thy compassion spares.

PHILIP DODDRIDGE (1702–1751)

We have lost, O God, that sense of reverence, which is becoming of Thee.
We only know the frivolousness of life. So help me to enter into
that holy reverence that is worthy of Thee. Amen.

So will I make my holy name known in the midst of my people Israel;
and I will not let them pollute my holy name any more:
and the heathen shall know that I am the Lord, the Holy One in Israel.
EZEKIEL 39:7

Often people complain about my constant preaching on the person of God. They say that I am only seeing a part of the great truth, and that there is much more. They accuse me of being narrow in my thinking and preaching.

If you are going to be narrow, and I think we ought to be narrow in the right thing, I am going to continue focusing on the person of God. If I am going to emphasize God, and the holiness of God, and the unapproachable quality that can be called that awful thing, that Holy One, I think I am on the right track. I do not take my orders from men, but from God.

The problem with ministry today is that it is fashioned for men and women. What is the latest topic? Let us go after that and the people will come in by the droves. Many churches focus on cultural topics so they can be culturally relevant.

Once, in Charles Spurgeon's church—the Metropolitan Tabernacle in London, England—somebody stole the clock that hung in the back of the sanctuary. They thoughtfully put a note where the clock had been, which read, Since the pastor is more interested in eternity than time, he will not miss this clock.

Forgive me as I put all my focus on God.

Begin, my tongue, some heavenly theme
And speak some boundless thing;
The mighty works, or mightier name,
Of our eternal King.

ISAAC WATTS (1674-1748)

Heavenly Father, forgive me when I am drawn by the things of the
world. Help me today to focus on Thee to the exclusion of everything else.
And may Jesus Christ bless my pursuit today. Amen.

If my people, which are called by my name, shall humble themselves,
and pray, and seek my face, and turn from their wicked ways; then will I hear
from heaven, and will forgive their sin, and will heal their land.
2 CHRONICLES 7:14

In the book of Revelation, we read of people in the presence of God, but not by some technical connection.

What I worry about today is that we are technical Christians, and we can prove it. We can prove we are Christians by technical analysis. Anybody can flip open a Greek lexicon and show you that you are a saint. I am afraid of that kind of Christianity, because if I have not felt any sense of vileness by contrast with that sense of unapproachable and indescribable holiness, I wonder if I have ever been hit hard enough to really repent. If I do not repent, I cannot believe.

We are told, "Just believe it, brother, just believe it." Then they smile, ask for our name, address and what church we would like to go to. We have it all fixed up technically. I'm afraid that our fathers knew God in a different manner than that. They knew God other then by technical analysis.

There was a bishop who would go down by the riverbank, kneel down by a log and spend Saturday afternoon repenting of his sins. There probably was not a holier man in the entire region round about. He felt the vileness of his sin and could not stand the dingy gray over against the unapproachable shining whiteness that was God.

Lord Jesus, before You I patiently wait;
Come now and within me a new heart create.
To those who have sought You, You never said, "No."
Now wash me and I shall be Whiter than snow.

JAMES L. NICHOLSON (1828–1876)

Holy Spirit of God, let me feel the vileness of my sin. Do not let me
think lightly of my sin, but allow me to think of it as Thou dost think of
it. Wash me whiter than snow, dear Lord, I pray. In Jesus' name, amen.

The sinners in Zion are afraid; fearfulness hath surprised the hypocrites.
Who among us shall dwell with the devouring fire?
who among us shall dwell with everlasting burnings?
ISAIAH 33:14

In the book of Isaiah, we read of the fiery burners. These seraphim stood above the throne on high. As you look at them, you see nothing in these creatures before the throne that exhibits the flippancy and irreverence we see now in just about every church. These were creatures caught up in the awesome holiness of the God who was high and lifted up. There was a sense of presence, and these holy creatures covered their feet. Why?

They covered their feet in modesty; they covered their face in worship; and they used their wings to fly. These were the seraphim, called the fiery burners.

In Ezekiel 1 and 10, we see creatures coming out of the fire. These were the holy fiery burners Ezekiel saw, those magnificent creatures caught up in the atmosphere of worship because they were in the presence of the Holy One.

I have often heard this text used by preachers to ask which ones are going to go to hell. But if you read the text in its context, it is not describing hell at all.

Who among us shall dwell in the fiery burnings? The next verse answers the question. It is not hell, but the presence of God.

Lift up your heads, ye gates of brass, ye bars of iron, yield,
And let the King of Glory pass; the cross is in the field.
That banner, brighter than the star that leads the train of night,
Shines on the march, and guides from far His servants to the fight.

JAMES MONTGOMERY (1771-1854)

Heavenly Father, I envy those creatures coming out of the fire. I long to know
Thee in the passion of Thy presence. Burn deep within me holy desires that
nothing in this world can ever put out. I pray this in Jesus' name. Amen.

And I looked, and, behold, a whirlwind came out of the north, a great cloud, and a fire infolding itself, and a brightness was about it, and out of the midst thereof as the colour of amber, out of the midst of the fire.
EZEKIEL 1:4

The awesome, holy creatures described by Ezekiel, about which we know so little but ought to know more, came out of the fire having four faces. They went straight ahead and let down their wings to worship; and at the word of God's command, they leapt to do His will.

God spoke to Moses out of the burning bush. When God went with Israel, it was in the cloud by day and the pillar of fire by night. On the day of Pentecost, the Holy Spirit rested upon each of the disciples as a tongue of fire.

What is God saying in all of this?

God dwells among men in that awesome fire. He took not away the pillar of the cloud by day or the pillar of fire by night so that He might lead them in all their journeys. It was God dwelling among them. It was His presence in the fire that brought to Israel the protection and guidance needed in her journey.

When the tabernacle was made, the cherubim of gold overshadowed the mercy seat. What was it that came down between the cherubs' wings? It was the fire of God's presence.

O for the living flame
From His own altar brought,
To touch our lips, our minds inspire,
And wing to heav'n our thought.
JAMES MONTGOMERY (1771-1854)

We praise Thee, O God, and worship Thee with an intensity that comes from the fire from off the altar. Burn, fire, burn within me holy desires until I want nothing more. Amen.

As for the likeness of the living creatures, their appearance was like burning coals of fire, and like the appearance of lamps: it went up and down among the living creatures; and the fire was bright, and out of the fire went forth lightning.
EZEKIEL 1:13

I read in Ezekiel that the seraphim covered their faces; and when Moses encountered God, he hid his face, for he was afraid to look upon God. In the book of Revelation, John the beloved fell down when he saw the Savior and had to be raised up almost from the dead. Paul went blind on the Damascus Road. Every encounter with God has been such that the man went flat down on his face and could not see.

What was the light that blinded them? Was it the cosmic ray coming down from some exploding body or two colliding galaxies that they talk about so much?

No, no, no—a thousand times no. It was the God of Abraham, Isaac and Jacob. The God that dwelled in the Bush; the God that dwells in the Shekinah between the presence, between the two wings of the seraphim.

What was it on that day in the early church when suddenly there came a sound from heaven as of a rushing mighty wind, and fire appeared and sat as a tongue of flame upon each one of them? What did that mean, and what could it mean but that God was branding them and therefore said, with His fiery holiness, you are mine.

> 'Tis burning in my soul, 'tis burning in my soul;
> The fire of heav'nly love is burning in my soul,
> The Holy Spirit came, all glory to His Name!
> The fire of heav'nly love is burning in my soul.

DELIA T. WHITE (1838–1921)

O Holy Spirit, bring to bear upon my life today the divine fire of holiness that will burn from me the dross of sin and bring me into the presence of the Holy One. In the blessed name of Jesus I pray. Amen.

But the heavens and the earth, which are now, by the same word are kept in store,
reserved unto fire against the day of judgment and perdition of ungodly men.
2 PETER 3:7

The church of Jesus Christ was born out of fire, just as the creatures in Ezekiel came out of fire. The church was born out of fire; but we have gray ashes today where the fires seem to have gone out. We are to be men and women of fire, for that is our origin.

What fire is that?

Is it to be the atomic fire? Fire from a hydrogen bomb?

Do not allow yourselves to be fooled by the scientist. Do not allow your spiritual perceptions and concepts to be dragged down to their level. Do not think in terms of science.

That awesome fire, out of which the seraphim moved, is that fire that dwelt between the cherubim; and that blazing light that knocked all flat is the same fire that shall dissolve the heavens and the earth. It is the awful presence of the Holy One.

God does not need anything exterior to Himself to do any work He has decreed. It is the awesome presence of God, the fire of the Holy One, which will accomplish the presence of God. All who cannot stand in His presence will be destroyed.

> Burn, burn, O love, within my heart,
> Burn fiercely night and day,
> Till all the dross of earthly loves
> Is burned, and burned away.
>
> FREDERICK W. FABER (1814–1863)

I stand in Thy fiery presence, O Lord, filled with fear and awe.
I know Thy presence is where I long to be.
Burn the dross that comes between Thee and me. Amen.

May 19

Art thou not from everlasting, O Lord my God, mine Holy One?
we shall not die. O Lord, thou hast ordained them for judgment;
and, O mighty God, thou hast established them for correction.
HABAKKUK 1:12

It is the presence of the Holy One the Scriptures describe in terms of fire that we must deal with finally.

Some have the mistaken notion that their destiny is in their hands. They are going to decide when they serve Christ. They are going to make the decision. They are going to push God around. They are going to accept Jesus or not accept Jesus. They can lay their heads on the pillow tonight with a heartbeat between them and eternity and tell themselves, *I'll decide this question. I am a man of free will. God is not forcing my will.*

We have brought God down to the level of being our personal manager. Jesus will handle all of our problems.

I have a word for you.

God will help you, all right, but oh, how far this thought is from biblical religion! There was God in the midst, and what was it that gathered the people together in the book of Acts? As they ministered unto the Lord, as they fasted and prayed in the awesome Presence, they heard the voice of the Holy Ghost say, *separate me Barnabas and Saul.*

Today we are thrown back on our planning, our reasoning and our thinking, forgetting the fact that the great and holy God is in our midst.

What will you do with Jesus? Neutral you cannot be;
Someday your heart will be asking, "What will He do with me?"
A. B. SIMPSON (1843–1919)

O heavenly Father, forgive me for trying in my own strength to serve.
I have exhausted my humanity in fruitless endeavors. Let me rest in
Thee and trust my life to the wisdom that brought all things into being.
I pray this in the blessed name of Jesus. Amen.

Thou art of purer eyes than to behold evil, and canst not look on iniquity:
wherefore lookest thou upon them that deal treacherously, and holdest thy tongue
when the wicked devoureth the man that is more righteous than he?
HABAKKUK 1:13

This phrase—"Thou art of purer eyes than to behold evil, and canst not look on iniquity"—has always fascinated me.

The question I have to ask myself is simply this: Dare I think of iniquity any less than God thinks of iniquity? I have a way of excusing iniquity and downplaying the horribleness of it. I must come to the point where I view iniquity as God views it, and treat it as God treats it.

I am not thinking of looking on other people's iniquity, but on the iniquity that haunts the corridors of my own soul. It is one thing to point out iniquity in someone else's life, and tell him what God thinks of it; but it is another thing altogether to point out the iniquity in my own life and understand that God cannot look on that iniquity.

I wonder about the person who can listen to a sermon that has outlined the iniquity of mankind and then go home without being bothered by it. Does that person have the knowledge of the Holy One?

> When penitence has wept in vain
> Over some foul, dark spot,
> One only stream, a stream of blood,
> Can wash away the blot.

CECIL FRANCES ALEXANDER (1818-1895)

O Heavenly Father, help me to view my sin from Thy point of view.
Do not allow me to underestimate the horror of my sin. Let me never
become adjusted to the error of my way, but may I lean heavily
upon Thy grace. Amen.

Therefore say unto the house of Israel, Thus saith the Lord God;
Repent, and turn yourselves from your idols;
and turn away your faces from all your abominations.
EZEKIEL 14:6

The one thing I cannot get over, and it bows me down in penitent prayer each day, is my own iniquity.

That I am born again, I know. That I am bound for heaven, I know. That Jesus Christ died for all my sins on the cross, I know.

Deep within me is petulance toward personal iniquity. The closer I get to the knowledge of this Holy One, the more horrible my iniquity becomes. As I begin to view myself as God views me, and look at myself through His eyes, those holy eyes, I begin to feel about my iniquity as God feels about it.

I look back and remember a day when it was common for men and women to come to an altar of prayer and kneel there, shake, tremble and weep in agony of conviction over their iniquity.

We do not see it now because the God we preach is not the everlasting, awful Holy One who cannot look upon iniquity.

When we get a vision of the Holy One, as He desires to reveal Himself, this will come back as a mighty power to change us into His likeness.

Lord, incline me to repent;
Let me now my fall lament,
Deeply my revolt deplore,
Weep, believe and sin no more.
CHARLES WESLEY (1707-1788)

My sin, O God, my sin is ever with me. The closer I come to Thee
the more horrid my sin becomes. I will praise the name of Jesus for
the blood that has cleansed me, enabling me to come boldly
into Thy presence. Praise the name of Jesus. Amen.

O Lord, thou hast brought up my soul from the grave: thou hast kept me alive,
that I should not go down to the pit. Sing unto the Lord, O ye saints of his, and give
thanks at the remembrance of his holiness. For his anger endureth but a moment;
in his favour is life: weeping may endure for a night, but joy cometh in the morning.

PSALM 30:3-5

We come into the presence of God with our concept of morality, having learned it from books, newspapers and schools. We come dirty, and everything we have is dirty; our whitest white is dirty, and our church is dirty and our thoughts are dirty. We come to God dirty and do nothing about it.

If we come to God dirty but trembling in shock and awestruck, and we kneel in His presence, and at His feet cry like Isaiah, "I am undone, I am a man of unclean lips," then we would be coming properly and in reverence to God. The way it is today, we skip into God's awful presence, and somebody who is dirty comes with the latest book, *Seven Steps to Salvation,* and gives out seven verses that get a fellow out of his problems and troubles.

Each year more people are going to church, giving more money, but with less spirituality and less holiness, forgetting that without holiness no man shall see God.

I want God to be what God is, and I want God to remain what God is—the impeccable holy, the unapproachable holy thing, the Holy One. I want Him to be and remain holy, in capital letters. I want His heaven to be holy; I want His throne to be holy; and I do not want Him to change or modify His requirements. Even if it shuts me out, I want something holy left in the universe.

I have found the joy no tongue can tell, how its waves of glory roll!
It is like a great o'erflowing well springing up within my soul.

BARNEY E. WARREN (1867–1951)

O Holy God, Thy holiness prevents me from coming into Thy presence.
Thy grace invites me in by the blessed name of the Lord Jesus Christ.
Amen and amen!

And the men of Bethshemesh said,
Who is able to stand before this holy Lord God?
and to whom shall he go up from us?
1 SAMUEL 6:20

The church doors are wide open for anyone who has a mind to come and join. I honestly believe some think that an open door into the church is an open door into heaven. Just walk through the open church door and down the corridor on the right is the doorway into heaven. Repentance is not necessary anymore to join the church. Living a holy life is certainly not required by most these days.

Our problem is that we keep or allow our churches to stay dingy gray instead of pleading for holy whiteness. We are willing to accept something off-color as long as it does not offend anybody.

Whenever I mention this, somebody comes along and says, "Now, my brother, don't get excited about this and don't become a fanatic, for don't you understand that God understands our flesh and knows we are but dust?"

It may be a hard stand, but I believe that what God cannot look at is something we should not be involved in. The qualification to join the church should be similar to the qualifications of entrance into heaven. Remember what the Word says: Without holiness it is impossible to please God.

This is the day to please God.

Lord Jesus, for this I most humbly entreat;
I wait, blessed Lord, at Thy crucified feet;
By faith, for my cleansing, I see Thy blood flow,
Now wash me, and I shall be whiter than snow.

JAMES L. NICHOLSON (1828–1876)

O heavenly Father, it is my desire to please Thee in all I do.
Whatever pleases Thee, O Lord, will be my pleasure.
I pray this In Jesus' name. Amen.

God reigneth over the heathen: God sitteth upon the throne of his holiness.
The princes of the people are gathered together, even the people of the God of
Abraham: for the shields of the earth belong unto God: he is greatly exalted.
PSALM 47:8-9

This is the day for jolly joke telling, for banqueting Christians. Few take anything seriously, especially their Christianity. If you cannot get the people to laugh, you are not going to get them to come back again. Our motto is: Give them what they want and they will give us what we want. Unless you can give them a laugh a minute, they are bored and will not return.

What bothers me about all this is that each of us will be called before the Ineffable to appear and give an account of our life. The atmosphere will not be suitable for jolly joke telling. God is always serious and will be even more so at that moment. How are we going to do it?

There is a way for man to rise to that sublime abode, a way to prepare us for the sight of holiness above. Our hymnody encourages us to follow that path that will bring us right in to the awesome presence of God. Maybe that is why hymns are not so popular today.

But how can I, a son of ignorance and night, come into the holiest of holies in heaven and encounter God?

Only by bowing in humble reverence to this awesome Holy One.

These, these prepare us for the sight
Of holiness above;
The sons of ignorance and night,
May dwell in the Eternal Light,
Through the Eternal Love.

THOMAS BINNEY (1798-1874)

O God, Thou sittest on Thy throne with seraphim, cherubim,
angels, archangels, principalities, powers and unfallen creatures.
They can bear the burning bliss, but that is because they never
have known a fallen world like this. Amen.

For he hath said, I will never leave thee, nor forsake thee.
HEBREWS 13:5

We have all kinds of psychology and therapy to comfort people so they do not feel bad. Nothing wrong with trying to comfort someone who is going through some hard times, but sometimes we take it too far.

I do not want to be comforted from the human standpoint. I do not want anybody downplaying the iniquity in my own heart. I need to allow myself to be broken before God, and out of that brokenness will come God's strength and His presence. The presence of God is what I yearn for each day.

My family and friends cannot help me in that awful hour when I appear before God. When the Uncreated Being impinges on my naked spirit, I am beyond the help of anything human.

There is only one way, and that is through the offering sacrifice and the Advocate with God; but do not take that lightly. Conversion used to be a revolutionary, radical, wondrous, terrible, glorious thing. Not much of that left anymore. We have forgotten that God is the Holy One.

God's presence in my life now is preparing me for that awful day to come. It is the presence of God now invading my spirit that is preparing me for that day.

> How did my heart rejoice to hear
> My friends devoutly say,
> "In Zion let us all appear,
> And keep the solemn day!"
>
> ISAAC WATTS (1674-1748)

I rejoice, O God, in that mysterious presence that is now preparing me to come into Thy presence in the heavens. Each day my heart pants for that glorious day. Hallelujah For the Lamb of God! Amen.

*Now for a long season Israel hath been without the true God, and without
a teaching priest, and without law. But when they in their trouble did turn
unto the Lord God of Israel, and sought him, he was found of them.*
2 CHRONICLES 15:3-4

Grace is God's good pleasure flowing out of the goodness of God and
is what God is like. If you were to meet God, you would find that this is
what God is like.

Grace is that which in God brings into favor one that was unjustly
in disfavor. Grace and favor, incidentally, are used interchangeably in the
English Bible.

Grace is the goodness of God confronting human demerit. When justice confronts a moral situation, it pronounces death. Still, the goodness
of God yearns to bestow blessedness; and that is grace even to those who
do not deserve it but who have specific demerit.

A difference exists between no merit and demerit. No merit simply is
a negative thing; it is vacuity. Demerit is a positive thing that means there
is not only no merit, but there is also the opposite of merit. We have gone
beyond having no merit to a position of owing more than we could ever
pay. We start out owing and it only gets worse. Try as we might, we could
do nothing to wipe the slate clean.

God's grace overrides all of that and brings us into His favor.

Marvelous grace of our loving Lord,
Grace that exceeds our sin and our guilt,
Yonder, on Calvary's Mount out poured,
There where the blood of the Lamb was spilt.
JULIA H. JOHNSTON (1849–1919)

*Dear Lord Jesus Christ, what Thou did on Calvary is beyond my wildest
understanding. I contemplate it but cannot understand it; but what Thou
did there brought into my life the marvelous grace of God. Amen and amen.*

Thou in thy mercy hast led forth the people which thou hast redeemed:
thou hast guided them in thy strength unto thy holy habitation.
EXODUS 15:13

Four times as much is said about mercy in the Old Testament as in the New. On the other side, strangely and wondrously, there are more than three times as much said about grace in the New Testament as in the Old.

We read that the law was given by Moses; grace and truth came by Jesus Christ (see John 1:17). Christ is the blessed channel through which grace flows, but it is possible to misunderstand this. Unfortunately, a great many have.

Never underestimate the ability of good people to misunderstand. For the most part, many have made this to mean that Moses knew only law and Christ knows only grace. This was not the teaching of our fathers, and you will not find it in any of the writings of the Puritans, nor even of John Calvin or the great revivalists and reformers.

It cannot be said too often that it takes all of the Word of God to make it the Word of God. To divide it, even rightly, is to run the great risk of misunderstanding. When we divide and categorize Scripture, we run into the danger of misinterpreting the mind and heart of God. Leave this work to the Holy Spirit who breathes truth into our hearts.

> For why? the Lord our God is good;
> His mercy is forever sure;
> His truth at all times firmly stood,
> And shall from age to age endure.
>
> WILLIAM KETHE (?–1594)

Thy Word, O God, is my environment day by day.
May Thy blessed Holy Spirit open up my heart so that I may nourish
my soul on the delicacies of Thy grace. In Jesus' name, amen.

For the Lord God is a sun and shield: the Lord will give grace and glory:
no good thing will he withhold from them that walk uprightly.
O Lord of hosts, blessed is the man that trusteth in thee.

PSALM 84:11-12

To believe that God gave the law through Moses, therefore, Moses knew no grace is to misread or fail to read that passage properly. Does not the Bible say that before the Flood, Noah found grace in the eyes of the Lord? Where did he find that grace?

After the law was given, Moses had been on the mountain 40 days and 40 nights when God reached down out of the fire and storm and with His finger chiseled the 10 words on the tablets of stone. That was an important point in history, but it did not in any way negate the grace of God.

The Bible says, Thou hast found grace in my sight and I know thy name (see Exod. 33:12). God did not deal with Moses based on law. He dealt with Moses based on grace.

Moses knew it, and said, If I have found grace in thy sight . . . (see v. 13). How could it be otherwise? How could it be that God should act only in law in the Old Testament and only in grace in the New if God does not change? If immutability is an attribute of God, then God must always act like Himself.

All needful grace will God bestow,
And crown that grace with glory too.
He gives us all things, and withholds
No real good from upright souls.

ISAAC WATTS (1674-1748)

How I praise Thee, O God, that Thou dost always act like Thyself! My
great comfort is that when I come to Thee, I know that Thou will always be
the same. I bless Thee in the precious name of the Lord Jesus Christ. Amen.

For this my son was dead, and is alive again; he was lost, and is found.
And they began to be merry.
LUKE 15:24

The parable of the prodigal son has some very fascinating aspects to it. After the prodigal son had spent all that he had, he found himself among the swine, and Scripture says that he came to himself.

What a beautiful idiom; it's as if God understood that the man had not been himself, but now through the wisdom taught him by loss and homesickness, he comes to himself.

You do not find people always the same. They wander away as the prodigal did; then something happens, causing them to come to themselves.

Grace does not come like the weather, like a great surge of hot grace and then no grace at all. Since grace is what God is, God must always act like Himself. He must act like Himself before the Flood and after the Flood. Like Himself when the law was given, and after. God must always act like Himself; and since grace is an attribute of God, it is that which God is, and it cannot be removed from God if God remains God. There has been and always will be grace in the heart of God; and there is not any more grace now than there ever was, and there never will be any more grace than there is now.

No more a wandering sheep, I love to be controlled;
I love my tender Shepherd's voice, I love the peaceful fold:
No more a wayward child, I seek no more to roam;
I love my heavenly Father's voice, I love, I love his home!

HORATIUS BONAR (1808–1889)

Dear heavenly Father, I find great comfort in coming to Thee and finding Thy grace always sufficient. I change, but Thy grace never changes. It always brings me to where Thou want me to be. Amen.

*According as he hath chosen us in him before the foundation of the world,
that we should be holy and without blame before him in love.*
EPHESIANS 1:4

Prior to Moses, nobody was ever saved except by grace. During Moses' time,
nobody was ever saved except by grace. After Moses, and before the cross
and after the cross and since the cross, and all during every dispensation
anywhere, any time since Abel offered his first lamb before God on the
smoking altar, nobody was ever saved in any other way than by grace.

Grace is the only way then as it is now.

Remember, grace always comes by Jesus Christ, and by no other way.
This does not mean that before Jesus was born of Mary there was no grace,
because God dealt in grace with mankind looking forward to Christ. Now
that Christ is come and has ascended to the Father's right hand, God looks
back upon the cross, as we look back upon the cross. Everyone saved, from
Abel on was saved by looking forward to the cross. Grace came by Jesus
Christ, and everybody that has been saved since the cross has been saved
by looking back at the cross. Grace always comes by Jesus Christ. It did
not come at His birth; it came in God's ancient scheme.

Grace always has been in the mind of God when He was thinking
about you and me.

Grace first contrived the way
To save rebellious man;
And all the steps that grace display
Which drew the wondrous plan.

PHILIP DODDRIDGE (1702–1751)

*Thy Grace, O Lord, has rescued me from the depravity of humanity.
From everlasting to everlasting Thy grace has reigned throughout
Thy creation. I praise Thee that I found that grace I need.
Praise be the name of Jesus. Amen.*

May 31

Let us therefore come boldly unto the throne of grace,
that we may obtain mercy, and find grace to help in time of need.
HEBREWS 4:16

God's redemptive plan was carefully wrought out and thought out, and came according to God's ancient plan in Christ Jesus.

Grace did not come when Christ was born in a manger or when He was baptized or anointed of the Spirit. It did not come when He died on the cross or when He rose from the dead or went to the Father's right hand.

Grace came from the ancient beginning, through Jesus Christ, the Eternal Son, and was manifest on the cross at Calvary. It had been always operative, from the beginning.

If God had not operated in grace, He would have swept away the human race, he would have crushed Adam and Eve under His heel in awful judgment, for they had it coming. Because God was a God of grace, and because He had already planned eternity, the Lamb of God had been slain before the foundation of the world. There was no embarrassment in the divine scheme; God did not have to back out and say, I'm sorry, but I've mixed things up here. He simply went on with His redemptive scheme.

O wondrous love! To bleed and die,
To bear the cross and shame,
That guilty sinners, such as I,
Might plead Thy gracious name!

JOHN NEWTON (1725-1807)

Precious Lord Jesus, I bow before Thee, thanking Thee for the grace that
has made my redemption possible. Praise be to Thy name. Amen.

For as in Adam all die, even so in Christ shall all be made alive.
1 CORINTHIANS 15:22

In the Garden of Eden, when the first Adam slipped and fell, the second Adam was already there. Adam's failure was not a shock to God, so that He had to scramble around to try to find a solution. Beyond our comprehension is the fact that the second Adam preceded the first Adam; and that is a tribute to God's amazing grace.

Anything God has ever done for anybody is because of His amazing grace. God's grace is for everybody, and everybody—the lowest woman in the world; the most sinful, bloody man in the world; a Judas, a Hitler—receives it in some degree. If it had not been that God was gracious, we all would have been cut off.

After all, there is not much difference in sinners. When a woman sweeps the house, it is dirty—black, gray and different colors—but it is all dirty and filthy before the broom. When God looks at humanity, He sees some that are very white, but still dirty. He sees some that are very black, and they are dirty. He sees some that are morally speckled, and it is all dirty, and it all goes before the moral broom.

Everybody falls under the grace of God.

> Come, ye weary, heavy laden,
> Bruised and ruined by the fall;
> If you tarry 'til you're better,
> You will never come at all.
> Not the righteous, not the righteous;
> Sinners Jesus came to call.
>
> JOSEPH HART (1712–1768)

O gracious heavenly Father, full of mercy and grace,
how I praise Thee that although my life was wrecked and ruined with sin,
Thy grace has set me free. Praise the name of Jesus. Amen.

Surely he scorneth the scorners: but he giveth grace unto the lowly.
The wise shall inherit glory: but shame shall be the promotion of fools.
PROVERBS 3:34-35

Everybody, regardless of who they are or what they have done, falls under the grace of God. Not everybody experiences the saving grace of God, and here is the big difference. God's grace extends to everyone; but when the grace of God becomes operative through faith in Jesus Christ, there is the new birth.

Not everyone experiences this grace; nevertheless, God holds back any judgment that would come to a man until God, in His kindness, has given every man a chance to repent.

Grace is God's goodness; it is the kindness of God's heart, His good-will and cordial benevolence. It is what God is like.

God is kind and gracious, filled with goodwill, cordiality and benevolence—all the time. You will find God to be gracious always, and at all times and toward all people forever. Nobody will ever run into any meanness in God, any resentment or ill will, for there is none in Him.

All of these aspects of God work in perfect harmony with God's justice and judgment. I believe in hell and in judgment, but I also believe that those whom God must reject He will still feel gracious toward and cannot do anything else.

Hast thou not given Thy word
To save my soul from death?
And I can trust Thee, Lord,
To keep my mortal breath;
I'll go and come, nor fear to die,
Till from on high Thou call me home.

ISAAC WATTS (1676-1748)

Heavenly Father, I have experienced the graciousness of Thy love.
I praise Thee that Thou did not leave me in my sin, but rescued me and
set me upon that Rock, even the Lord Jesus Christ. Amen.

Moreover the law entered, that the offence might abound. But where sin abounded, grace did much more abound: That as sin hath reigned unto death, even so might grace reign through righteousness unto eternal life by Jesus Christ our Lord.
ROMANS 5:20-21

God measures His grace against our sin. Grace has abounded unto many, and where sin abounded, grace did much more abound. When God said, "much more abound" it does not mean there are any degrees in God's grace or any progressiveness in God's grace. God has no degrees, but man does. This terminology is for us to grasp and understand that God's grace is bigger than our ability to sin.

For example, we give degrees to sin. We believe that one sin or act of sin is greater than another act of sin. As far as God is concerned, sin is sin and has no degrees. To put it in our understanding, it does not take any more of God's grace to deal with one act of sin than it does another act of sin. Sin is sin as far as God is concerned, and His grace is greater than all of our sins put together.

Sometimes people feel that they are better than someone else because their sin is not quite as terrible. When it comes to God and His evaluation of sin, sin is still sin, and every sin is covered by God's grace. The only way into God's grace is through Jesus Christ.

Marvelous, infinite, matchless grace,
Freely bestowed on all who believe!
You that are longing to see His face,
Will you this moment His grace receive?
JULIA H. JOHNSTON (1849-1919)

My heavenly Father, I praise Thee for the grace that has been poured out in my direction. Hallelujah! Thy grace is bigger than all my sin. I only need to know that Thy grace has me covered. Praise the name of Jesus! Amen.

*But not as the offence, so also is the free gift. For if through the offence of one
many be dead, much more the grace of God, and the gift by grace,
which is by one man, Jesus Christ, hath abounded unto many.*

ROMANS 5:15

John Bunyan wrote his life story and called it, "Grace Abounding to the Chief of Sinners." Bunyan honestly believed that title represented his life. He believed that he was the man who had the least right to the grace of God. Not that anybody ever had a right. But he so deeply felt his own sinfulness, and it was only the abounding grace of God that brought him through.

Our biggest mistake is in thinking that God is just like us. One day a person will be kind and gracious, and the next day he or she will be full of anger and resentment. When the Bible says that God's grace does much more abound, it does not mean that it abounds more than anything else in God. It means that it abounds more than anything in us. No matter how much sin a man has done, grace abounds unto that man.

The higher a man thinks of himself, the less he appreciates the grace of God. When a person begins to see himself as John Bunyan saw himself, completely under the sentence of death, the grace of God becomes that much more amazing. When I compare God's grace with my sin, God's grace always wins.

Sing, my soul, His wondrous love,
Who from yon bright throne above,
Ever watchful o'er our race,
Still to man extends His grace.

ANONYMOUS

*Dear heavenly Father, like Bunyan and the apostle Paul, I feel that
I am the chief of sinners. Thy grace is so amazing because it covers
sinners like me. Praise the name of Jesus. Amen.*

*But will God indeed dwell on the earth? behold, the heaven and heaven
of heavens cannot contain thee; how much less this house that I have builded?*
1 KINGS 8:27

God's grace in my life is an overwhelming plenitude of kindness and
goodness. If I could only remember and get hold of that, I would not have
to be pandered to and entertained so much. If I could only walk around
remembering the grace of God toward me, who has nothing but demerit,
and is in an incomprehensible mess, I would have nothing but gratitude
in my heart for God.

God's grace is so vast, so huge, so overwhelming that nobody can
ever grasp it or hope to understand it. Grace is the loving-kindness of
God toward people.

Just think of it, would God have put up with us for this long if He
had only a limited amount of grace? If He had only a limited amount
of anything, He would not be God, because for God to be God, He must
be infinite.

You cannot use the word "amount" when referring to God, because
"amount" means a measure, and God cannot be measured. You cannot
measure God in any direction. God dwells in no dimension and cannot
be measured in any way.

'Tis not by works of righteousness
Which our own hands have done,
But we are saved by sovereign grace
Abounding through His Son.
ISAAC WATTS (1674-1748)

*I praise Thee, O God, for Thy saving grace abounding to me
through Thy precious Son, even the Lord Jesus Christ, my Savior.
May His name be praised. Amen.*

And God is able to make all grace abound toward you;
that ye, always having all sufficiency in all things,
may abound to every good work.
2 CORINTHIANS 9:8

God's infinitude means that the grace of God must always be measureless. When we sing of the grace of God, of course it is amazing. Look at yourself, see how sinful you are, and say, "God's grace must be vast, as huge as the space to forgive such a sinner as I am."

When God shows grace to a sinner, He is not being dramatic; He is simply acting like God. He will never act any other way but like God.

Take, for example, a man that justice has condemned. When that man turned his back on the grace of God in Christ and refused to be rescued, the time comes when God must judge the man; when God judges the man, He acts like himself. When God shows love to the human race, He acts like Himself. When God shows judgment to the angels that kept not their first estate, He acts like Himself. God always acts in conformity with the fullness of His own holy, perfect symmetrical nature. God always feels His overwhelming plenitude of goodness and feels it in harmony with all His other attributes.

Nothing should create praise in us more than knowing that God will always act like Himself.

Amazing grace, how sweet the sound
That saved a wretch like me!
I once was lost, but now I'm found,
Was blind, but now I see.

JOHN NEWTON (1725-1807)

Dear Lord Jesus, my wonderful Savior, how I bless Thee for the grace
that was able to save a wretch like me! I worship Thee because Thou
hast made my worship worthy of Thee. Amen and amen.

For the Lord your God is God of gods, and Lord of lords, a great God, a mighty, and a terrible, which regardeth not persons, nor taketh reward.
DEUTERONOMY 10:17

One important consideration when thinking about God is that God never gets frustrated. Humans do, and for good reason. We are not infinite. But God has no good reason to become frustrated with anything or anybody, at any time.

God does not get frustrated because He is infinite. The infinitude of God means that God always remains God, and never changes. Everything God is remains in complete harmony. All of this, He bestows on His Eternal Son.

Many people talk about the goodness of God and then become sentimental about it and say that God is too good to punish anybody. Therefore, they have ruled out hell.

The man who has an adequate conception of God will not only believe in the love of God, but he will also believe in the holiness of God. He will not only believe in the mercy of God, but in the justice of God.

When you see the everlasting God in His holy perfect union, acting in judgment, you know that the man who chooses evil must never dwell in the presence of this holy God.

Great God, how infinite art Thou!
How poor and weak are we!
Let the whole race of creatures bow,
And pay their praise to Thee.
ISAAC WATTS (1674-1748)

Eternal God and Father of our Lord Jesus Christ, praise for Thee wells up within my heart. To know my own wretchedness is to truly appreciate Thy grace. Amen.

And be ye kind one to another, tenderhearted, forgiving one another,
even as God for Christ's sake hath forgiven you.
EPHESIANS 4:32

God is so kind that infinity will not be able to measure it. He is so immeasurably loving; but he is also holy and just. This we must keep in mind all the time. The grace of God comes only through Jesus Christ. The second Person of the Trinity opened the channeling grace, and it flows through Him. It flowed through Him from the day that Adam sinned, all through Old Testament times, and it never flows any other way.

Some people do not quite grasp this God. They get dreamily poetic about the goodness of our heavenly Father who is love. They write, "Love is God, God is love, love is all in all, and everything will be okay." That sums up a lot of teaching today, but it is false teaching.

If I want to know this immeasurable grace, this overwhelming, astounding kindness of God, I have to step under the shadow of the cross. I must come to where God releases His grace. Either I must look forward to it or I must look back at it. I must look one way or the other to that cross where Jesus died.

> Almighty God, Thy grace impart;
> Fix deep conviction on each heart;
> Nor let us waste, on trifling cares,
> That life which Thy compassion spares.
>
> PHILIP DODDRIDGE (1702–1751)

I praise Thee, O God and Father of our Lord Jesus Christ, for channeling
Thy grace, through Christ, into my life so effectively. Thy grace is my
portion each and every day. Praise the name of Jesus! Amen.

And being found in fashion as a man, he humbled himself, and became obedient unto death, even the death of the cross. Wherefore God also hath highly exalted him, and given him a name which is above every name: That at the name of Jesus every knee should bow, of things in heaven, and things in earth, and things under the earth.

PHILIPPIANS 2:8-10

"No man cometh unto the Father but by me," said our Lord Jesus Christ. The grace that flowed out of Christ's wounded side as He hung on the cross and died, saves you and me today. We must remember that always.

Peter echoed this sentiment when he said that there is no name given under heaven among men whereby we must be saved. The reason for that of course is that Jesus Christ is God. He always was God and always will be. When Christ came in the flesh, it was only an incident in His existence. Nobody else could take on flesh and still be the infinite God. Do not ask how He did it; the simple truth is that He did.

The law could come by Moses, and only the law could come by Moses; but grace came by Jesus Christ, and He was from the beginning. Grace could only come by Jesus Christ, because nobody else but God could die for mankind.

When Jesus walked around on earth and patted the heads of babies, forgave harlots and blessed mankind, He was simply acting like God in a given situation. That is all . . . just acting like God.

Jesus is the sweetest name I know,
And He's just the same as His lovely name,
And that's the reason why I love Him so;
Oh, Jesus is the sweetest name I know

LELA LONG (1896-1951)

Our Father in heaven, the name of Jesus resonates in my heart, and I never tire whispering that name in the stillness of my worship and praise. May that wonderful name be the theme of my life. In that name of Jesus I pray. Amen.

*For there is one God, and one mediator between God and men, the man
Christ Jesus; Who gave himself a ransom for all, to be testified in due time.*
1 TIMOTHY 2:5-6

We need to remember and meditate on the truth that in everything God does, He always acts in perfect harmony with who He is. In Jesus' act of atonement, it could not have been a divine act alone, for it had to be for men. It could not be a human act alone, for only God could do it. Therefore, the act of atonement was a human act and a divine act in perfect harmony.

Atonement happened in history, a once-done act accomplished there in the darkness on the cross; hidden there—a secret act, and never repeated. This act was owned and accepted by God the Father Almighty, who raised Jesus from the dead the third day and took Him unto His own right hand. This is why it is important that we do not degrade ourselves by vulgarizing the atonement.

I believe that Jesus paid the price, all right; but I hope I know what I mean and do not make it less than what God intends it to be. We need to very carefully and prayerfully meditate on the marvelous doctrine of the atonement.

There is a fountain filled with blood
Drawn from Immanuel's veins;
And sinners, plunged beneath that flood
Lose all their guilty stains.

WILLIAM COWPER (1731-1800)

*Dear God, I am amazed by the atonement Thy Son,
even the Lord Jesus Christ, established on the cross. I know not how
it affects me, I just know that it does affect me,
and I praise the wonderful name of Jesus. Amen.*

And without controversy great is the mystery of godliness: God was manifest in the flesh, justified in the Spirit, seen of angels, preached unto the Gentiles, believed on in the world, received up into glory.

1 TIMOTHY 3:16

In meditating upon the atonement, I must confess that I do not know how it was accomplished; I only know that God did it. I can only stand in the valley of dry bones as Ezekiel did, raise my hand to God and say, "Oh, Lord God, thou knowest."

I can picture the angels looking over the shoulders of the prophets as they wrote concerning the atonement, desiring to look into it. Not even the sharp-eyed angels around the throne of God know how He did it.

In the shadow of the cross, in secret, God did a once-for-all act never done before and never done again—an historic act done once, finished and complete. Even the apostle Paul said that this is the mystery of God manifested to men. Because He did all that, the amazing grace of God flows to all men.

Paul, one of the greatest minds of all time, could not fathom the mystery of this work of atonement. Praise God, we do not have to understand it to benefit from it! This amazing grace of God flows to us through the Lord Jesus Christ who finished the work of atonement for time and eternity.

Blessed be the Fountain of blood, to a world of sinners revealed;
Blessed be the dear Son of God, only by His stripes we are healed.
Though I've wandered far from His fold, bringing to my heart pain and woe,
Wash me in the blood of the Lamb, and I shall be whiter than snow.

EDEN R. LATTA (1839-1915)

Dear Lord Jesus, how I praise Thee for the blood Thou did shed on Calvary's cross. I don't understand all of the ramifications of Thy sacrifice, but I have benefited in every area of my life because of it. I thank Thee for the sacrifice Thou did make for me. Amen.

*And I beheld, and I heard the voice of many angels round about the throne
and the beasts and the elders . . . Saying with a loud voice,
Worthy is the Lamb that was slain to receive power, and riches, and wisdom,
and strength, and honour, and glory, and blessing.*

REVELATION 5:11-12

If angels can be envious, they might look upon ransomed sinners and desire to look into the mystery of God's atonement. The angels, who can bear the burning bliss before the throne, have never known a sinful world like this. God merely tells them to go help His people and sends them out to be ministering spirits to those who shall be heirs of salvation, but He never explains the atonement to them.

I doubt there is an angel or archangel anywhere in heaven that understands what happened on the cross. I can picture them standing around the cross, wondering what was going on. We know more than they do. We know that He died. We know that because He died, we do not have to. We know that He rose from the dead; and because He rose from the dead, we, too, shall rise from the dead to believe on Him. We know He went to the right hand of God and sat down in perfect approval; and we know that because He did that, we will go there to be with Him.

God buried the secret of the atonement in His own great heart, forever, and we can only say, "Worthy is the Lamb."

Thou art worthy, Thou art worthy, Thou art worthy, O Lord,
To receive glory, glory and honor, glory and honor and pow'r;
For Thou hast created, hast all things created, Thou hast created all things;
And for Thy pleasure they are created, Thou art worthy, O Lord!

PAULINE M. MILLS (1898-1991)

*Dear Lamb of God, the mysteries surrounding Thy work fascinate me.
The more I meditate upon them, the more mysterious they seem.
All I can do is say, "Worthy is the Lamb that was slain." Amen and amen.*

But God, who is rich in mercy, for his great love wherewith he loved us,
Even when we were dead in sins, hath quickened us together with Christ,
(by grace ye are saved;).
EPHESIANS 2:4-5

The apostle Paul never tried to explain the atonement. None of the apostles in their epistles tried to explain it. The early church fathers never tried. It was only when the Greek influence came in that they began to think their way through and give us an explanation.

I appreciate those explanations; but, for my part, I stand and gaze on Him and say, "I don't know. I don't know." I do not know how He did it, or what it all means any more than a two-year-old baby who stands gazing into his mother's face and says, "Mother, how did I get here?" The mother simply smiles and says, "You'll know later." She does not try to explain to a two-year-old intellect.

I do not believe God will ever say, "You will know later." I think He will say, "Believe on my Son."

What is of the earth, God lets us know. What is of heaven, He holds in His own great heart and will not tell even the angels, and maybe He will not tell us.

Maybe we should cease to strain to understand and should just stand in wonder and amazement at the amazing grace of God in the atonement.

Wonderful grace of Jesus, greater than all my sin;
How shall my tongue describe it? Where shall its praise begin?
Taking away my burden, setting my Spirit free,
For the wonderful grace of Jesus reaches me.

HALDOR LILLENAS (1885-1959)

My heavenly Father, all I can say is, Oh, the wonder of the atonement,
and the awesomeness of it all! Can I talk too much about it?
Can I sing too much about it? Can I pray too much about it?
I think not, and I will continue to pursue this throughout the rest of my days.
In Jesus' name, amen.

And when he came to himself, he said, How many hired servants of my father's have bread enough and to spare, and I perish with hunger!
LUKE 15:17

Probably one of the greatest stories in all of literature is the story of the prodigal son.

The younger son grew bored with his life and looked at the hills in the distance, longing for adventure and excitement. He took his share of his inheritance, went out into the world and filled his days with riotous living. How long he was there is anybody's guess, but he ended up asking for a job to feed hogs, which was as far down as you possibly could get for a Jewish man.

It got so bad for him that he had to eat some of the pig's food to stay alive. Then one day, he got to thinking. That is where the Scripture says that he came to himself. Up to this point, he had been somebody else; but now he had come to himself.

That is the definition of repentance. This young man had explored all of the excitement and the pleasures of the world, and none of it satisfied him. That is the plight of those who are looking for enjoyment but are not able to find fulfillment.

When he came to himself, he began to remember from whence he came.

I was a wandering sheep, I did not love the fold;
I did not love my Shepherd's voice, I would not be controlled:
I was a wayward child, I did not love my home;
I did not love my Father's voice, I loved afar to roam.

HORATIUS BONAR (1808–1889)

Dear God, I well remember my prodigal days and the searching for that which is true. How I praise Thee that I came to myself and returned to the Father's home. Praise the name of Jesus. Amen.

And the younger of them said to his father, Father, give me the portion of goods that falleth to me. And he divided unto them his living. And not many days after the younger son gathered all together, and took his journey into a far country, and there wasted his substance with riotous living.

LUKE 15:12-13

Many have tried to explain the prodigal son. Some say he was a backslider. Some say he was a sinner. However, I can imagine God saying of the sinner, "This my son was dead and is alive again."

I could not accept all of this, so I went to God and said, "God, will you show me?"

I went to a place all by myself; I used to spend days in praying all alone, and I went there. Suddenly there flashed over me an understanding. I have never had reason to doubt God in teaching me His Bible, and I believe God said to my heart, "The prodigal son is neither a backslider nor a sinner; the prodigal son is the human race. The human race went out to the pigsty, to the far country in Adam, and came back in Christ my Son."

The prodigal son is part of a trio of parables. There is the parable of the lost sheep, the lost coin and the lost son. The sheep that wandered away was a part of the human race that will be saved, and when he comes back, he is that part of the human race that is redeemed and will accept redemption.

Jesus my Shepherd is; 'twas He that loved my soul,
'Twas He that washed me in His blood, 'twas He that made me whole.
'Twas He that sought the lost, that found the wand'ring sheep;
'Twas He that brought me to the fold, 'tis He that still doth keep.

HORATIUS BONAR (1808-1889)

Dear God and Father, I appreciate Thy persistence in bringing me back into the fold. My redemption is what brought me into fellowship with Thee, and that fellowship I cherish more than anything else in this world or the world to come. I praise Thee and thank Thee In Jesus' name. Amen.

*But the father said to his servants, Bring forth the best robe, and put it on him;
and put a ring on his hand, and shoes on his feet: And bring hither the fatted calf,
and kill it; and let us eat, and be merry: For this my son was dead, and is alive
again; he was lost, and is found. And they began to be merry.*

LUKE 15:22-24

When the prodigal son returned, what did he find his father to be like?

Irrespective of how the prodigal treated his father, and how the neighbors pitied him and said, "Oh, isn't that a terrible way that boy treated his poor old father," the father had not changed. His father was humiliated, shamed, grieved and heartbroken, but when the boy came back, he had not changed at all.

Jesus is saying to us, "You went away in Adam, but you are coming back in Christ. When you come back, you will find the Father has not changed. He is the same Father He was when you all went out—every man to his own way." When we come back in Jesus Christ, we will find Him exactly the same as we left Him—unchanged.

That is the story of the prodigal son. The father ran, threw his arms around him, welcomed him, put a robe on him, a ring on his finger and said, "This is my son which was dead, and he is alive again."

This is the grace of God worth believing in.

O weary wanderer, come home,
Thy Savior bids thee come;
Thou long in sin didst love to roam,
Yet still He calls thee, come.

JOHN S. COFFMAN (1848-1899)

*Dear Father of all prodigals, of all generations, how thankful I am
that the invitation to come home reached me just in time.
How I praise Thee for the love Thou hast shown me, and others like me!
I praise the name of Jesus. Amen.*

And you, being dead in your sins and the uncircumcision of your flesh,
hath he quickened together with him, having forgiven you all trespasses;
Blotting out the handwriting of ordinances that was against us, which was
contrary to us, and took it out of the way, nailing it to his cross.
COLOSSIANS 2:13-14

After all that the prodigal son had experienced, he finally came to himself. That is a journey worth taking. As soon as he had come to himself, he knew what he had to do.

How many people wander in the far country, far away from the father, because they do not know what they need to do? Perhaps their circumstance is creating frustration for them. Perhaps they are trying to figure out what to do. Until they come to themselves, and the reality of who they are, they will never know what to do.

The prodigal had to realize where he was and where he had come from in order to really know where he had to go. When he went home, the father greeted him and said, "This my son was dead and is alive again."

God's grace flows free and is all the grace that anybody would ever need. If you set your teeth against Him, the grace of God might as well not exist for you, and Christ might as well not have died. If you yield to Him and come home, then all the overwhelming, incomprehensible plenitude of goodness and kindness and the great illimitable reaches of God's nature are on your side.

I've wandered far away from God,
Now I'm coming home;
The path of sin too long I've trod,
Lord, I'm coming home.

WILLIAM J. KIRKPATRICK (1838–1921)

O God, my heavenly Father, "home" is a very wonderful word. The fact that
Thou welcomed me home with open arms is more than I can truly comprehend.
But, oh, the welcome home is so wonderful! Praise the Lord. Amen.

Teaching them to observe all things whatsoever I have commanded you:
and, lo, I am with you always, even unto the end of the world. Amen.
MATTHEW 28:20

I believe it becomes increasingly harder for preachers to preach all the Word of God these days. So many specialists are occupying the pulpit today, but we just need the plain preaching and teaching of the Word of God.

Two important tenets of the Christian faith are the omnipresence and the imminence of God. Omnipresent means that God is everywhere. Imminent means that God penetrates everything. God's omnipresence and imminence are standard Christian doctrines and were believed back even in the Old Testament to the Jews.

All that is meant by this is that God is in everything even while He contains all things. I like to illustrate this by using a submerged bucket of ocean water. It is full of the ocean. The ocean is in the bucket, but the bucket also is in the ocean surrounded by it. This is the best illustration I can think of about how God dwells in His universe and yet the universe dwells in God.

God is in me, and I am in God; and even though I really cannot comprehend it, I can embrace it, believe it and trust God's wisdom in this.

O may these thoughts possess my breast,
Where'er I rove, where'er I rest;
Nor let my weaker passions dare
Consent to sin, for God is there. Amen.
ISAAC WATTS (1674–1748)

Precious heavenly Father, Thy nature is far beyond my comprehension.
I praise Thee that Thou art in me, and I am in You. How that works
is beyond my comprehension, but it is not beyond my ability
to embrace it. Amen and amen.

Surely he hath borne our griefs, and carried our sorrows:
yet we did esteem him stricken, smitten of God, and afflicted. But he was wounded
for our transgressions, he was bruised for our iniquities: the chastisement of
our peace was upon him; and with his stripes we are healed.
ISAIAH 53:4-5

In meditating on the doctrine of the atonement, we must keep in mind that it is the objective work of Christ, the thing He did on the cross. He did this before any of us today were living. This work was accomplished alone, in the shadow of the cross.

Jesus accomplished the work of atonement there on the cross. The spear went into His side; the nails went into His hands and feet. The pain associated with this is beyond our ability to comprehend. Yet, Jesus separated Himself from the Father for that moment, which was more painful to Him than any of the physical pain He endured.

Separation from the Father was the cost of atonement.

Atonement could have been done without affecting anybody. The truth of the matter is, it was done, and still there are millions who die unaffected by it. It was an external act, an objective act, something done beyond and outside of us. Here is the beauty of it: This act, which He did alone, in the darkness, makes justification possible, bringing reconciled men and women to God.

Blessed be the glorious tidings
To a suffering world revealed.
Christ has made a full atonement;
By His stripes we may be healed.

A. B. SIMPSON (1843-1919)

O God, how precious the atonement is to me. No matter my
circumstances, no matter my problems, the blood of the Lord Jesus
Christ has set me free—free to worship and adore Thee all the rest
of the days of my life. Amen and amen.

But this man, after he had offered one sacrifice for sins for ever, sat down on the right hand of God; From henceforth expecting till his enemies be made his footstool. For by one offering he hath perfected for ever them that are sanctified.
HEBREWS 10:12-14

Justification declares the sinner righteous, but it is external to the man. That is, the justified man may be no better off for his justification if that is all that happened to him. Justification is a judicial thing. Just as a man may stand before the court and be declared innocent of a crime—not guilty, and yet it does not change the man inside. He weighs exactly the same as he weighed before; stands at the same height, with the same color of hair and eyes as before. He has the same relationships and in every way is the same man he was before. The only difference, he is judicially free, declared not guilty before the law.

When a man finds out that he is declared not guilty, he will rejoice in that fact. But he did not do the work. The work was done in the minds of the jurors and before the law.

Justification is the act God performs to reconcile us with Him.

God first established atonement, and based on that is the work of justification. Because Jesus died on the cross and purchased our atonement, God now can justify us in His sight, because it is not us that are in His sight, but rather Christ.

Free from the law—oh, happy condition!
Jesus hath bled, and there is remission;
Cursed by the law and bruised by the fall,
Grace hath redeemed us once for all.
PHILIP P. BLISS (1838-1876)

O Father, to know that I'm justified and set free from the penalty of my sin is to bring me to a point of great rejoicing. How I praise Thee for the finished work of Christ on my behalf. In the blessed name of Jesus I pray. Amen.

Ye were not redeemed with corruptible things, as silver and gold,
from your vain conversation received by tradition from your fathers;
But with the precious blood of Christ, as of a lamb without blemish and without spot:
Who verily was foreordained before the foundation of the world.
1 PETER 1:18-20

Atonement is the basis upon which God acts toward humanity. Atonement makes justification possible, and justification leads to regeneration. This is the work of God outside of a man that has the potential to change the inside of a man.

Regeneration takes place at the same time justification takes place. When God justifies a man, He also regenerates that man so that nobody ever was justified and not regenerated. You can think of them apart, though they cannot actually be separated.

Justification is an objective judicial thing. But regeneration takes place within the life and heart of the man, and it is a subjective thing. It deals with man's nature. It gets inside the man, because Jesus died in the darkness and God accepted that atonement for that man's sin.

Any man who believes in Christ, God can justify, declare him righteous and then regenerate him by imparting to him the nature of God. God's promise is that we are partakers of the divine nature through His promises. A regenerated man is a man who partakes of the divine nature, a man who has a new relation to God, which gives him eternal life.

Nor silver nor gold hath obtained my redemption;
No riches of the earth could have saved my poor soul.
The blood of the cross is my only foundation;
The death of my Savior now maketh me whole.

JAMES M. GRAY (1851–1935)

O God, I rejoice today in my redemption. Nothing I could do, but
everything Thou hast done has brought me into a right relationship with
Thee. For this, I praise the name of the Lord Jesus Christ. Amen.

In my distress I called upon the Lord, and cried unto my God: he heard my voice out of his temple, and my cry came before him, even into his ears.
PSALM 18:6

One of the great Bible truths we should revel in is that the newest convert born again today, has a degree of moral likeness to God, which gives him a measure of compatibility. Heaven is a place of complete compatibility. Sin introduced an incompatibility between God and the sinner.

Sin disrupts the communion between God and man. Sin introduces that quality which throws men and God out of accord with each other. As it is, there is no accord, no congruity. But when that sinner believes in the blood atonement, which is trust in Christ, and is justified in heaven and regenerated on earth, there is complete compatibility and communion.

We are justified in heaven and regenerated on earth because earth is the only place where you can get regenerated. You cannot wait until you die. That is too late. There is no place to be regenerated after you are dead. When you are regenerated, you are given a measure of the character of God so that there is a likeness of the image of God restored to the man or woman, and regeneration creates a measure of compatibility. That compatibility allows God to draw feelingly near to the man or woman, and it makes communion morally consistent.

Lead me through the vale of shadows,
Bear me o'er life's fitful sea;
Then the gate of life eternal
May I enter, Lord, with Thee.
FANNY J. CROSBY (1820-1915)

Dear Father and God, how I praise Thee for the wondrous yet mysterious union I can have with Thee today. My walk today with Thee is the great joy of my life. Amen and amen.

There is none like unto the God of Jeshurun, who rideth upon the heaven
in thy help, and in his excellency on the sky. The eternal God is thy refuge,
and underneath are the everlasting arms: and he shall thrust out the
enemy from before thee; and shall say, Destroy them.
DEUTERONOMY 33:26-27

You cannot have communion where there is complete unlikeness. Communion is possible only where there is absolute likeness. You can go to any creature that has a nature other than yours and you cannot have communion. You pat your dog on the head, but you really cannot commune with that dog. The dog cannot commune with you, because there is too great of a dissimilarity of nature.

For the same reason, God cannot commune with the sinner, because there is a violent unlikeness, a dissimilarity that makes communion impossible.

The new man within you is the regenerated man. You have started on your way toward God's likeness, and there is enough of it there, even in the new convert, that God can commune without incongruity. He finds some of His image in the regenerated man. God, being the God He is, can never commune with anything except His own likeness. Where there is no likeness, there can be no fellowship between God and that unlike thing. When that is restored to a person, God begins communion and, of course, He can commune to a deeper extent depending upon the fullness and completeness of that compatibility.

> What a fellowship, what a joy divine,
> Leaning on the everlasting arms;
> What a blessedness, what a peace is mine,
> Leaning on the everlasting arms.
>
> ELISHA A. HOFFMAN (1839–1929)

Dear Lord Jesus, how warm my walk is today, as I fellowship with Thee
all along the way. I praise Thee for this fellowship that has made
my life the joy it has become. Amen.

*And have put on the new man, which is renewed in knowledge
after the image of him that created him.*
COLOSSIANS 3:10

The apostle Paul says in the book of Colossians that the Christian is the one who has put on the new man. He told the Colossians that the seed was in them, the root of the matter was in their hearts. They were regenerated; so God could commune with His image in them and see a little bit of His own face there, and hold communion with His people.

That is exactly why we can say, "Abba Father."

A new father goes to the hospital to see his first baby. He goes to the window to look at all of the babies, but what he is looking for is one that looks like him. The babies may be cute, but he has no interest in any of them except his own.

When he sees his own baby, what he is looking for is himself. The little baby has his ears, his nose, his eyes and so forth. The thing that drove him to that little baby is his own image in that baby.

The thing to draw God to us is His image in us. Sin has destroyed it. Regeneration puts it back in. Now that new man in Christ can have communion and fellowship with the Father of whose image He is.

Father of heaven, whose love profound
A ransom for our souls hath found,
Before thy throne we sinners bend;
To us Thy pardoning love extend.
EDWARD COOPER (1770-1833)

*O Abba Father, through regeneration I have come back to the place
where Thee can see in me Thy blessed divine image.
How I praise Thee through Jesus Christ my Savior! Amen.*

But it is good for me to draw near to God:
I have put my trust in the Lord God, that I may declare all thy works.
PSALM 73:28

A new convert certainly may not be much like God, but he has something of the resemblance to the deity, and so God can own Him as he is, and the angels recognize the family resemblance.

This being so, there is a serious problem among Christians. The problem is a feeling that God is far away or vice versa. It is hard to rejoice if you do not feel, for feeling is rejoicing. It is hard to rejoice when you are suffering from that sense of remoteness. Most Christians suffer from this sense of divine remoteness.

They certainly know that God is with them; they are sure they are God's children, and they can take you to their marked New Testament and prove to you seriously and soberly that they have been justified and regenerated. They can testify that they belong to God, and heaven is going to be their home. They've got the theology in their heads, but they suffer from a sense of remoteness.

To know a thing in your head is one thing, but to feel it in your heart is something altogether different. Most Christians are trying to be happy apart from having a sense of God's presence.

I am thine, O Lord, I have heard Thy voice,
And it told Thy love to me;
But I long to rise in the arms of faith
and be closer drawn to Thee.
FANNY J. CROSBY (1820-1915)

O God, I long to draw closer to Thee. I hunger and thirst for Thy presence in my life today. May Thy presence be a reality to me today. Amen.

That I may know him, and the power of his resurrection, and the fellowship
of his sufferings, being made conformable unto his death.
PHILIPPIANS 3:10

Most Christians suffer from a sense of divine remoteness. They have no sense of God's presence.

They know He is there; the Bible says He is there. They can quote Bible verses substantiating this truth. Yet, there is still a sense of remoteness when it comes to their fellowship with God.

It is like trying to have a bright day without having the sun. Somebody could say, "It is now 12 o' clock noon, therefore the sun is up. Let's rejoice in the sun. Isn't it beautiful and bright? Let's just take it by faith and rejoice that the sun is up, and all is well."

The sun is up according to the calendar. You can point upward and say, "The sun is up," but you are just kidding yourself. As long as it is gloomy and rainy, the wet, soggy leaves keep dripping down, and it is dark; you are not having a bright day. When the sun comes out, then you can rejoice in the presence of the sun.

The sun is always there. However, the presence of the sun is what I am talking about. God is always there, but it is His presence that makes my day a day to rejoice in God.

Lord of our life, God whom we fear,
Unknown, yet known; unseen, yet near;
Breath of our breath, in Thee we live;
Life of our life, our praise receive.
SAMUEL F. SMITH (1808–1885)

Dear God, my life consists of Thy life. I live because Thou livest.
My joy is experiencing the nearness of Thy presence. May I revel in
the manifest presence of Thee today. In all this, I praise Thee through
Jesus Christ my Lord. Amen.

In thee, O Lord, do I put my trust; let me never be ashamed:
deliver me in thy righteousness. Bow down thine ear to me; deliver me speedily:
be thou my strong rock, for an house of defence to save me.
PSALM 31:1-2

Most Christians are theological Christians. They know they are saved. Somewhere, somebody has given them a marked New Testament, and it is proper that we should until they get their theology straight. The problem here is that they are trying to be happy without a sense of God's presence. That yearning desire to be near to God, to have God near to us, is found everywhere among God's people. You will find it in prayers, songs and hymns.

If you think I am merely spinning this out of my head, go to the next prayer meeting, kneel down with the brethren and listen to them pray. We all pray alike. It's, "Oh, Lord, come. O Lord, draw near. O Lord, show Thyself. Be near to me, Lord."

If that is not enough, we sing songs with words such as, "Come thou fount of every blessing," and, "Draw me nearer, nearer blessed Lord."

This yearning to be nearer to God and have God come nearer to us is universal among born-again Christians; and we think of God as coming from across some distance to where we are. God is within.

Come, Thou Fount of every blessing,
Tune my heart to sing Thy grace;
Streams of mercy, never ceasing,
Call for songs of loudest praise.
Teach me some melodious sonnet,
Sung by flaming tongues above;
Praise the mount, I'm fixed upon it,
Mount of thy redeeming love.

ROBERT ROBINSON (1735-1790)

Eternal God, who dwellest in eternity, come near me and bless my life today
with Thy presence. Tune my heart to sing Thy praise throughout this day. Amen.

And Jacob awaked out of his sleep, and he said,
Surely the Lord is in this place; and I knew it not.
GENESIS 28:16

God does not dwell in space; therefore, God does not move like a rocket or ray of light and come from some remote place or start toward some remote place. God contains all remoteness and all distances in His own great heart. Then why do we feel Him at a distance?

It is because of a dissimilarity to Him in our nature. We have an unlikeness with which God cannot commune and call us His children. In the practical working out of it, we sense our dissimilarity, which is why God seems remote.

Nearness to God is not a geographical or astronomical thing. It is not a spatial thing, having to do with space. Rather, it is a spiritual thing, having to do with nature. That is why we can pray, "Draw me nearer."

We are not praying for God to come down from some remote distance. We know that God is here now. Jesus said, "Lo, I am with you always."

I think of Jacob when he first encountered God in what is known as Jacob's Ladder. When he arose from that dream, he said, "God is in this place and I didn't know it." He did not say God came to this place. He said, "God is in this place."

O Thou, in whose presence my soul takes delight,
On whom in affliction I call,
My comfort by day and my song in the night,
My hope, my salvation, my all!
JOSEPH SWAIN (1761–1796)

Dear God, to know Thou art with me now and ever shall be brings joy
and pleasure to my life. I need not fear anything, for Thou art near.
Hallelujah! Hallelujah! Amen.

Yet I am the Lord thy God from the land of Egypt,
and thou shalt know no god but me: for there is no saviour beside me.
I did know thee in the wilderness, in the land of great drought.
HOSEA 13:4-5

A yearning to be near God is in fact a yearning to be like Him. It is the yearning of the ransomed heart to be like God so that there can be perfect communion—so the heart and God can come together in divine fellowship.

There is a similarity that makes it compatible and proper for God to commune with His children, even the poorest and weakest of his born-again children. However, there are dissimilarities as well, and those dissimilarities are such that there is not the degree of fellowship there ought to be.

There is not a perfection of the sense of God's presence that we want and yearn for and pray for and sing about. How are we going to know what God is like so that we may know whether we are like God?

The answer is simple: God is like Christ, for Christ is God. Christ is God manifested to mankind. Our focus needs to be on Jesus. By looking at our Lord Jesus, we will know what God is like; and then we will know what we have to be like if we are going to experience the unbroken and continuous presence of God.

Oft I hear a gentle whisper o'er me stealing,
When my trials and my burdens seem too great;
Like the sweet-voiced bells of evening softly pealing,
It is saying to my spirit, "Only wait."
A. B. SIMPSON (1843-1919)

O Lord God, who art ever so near me, I praise Thee that Thy presence is
a refuge. No matter how dire my situation seems to be, I can rest
in Thy presence. In the name of Jesus I pray. Amen.

*Yea, though I walk through the valley of the shadow of death, I will fear no evil:
for thou art with me; thy rod and thy staff they comfort me.*
PSALM 23:4

As Christians, we know God is present. Yet, for many there is a sense of His absence. Yes, we are born again and destined for heaven for all eternity. And yes, we believe in the omnipresence of God. In spite of that, there is deep inside of us an indefinable sense of God's absence. Something is missing. We are yearning for something that does not seem to be there.

As the man feels the sun is gone on dark days, never to return, he knows better and yet he is not happy, because he cannot see the sun. The sun is there, but there is a sense that it is not there.

At times, we feel that God is away even when we know He is present. But for some reason God cannot manifest himself to us as He wants to, for a variety of reasons. We need to find out those reasons and clear our hearts from any spiritual debris hindering us from experiencing the awesome presence of God.

Draw nigh to us, Thou Lord of Hosts,
And send on us Thy Holy Ghost;
With love and grace our lives command,
Give us Thy truths to understand.
JOHANN MICHAEL ALTENBURG (1584-1640)

O blessed Holy Spirit, I yield to the gracious leading of Thy hand as You bring me closer to the heart of God my Father. Illuminate my heart with the truth of Thy Word. I pray In Jesus' name. Amen.

*For I am the Lord your God: ye shall therefore sanctify yourselves,
and ye shall be holy; for I am holy. . . . For I am the Lord that bringeth you up out of
the land of Egypt, to be your God: ye shall therefore be holy, for I am holy.*
LEVITICUS 11:44-45

If we are to know God, we must know Jesus. The more we get to know Jesus, the more we will understand God and ourselves as Christians.

The first thing I need to understand about Jesus is His holiness. Our God is holy; our Lord Jesus Christ is holy; and we call the Spirit the Holy Spirit. Holiness also needs to be one of our qualities as Christians. As God is holy, so are we to be holy.

I have noticed how stained, spotted and carnal the average Christian is. It is something altogether different from the person of the Lord Jesus Christ. For some reason, the average Christian allows spiritual stains in his life.

Months go by without repentance. Years go by without asking for cleansing or taking the spots off our garments; without asking to be cleansed of our carnality and unlikeness to God's image within our heart. Then we sing, "Draw me nearer, nearer blessed Lord," or we pray, "Come Lord. Come to this meeting." The truth is, the Lord is there, and what we are praying is, "Oh Lord, show Thyself."

The holy Lord cannot show Himself in full communion to an unholy Christian. To truly experience God, we must be godly in every aspect of our life. We must be like Christ, and as holy as Christ.

Holy, holy, holy! All the saints adore Thee,
Casting down their golden crowns around the glassy sea;
Cherubim and seraphim falling down before Thee,
Which wert, and art, and evermore shall be.
REGINALD HEBER (1783–1826)

*Blessed Holy Spirit, I shrink from Thy holiness, and yet that is exactly
what draws me to Thee. Cleanse my heart in such a way that Thy holiness
will be the desire of my heart. I pray this in Jesus' name. Amen.*

July 2

O Lord, I have heard thy speech, and was afraid: O Lord, revive thy work in the midst of the years, in the midst of the years make known; in wrath remember mercy.
HABAKKUK 3:2

What we need today more than anything is revival. A revival, among other things, is a sudden manifestation of God's presence. It is not the coming of the sun, but the sun breaking through the clouds. Although the sun may be hidden, it is still there until it breaks through the clouds.

A revival is not God coming to us; rather, it is God breaking through obstacles hindering us from experiencing Him. The biggest thing hindering us from really experiencing such a move of God is our selfishness. We want God to do something in someone else's life, but we do not plan to make any changes in our own life. We are happy with the way we are, even though we are not experiencing the presence of God deep within our hearts.

If we are to have fellowship with God and communion with Him, we need to be like Him, as Jesus is. The selfishness that grips our heart, the self-indulgence that rules our life ,need to be repented of and confessed to God as sin. Once this spiritual debris is cleansed from our hearts, the sun of God's presence will break through and shine deep within our hearts.

Revive Thy work, O Lord!
And give abounding joy;
Oh, fill our hearts with perfect love
And burn out all alloy!
OSWALD J. SMITH (1889-1986)

O Holy Spirit of Pentecostal power, break through the clouds of despair and discouragement, and shine upon my heart in the brilliance of Thy holiness. Fill me with the holy light of Thy presence. In Jesus' name I pray. Amen.

Who, when he was reviled, reviled not again; when he suffered,
he threatened not; but committed himself to him that judgeth righteously.
1 PETER 2:23

I am sick in my own heart; sick about myself, about my friends and about the preachers in the ministry today. How utterly self-centered we have become, and yet we talk loudly about glorifying God, and boastfully say, "This is the glory of God."

How do you know that you are self-centered?

This is very simple. If anybody crosses you, your hackles go up immediately because you are self-centered and self-indulgent. You are very quick to defend yourself against all so-called enemies. Just let anybody cross you, and they will know it immediately.

Christ was not like that. He gave Himself and poured Himself out without one bit of selfishness. He was reviled against but reviled not against His enemies.

Any Christian's heart that is self-indulgent and self-centered cannot be warmed up. The Christian who is defending himself is one who will never experience a depth of fellowship and communion with God.

Christ loved us; He is our Shepherd. He is our Advocate above, pleading our cause. We are His brethren and He is our God. But the changes of fellowship and sweetness in the saints while they walk on earth, are more than just technical changes.

Gracious gales of heavenly blessing
In Thy love to us afford;
Let us feel Thy Spirit's presence,
Oh, revive us by Thy Word!
DANIEL W. WHITTLE (1840–1901)

My heart, O God, needs a blast from on high. Change in me
that which needs changing to bring me into the sweetness of Thy fellowship.
I pray this in Jesus' name. Amen.

For even Christ pleased not himself; but, as it is written,
The reproaches of them that reproached thee fell on me.
ROMANS 15:3

It is amazing to me how much people allow doctors to push them around. Whatever the doctor says is gospel. Some people's lives would drastically change if they would obey God as strictly as they obey their doctors. The doctor only influences your health; God influences all your eternity.

Many people have put their spiritual life on a budget and will not spend anything for God unless they can justify it in the columns of a "spreadsheet." What a cheap carnal way of living, and yet many people do so.

The love of the Lord Jesus Christ was a great, passionate outpouring, causing Him to give Himself completely. He pleased not Himself.

What is wrong with the majority of Christians today is that we are self-pleasers. We live for ourselves. Even though we are saints; even though we are born again and have our marked-up New Testament, the love we have is a calculating and narrow love. It is a love that does not give itself, so how can He give Himself and fellowship with us? Our absolute surrender to Jesus Christ paves the way for Him to pour out His love on us and for us to fellowship with Him.

> The love of God is greater far
> Than tongue or pen can ever tell;
> It goes beyond the highest star,
> And reaches to the lowest hell;
> The guilty pair, bowed down with care,
> God gave His Son to win;
> His erring child He reconciled,
> And pardoned from his sin.
>
> FREDERICK M. LEHMAN (1868–1953)

Dear God, Thy love is far more than I can truly comprehend.
I open up my heart and life to receive from Thee that which will bring me
into fellowship with Thee. I pray this in Jesus' name. Amen.

Then said Jesus, Father, forgive them; for they know not what they do.
And they parted his raiment, and cast lots.

LUKE 23:34

The kindness of Jesus is at odds with the harshness, severity, sharpness, acerbity, bitterness and acidity in so many people's lives. What a contrast! How can a kind Savior feel perfectly at home with a harsh Christian? And another thing: Our Lord was a forgiving Lord and even forgave them while nailing Him to the cross.

But how hard and vengeful are so many of the Lord's children. People remember things that happened 20 years ago, and cannot get over it. "Oh, I've forgiven it all right, but I can't forget it." Jesus was forgiving, and He proved He was forgiving by dying. We prove that we are vengeful and hard by many, many proofs and demonstrations.

If we are to have the kind of fellowship and communion with God that He desires us to have, we can only come near in the spirit of Jesus. What God accepts is what I see and discover in the Lord Jesus Christ—His Holiness, His love, His forgiving spirit. As this becomes a part of my life, and grips me, it prepares me for fellowship and communion with God Almighty.

I would love thee, God and father!
My Redeemer and my King!
I would love Thee, for without Thee
Life is but a bitter thing.

MADAME GUYON (1648–1717)

Dear Father in heaven, because of the forgiving spirit of the Lord Jesus Christ, I am able to have a forgiving spirit within me toward all who would offend me. Cleanse me to the point of absolute forgiveness and bring me to the point of absolute love. In Jesus' name, amen.

July 6

*Therefore as by the offence of one judgment came upon
all men to condemnation; even so by the righteousness of one the
free gift came upon all men unto justification of life.*
ROMANS 5:18

An amazing quality of Jesus was His humility. Although he was the high, Holy One, He came down and lived like a man. On the other hand, we who are the lowest, sometimes act the proudest and the most arrogant. How completely unlike Jesus we are in our everyday living.

Someone might ask, "Am I justified by being like God?"

We are justified by being declared righteous by Almighty God who passed His sentence upon the cross of Jesus, and by the dying of the Savior in the darkness there on the hill. Because He made atonement, God justifies; and when God justifies, He regenerates. That is the process of salvation.

Regeneration does not freeze the image of God in you. That image of God must continue to grow and come in and then come out. As an artist works on a picture, first it's only an outline in the general drawing, but he knows what is there and slowly it comes out. God seems far from us because we are so unlike God. It is not distance that separates us, but our hearts. The purpose of God in regeneration is to make us, step-by-step, into the likeness of Jesus. The characteristic humility of Jesus is to shine forth in our life day by day.

'Tis so sweet to walk with Jesus,
Step by step and day by day;
Stepping in his very footprints,
Walking with Him all the way.

A. B. SIMPSON (1843–1919)

*Dear Lord Jesus, I claim for my life that humility that was so predominant
in Thy life. Whatever it takes to bring me to that point in my life,
I ask Thee to do it today. Amen.*

Blessed be the God and Father of our Lord Jesus Christ,
who hath blessed us with all spiritual blessings
in heavenly places in Christ.

EPHESIANS 1:3

One thing that delights my spirit in reading the Gospels is the heavenly-mindedness of Jesus. He was in the bosom of the Father while He was on earth. He never left the bosom of the Father. And all through His public ministry the heavenly-mindedness seemed to be the framework in which He mingled with humanity.

The only time Jesus ever left the bosom of the Father was in the awful, wrenching agony when God turned away from Him on the cross that He might die for mankind. It was the only time He was separated from the bosom of the Father.

All through His earthly ministry He talked about heavenly things. The parables He established with His disciples had a heavenly bearing. Often Jesus would say, "I came from above." Then He would say, "I tell you things from above."

He lived in the heart of God, and the world above this world is the world in which He inhabited. We could rightly say that Jesus was "other-worldly-minded." This is the example for us to follow—to be so engrossed with heavenly things that our focus is always upward.

Lord, my sins they are many, like the sands of the sea,
But Thy blood, O my Savior, is sufficient for me;
For Thy promise is written, in bright letters that glow,
"Though your sins be as scarlet, I will make them like snow."

MARY A. KIDDER (1820-1905)

Our Father, although I live in this world, my heart is in the world
above this world. I want to be so focused on Thee that nothing else
really matters. I pray this in Jesus' name. Amen.

The Lord reigneth; let the earth rejoice; let the multitude of isles
be glad thereof. Clouds and darkness are round about him:
righteousness and judgment are the habitation of his throne.
PSALM 97:1-2

In thinking about the average Christian experience, most are not really focused on heavenly things. We sing, "Draw me nearer," but there still is distance between God and us. Every Christian is as near to God as any other Christian, except for one problem. God cannot manifest Himself to many Christians because there is a dissimilarity of nature.

They have enough of God's nature to be justified and regenerated, but not enough to provide that fellowship. What is so desperately needed today is a perfection of fellowship with God—a fellowship that will lift us up above the carnal accoutrements of this life. We have become so distracted by religious toys, almost to the point of obsession.

There has been a great movement in the last several generations toward external religion and what I refer to as technical Christianity. It is hard for some Christians to put down their religious toys and concentrate on communion with God. Yet, everything about our regenerated heart is focused in the direction of heaven. The thing that nourishes our communion with God is the rarefied atmosphere of heaven. This, however, is never satisfied in external things. It is time to lay down the religious toys and establish our focus in the heavenlies where God reigns supreme.

There are depths of love that I cannot know
Till I cross the narrow sea;
There are heights of joy that I may not reach
Till I rest in peace with Thee.

FANNY J. CROSBY (1820–1915)

O Father in heaven, how easy it is to become preoccupied with toys
and entertainment. Deliver me from this obstruction and distraction
from my communion with Thee. I ask this in Jesus' name. Amen.

*Moreover he said, I am the God of thy father, the God of Abraham,
the God of Isaac, and the God of Jacob. And Moses hid his face;
for he was afraid to look upon God*
EXODUS 3:6

Many Christians have learned to live following the Lord from afar. As we get older, we have learned to live in the twilight and shadows, and not mind it so much. We have learned to live in the chill, and not mind it.

Peter followed the Lord from afar, but when the Lord turned and looked at him, Peter went outside and wept bitterly.

Have you any tears for your unlikeness to Jesus? Have you any tears for that distance between you and God that in reality is no distance at all, and yet you feel it is there? You are grateful and thankful for every blessed thing, and for goodness, justification and the good grace of God in your life. God has been so gracious. Yet, you cannot escape the sense that God seems far from you. You know He is not, but you feel He is.

Maybe you have allowed self-indulgence, a vengeful spirit, a lukewarm attitude or worldliness to put a cloud over the face of God. What are you going to do about it?

When you deal with the cloud, the sun will shine as bright as ever. Nothing can take the place of basking in the manifest presence of God. Oh, to gaze upon His face in adoring wonder and worship!

Face to face—oh blissful moment!
Face to face—to see and know;
Face to face with my Redeemer,
Jesus Christ who loves me so

CARRIE E. BRECK (1855-1934)

*I long, O God, to gaze upon Thy face. I long to see Thee as Thou desireth
me to see Thee, without all of the hindrances of sin and rebellion. I can do
that only through Jesus Christ my Savior. In His name I pray. Amen.*

*For ye know how that afterward, when he would have
inherited the blessing, he was rejected: for he found no place of repentance,
though he sought it carefully with tears.*
HEBREWS 12:17

The average Christian thinks that because he has heard a truth he now owns that truth. Spirituality is not like education. In education you read the textbooks, memorize a few facts and you have mastered the subject. Not so with spirituality.

Only the Holy Spirit can give you the illumination that will make the words you hear become part of your spiritual nature. The Holy Spirit wants to open up our hearts so that the truth becomes part of us.

Things often stand in the way of the illuminating work of the Holy Spirit. It will be different things for different Christians. Clearing out spiritual debris is an ongoing process, and the tool to use is repentance.

We need to begin to repent of our lack of holiness in the presence of the Holy; repent of our self-indulgence in the presence of the selfless Christ; repent of our harshness in the presence of the kind and forgiving Christ. We must repent of our lukewarm attitude in the presence of the zealous Christ burning like a fiery flame.

The Holy Spirit will guide each of us in the area where we need to do our repentance.

Breathe on me, breath of God,
Until my heart is pure.
Until with Thee I will one will,
To do and to endure.
EDWIN HATCH (1835-1889)

O Spirit of the living God, how I need Thee to lead me in the way everlasting. I tend to become lukewarm, but I pray that Thou might touch me with the fire from off the altar above. In Jesus' blessed name I pray. Amen.

Why art thou cast down, O my soul? and why art thou disquieted within me? hope thou in God: for I shall yet praise him, who is the health of my countenance, and my God.

PSALM 42:11

The attributes of God rest upon the character of God, and they are guaranteed by the changeless attributes of the Lord God Almighty, the Ancient of Days.

We need to understand what the attribute of God's omnipresence is and what it means in human experience. This is not just cold doctrine to teach and then move on. Any doctrine not rooted in the character and nature of God is not a biblical doctrine; or we have not understood the doctrine correctly. Every doctrine begins in the heart of God and then flows into the heart of man, creating a godly atmosphere in that man.

The attribute of omnipresence simply means that God is all-present. God is close to, near to, everyone and everything. It means that He is here. He is next to you wherever you may be.

When we pray, "Oh God, where art thou?" the answer comes back, "I am where you are. I am here; I am next to you, and I am close to everywhere."

I am not sure I understand it, but I embrace it and believe it, and it has so affected my life that all I can say is, "Hallelujah, Thou art near me!"

How wonderful, how beautiful
The sight of Thee must be;
Thine endless wisdom, boundless power,
And awful purity!

FREDERICK W. FABER (1814-1863)

Dear God, I rest quite comfortably knowing that Thou will always be Thyself. I cannot fathom the depths of Thy nature, but I can accept You as my Lord and God. Hallelujah! Thou art near me. Amen.

The Lord reigneth, he is clothed with majesty; the Lord is clothed with strength,
wherewith he hath girded himself: the world also is stablished, that it cannot be
moved. Thy throne is established of old: thou art from everlasting.

PSALM 93:1-2

If we had only reason and not Scripture when supporting teachings such as the omnipresence of God, the teaching would be dubious. If we had Scripture and no reason, we still would believe it. But we have both Scripture and reason. We have Scripture to declare it, and we have reason to shout, "It's true, I know it's true!" We may be sure that God is omnipresent—that He is everywhere.

If there were any place where God was not, then that place would mark the confines, the limits of God. If God had limits, God could not be the infinite God that He is. Some theologians call the infinitude of God His immensity; but immensity is not quite a big enough word.

"Immensity" simply means that whatever you are talking about is hugely, vastly large. "Infinitude" means not only that it is hugely and vastly large but that there are no limits. If God were very hugely, vastly large, we could then say that He was immense; but since He is infinite, we can only say that God has no size at all. You cannot measure God in any direction.

O God, our Help in ages past,
Our Hope for years to come,
Be Thou my Guide while life shall last,
And our eternal Home.

ISAAC WATTS (1674–1748)

I love Thee, O God, even though I cannot fully fathom the length and
breadth of Thy nature and character. By faith, I acknowledge Thy
presence in my life. I cannot explain it, but I can certainly embrace it,
in the name of the Lord Jesus Christ. Amen.

*And in thy majesty ride prosperously because of truth and meekness
and righteousness; and thy right hand shall teach thee terrible things.*

PSALM 45:4

God is equally near to all parts of His universe. When we think about God
and spiritual things, we think correctly only when we rule out the space
concept altogether, because our infinite God does not dwell in space. He
swallows up all space.

God fills heaven and earth, just as the ocean fills a bucket that has
been submerged a mile down. The bucket is full of the ocean, but the
ocean also surrounds the bucket in all directions. So when God says, "I fill
heaven and earth," He does, and heaven and earth is submerged in God
as well. He further says that the heaven of heavens cannot contain God.

You see, God is not contained; God contains, and there is a difference.
In Him, we live and move and have our being.

We have this habit of trying to put God into our life. We have our own
little boundaries, and we think God should fit into them. That is contrary
to the very nature of God. Nobody can contain God; therefore, nobody can
control God; and therefore, God does not do the bidding of any person.
God is busy performing *His* purpose and will.

My stubborn will at last hath yielded;
I would be Thine, and Thine alone;
And this the prayer my lips are bringing,
Lord, let in me Thy will be done.

LELIA N. MORRIS (1862-1929)

*Eternal God and Father, I want to be so full of Thee that
there is no room for anything else. May my life overflow with Thy
presence every day. Amen and amen.*

Whither shall I go from thy spirit?
or whither shall I flee from thy presence?
If I ascend up into heaven, thou art there:
if I make my bed in hell, behold, thou art there.
PSALM 139:7-8

Sometimes we talk about God being close to us or far from us. We are not thinking right, because in this regard, we are thinking geographically or astronomically. We think in light years or in meters, inches, miles, leagues. We are thinking about God as being spatial—that is, dwelling in space, which He does not. God contains space, so that space is in God. We should never have any problem about God being anywhere, for the fact is that God is everywhere.

David said, "If I ascend up to heaven, thou art there: if I make my bed in hell, behold thou art there."

Do not ask me to explain it, but remember what John Wesley said: "Don't reject it because you can't understand it."

If a man made his bed in hell, the omnipresence of God would require that wherever there is anything, the presence of God must be. It is impossible to escape the presence of God. Wherever we are, God is there. The problem is in acknowledging the presence of God wherever we are now.

Thou my everlasting portion, more than friend or life to me;
All along my pilgrim journey, Savior, let me walk with Thee.
Close to Thee, close to Thee, close to Thee, close to Thee;
All along my pilgrim journey, Savior, let me walk with Thee.
FANNY J. CROSBY (1820-1915)

Dear God, although I cannot fully understand these deep things
about Thee, I take Thee at Thy Word. I don't understand everything,
but I love Thee, and I embrace Thee in all the manifest goodness
of Thy presence. Praise the name of Jesus. Amen.

*If I say, Surely the darkness shall cover me; even the night shall be
light about me. Yea, the darkness hideth not from thee; but the night shineth
as the day: the darkness and the light are both alike to thee.*
PSALM 139:11-12

Whenever the world prays, as a rule they pray without any sense of God's nearness. God is always somewhere else, usually somewhere far away.

The reason is that in spiritual things, closeness and likeness are the same. Remoteness means dissimilarity. When it comes to personality, when it comes to spirits, when it comes to that which is not material, distance does not mean one lonely thing in all this wide world. That is why Jesus could go to the right hand of God the Father and still say to the people on earth, "I am with you always." Jesus Christ as God, and God being spirit can be instantaneously everywhere at the same time without a problem.

Men are shut off from God, not because God is spatially far from them, not because He is remote like a far galaxy or star, but because there is dissimilarity in nature. When we project our human concept up into spiritual things, we fail to discover God.

A familiar phrase today is, "Somebody up there likes me." I cannot think of a more horrible phrase than that. The world does not have that intimate connection with God that comes through knowing Jesus Christ. The Christian says, "Christ in me likes me."

Sun of my soul, Thou Savior dear,
It is not night if Thou be near;
Oh, may no earthborn cloud arise
To hide Thee from Thy servant's eyes!
JOHN KEBLE (1792-1866)

*Dear Lord Jesus, it is through Thee that I have come into that awesome
and wonderful presence of God. I know Thee and Thou knowest me,
and our fellowship is sweet each day. Amen and amen.*

For my thoughts are not your thoughts, neither are your ways my ways,
saith the Lord. For as the heavens are higher than the earth, so are my ways
higher than your ways, and my thoughts than your thoughts.
ISAIAH 55:8-9

People have the habit of projecting human concepts upward or outward. For instance, your friends are the ones who are the nearest to you, and the closer the friend, the nearer that person is likely to be. Your enemy, on the other hand, wants to put as much space between you and him as possible. Everything else being equal, the enemy gets as far away as he can.

That is a human concept, and it has to do with material things. Everybody is glad when his enemy is a mile away, and he is more comfortable if he is 10 miles away or on some other continent. As the world sees it, the further away your enemy is, the better off you are, because the world thinks in spatial terms.

With God there is no near and far. God never changes and never moves. God patiently waits for us to acknowledge His presence, He will open up the gates and we will begin to enjoy the manifestation of His presence in our daily life. Oh, to know God in such a personal measure!

Oh! to be like Thee, Blessed Redeemer,
This is my constant Longing and prayer;
Gladly I'll forfeit All of earth's treasures,
Jesus, Thy perfect Likeness to wear.
THOMAS O. CHISHOLM (1866-1960)

I long, O Lord Jesus, to be like Thee in every way possible.
I invite the Holy Spirit into my life today to do just that.
May my heart beat as Thy heart;
may we be one, I pray. Amen.

O Lord, thou hast searched me, and known me.
Thou knowest my downsitting and mine uprising,
thou understandest my thought afar off.
PSALM 139:1-2

When Christians gather together in an assembly, what makes it a Christian assembly? The only thing that makes it a Christian assembly is that God is there in the midst.

Two creatures may be in the same room and yet be millions of miles apart. If it were possible to get an angel and an ape in the same room, there would be no compatibility, no communion, no understanding, no friendship; there would only be distance, because the shining angel and the slobbering, chipper ape would be infinitely removed from each other even though they were in the same room.

When we come to anything that is intellectual, spiritual or of the soul, then space, matter, weight and time have no meaning at all.

On a Sunday morning, if a nonbeliever comes to church and sits in the same pew with a believer, they are miles apart as far as spiritual things are concerned. There is no fellowship there. The core of Christian fellowship is the fact that God is present, but more than that, we actually experience the presence of God in our midst. An unsaved person can never experience that, but it should be the constant experience of the Christian.

What have I to dread, what have I to fear,
Leaning on the everlasting arms?
I have blessed peace with my Lord so near,
Leaning on the everlasting arms.
ELISHA A. HOFFMAN (1839-1929)

Dear God and Father of our Lord Jesus Christ, the fellowship I enjoy with
my fellow believers is because of my fellowship with Thee. May I continue
in that same fellowship until we all meet in heaven. Amen.

Wherein in time past ye walked according to the course of this world,
according to the prince of the power of the air, the spirit that
now worketh in the children of disobedience.
EPHESIANS 2:2

God made man in His image, but man sinned and became unlike God in his moral nature. Because he is unlike God, that communion is broken. The only reason there is any sense of remoteness is the dissimilarity between the moral character of God and man.

When two men hate each other, they are enemies; they are separated and apart, even though for a moment they are forced to be together.

Two brothers who hate each other come to the funeral of their father and yet they will stand at that coffin and be miles apart because there is dissimilarity within them; there is alienation there.

Alienation is exactly what the Bible calls that moral incompatibility between God and man. God is not far away, but He seems to be far away because He is far away in character. Man has sinned, and God is holy. Only Christ's atonement remedies the gap.

Praise ye the Father for His loving-kindness,
Tenderly cares He for his erring children:
Praise Him, ye angels, praise Him in the heavens,
Praise ye Jehovah!
ELIZABETH R. CHARLES (1828–1896)

O God, I recognize the distance between me and Thee and that only
Jesus Christ can truly bring us together. I thank Thee that Jesus has
done for me what I could never do for myself.
Hallelujah for the Lamb of God!

Because that, when they knew God, they glorified him not as God,
neither were thankful; but became vain in their imaginations,
and their foolish heart was darkened.

ROMANS 1:21

Our Lord Jesus Christ, who is God incarnate, is in character all that God is. He is perfectly, altogether, exactly what God is. Paul describes the alienated sinner as walking in the vanity of his mind and having his understanding darkened.

Does that describe Jesus? Does that describe the glorious Son of God? Does ignorance of mind, blindness of heart, past feeling, given over to lasciviousness, walking in uncleanness and greediness describe Jesus?

It describes exactly the opposite of Jesus. It shows that the sinner is so dissimilar to God that the distance is a distance of character, not of space. God is not 100,000 light years away from a sinner. He's not even 1 inch away from the sinner. And yet He is far from the sinner while close enough to snatch him from the flames of hell.

It must be terrible for God to be so close and yet be entirely ignored by the man once created in His image.

Christ's work on the cross was to destroy this dissimilarity and bring into the human heart that magnificent presence of God.

Jesus, keep me near the cross,
There a precious fountain,
Free to all, a healing stream,
Flows from Calvary's mountain.

FANNY J. CROSBY (1820-1915)

Heavenly Father, today I embrace the cross and all that Jesus
accomplished there for me. On that cross, He stood between Thee and me
and brought us together in a divine unity that was humanly impossible.
How I praise the name of Jesus! Amen.

God is faithful, by whom ye were called unto the fellowship
of his Son Jesus Christ our Lord.
1 CORINTHIANS 1:9

According to all theologians of every denomination anywhere, God is omnipresent, which means He is close to, next to, anywhere, everywhere. No matter where we gather together as believers, we are in the vicinity of God's presence.

Our fellowship with God has nothing to do with space, but rather with the dissimilarity of character.

Suppose a very godly man and a very ungodly, evil man were forced to sit together on a journey. Neither will budge one inch from his position. The godly man will not surrender one inch toward sin, and the sinner will not even allow the holy man to talk to him. They have been forced to sit together for some time.

What could they talk about? They would have to find some common ground. It might be the landscape or some pretty tree or something like that. They never could have fellowship. They would be miles apart even though they were of the same nationality, approximately the same age and traveling in the same vehicle to the same location.

Fellowship is not based upon proximity but upon the character of the heart. We can fellowship with God because we have something within us that responds to the person of God.

Since I, who was undone and lost,
Have pardon through His name and word;
Forbid it, then, that I should boast,
Save in the cross of Christ my Lord.

ISAAC WATTS (1674-1748)

I love Thee, Lord, and I love the fellowship of men of like faith. Our fellowship
is based upon the fellowship we have with You. Nothing else brings us together
in beautiful harmony than You. I pray this in Jesus' name. Amen.

*And they heard the voice of the Lord God walking in the garden
in the cool of the day: and Adam and his wife hid themselves from the
presence of the Lord God amongst the trees of the garden.*

GENESIS 3:8

The world searches after God if haply they might find Him, but they do not find Him, because God and man are dissimilar in their moral natures. This is why God seems so far away to so many people.

When Adam sinned, he ran and hid himself from the presence of God. God called, "Adam, where art thou?" God knew where Adam was. Adam was the one who did not know where God was. Adam was lost because he was alienated from God. He had once had intimate fellowship with God, but then sin came in and destroyed in Adam what corresponded in God's heart.

This is the lostness of the world today. There is a remnant in their hearts that yearns for God without any way to connect with God. And because man cannot really connect with God, the devil introduces many things to distract people from that unanswerable yearning in their hearts. The noise and the clatter and the ritual and the motions are replacing the God they are seeking.

> Lord, I have shut the door, speak now the word
> Which in the din and throng could not be heard;
> Hushed now my inner heart,
> Whisper Thy will, while I have come apart,
> While all is still.

WILLIAM M. RUNYAN (1870–1957)

Holy Spirit, the world outside of Jesus Christ is lost. They have lost that vital connection with the One who created them in His own image. Everything in the world is against them finding out Jesus. Work in hearts today to bring them back where they belong. Amen.

And he said unto them, I am an Hebrew; and I fear the Lord,
the God of heaven, which hath made the sea and the dry land.
JONAH 1:9

Jonah refused to obey God, broke away and alienated his heart from God, thinking he could get away from God.

Jonah put as much distance between him and God as he supposed he could possibly do. I am sure he probably felt he was escaping God. It is the heart that puts distance between God and us. Yet, God is nearer than you are to yourself, nearer than your thoughts; while the sinner is far from God.

God is not far away like a Roman god upon the holy mountain. No, God is not away like that, but God is far away in his holy unlikeness to everything simple.

Jonah ran as fast as he could and as far as he could, and he never put any distance between him and God.

The natural man can seek as much as his heart desires and never come near God.

There is a place of quiet rest,
Near to the heart of God;
A place where sin cannot molest,
Near to the heart of God.

CLELAND MCAFEE (1866-1944)

O God, I can relate to Jonah. I have tried to run away from Thee,
and my rebellion has cost me plenty. I want to thank Thee for never
giving up on me as Thou never gave up on Jonah.
I bless Thee in Jesus' name. Amen.

But the dove found no rest for the sole of her foot, and she returned unto him into the ark, for the waters were on the face of the whole earth: then he put forth his hand, and took her, and pulled her in unto him into the ark.

GENESIS 8:9

The presence of God is the bliss of all moral creatures, just as the shining of the sun is the bliss of all creatures that love the sun. All the creatures that love the sun come out and come to the surface. Therefore, the presence of that holy God is the bliss of all moral creatures; and it is the absence of God that is the terror and the grief and the sorrow of all fallen creatures.

I am not referring simply to God's presence, but to God's manifest presence. There is a vast difference. Even in hell, the presence of God can be found, but certainly not His manifested presence.

Therefore, a man can walk around on the earth and be so close to God that he could whisper to Him. And God will hear his whisper. Yet the man is so alienated and remote that he will go to the river and commit suicide, thinking there is no God anywhere in the universe.

I believe this is what accounts for man's busy activities and for practically all of the entertainment there is in the world. There is a restlessness within that cannot be satisfied until, as St. Augustine said, we rest fully in God.

"Nearer the cross!" my heart can say. I am coming nearer;
Nearer the cross from day to day, I am coming nearer;
Nearer the cross where Jesus died,
Nearer the fountain's crimson tide,
Nearer my Savior's wounded side,
I am coming nearer, I am coming nearer.

FANNY J. CROSBY (1820-1915)

Dear God, I have felt that restlessness within my own soul, which nothing could satiate, until I rested fully in Jesus Christ. His nearness has calmed my soul. Amen.

July 24

Lo, this only have I found, that God hath made man upright;
but they have sought out many inventions.
ECCLESIASTES 7:29

Behind every invention of instruments, and every sort of entertainment is a simple reason. Mankind, who was created to have fellowship with God, and is now alienated from God, is trying to deal with that alienation. Maybe, so they think, the noise and activity will drown out that inner longing for something they cannot explain. They know something is wrong, even though they may not be able to explain it.

There is a sense of remoteness between the man alienated from God and the God who was their life and sunshine. Hell will be hell because moral creatures are cut off from the sunshine of God's face.

If there were no golden streets, no jasper walls, no angels, no harps, no living creatures, no elders and no sea of glass, heaven would be heaven because we shall see His face and His name on our foreheads.

It is the manifest, conscious presence of God that makes heaven what it is; and it is the refusal of God to ever manifest His presence in hell or earth or anywhere where men are not good men, or not wanting to be good men, that makes hell what it is.

This is the reason our world is in such desperate straits today.

Since Christ my soul from sin set free,
This world has been a heaven to me;
And mid earth's sorrows and its woe,
'Tis heaven my Jesus here to know.

C. J. BUTLER (N.D.)

Eternal God, Thou who dwellest in all eternity, fill my heart with
Thy presence and this world will be heaven to me. I thank Thee
for Jesus who makes it possible. Amen and amen.

And he said, My presence shall go with thee, and I will give thee rest.
And he said unto him, If thy presence go not with me, carry us not up hence.
EXODUS 33:14-15

The manifest presence of God is what interests me. It is one thing to know that God is here, but it is something else altogether to experience His presence as only the Holy Spirit can do. Why are so many Christians willing to live at arm's length distance from the manifest presence of God?

If today God would only manifest Himself to men all over the earth, every nightclub would be empty and turned into a happy prayer meeting. Every house of ill repute would be emptied in five minutes, and everybody with deep repentance and sorrow of heart would be down on their knees before God, asking for forgiveness and weeping tears of happiness.

It is the manifest presence of God that gives bliss to moral creatures, and it is the absence of this manifest presence that brings everlasting woe to moral creatures.

The government can enact as many laws as they can possibly think up. No law on any book has ever been the source of bliss to the human heart. The only thing the law can do is tell you how bad you are.

The manifest presence of God reveals to us how good God is. That is what makes my heart filled with joyful singing and praise.

My spirit, soul, and body, Jesus, I give to Thee,
A consecrated offering, Thine evermore to be.
My all is on the altar; Lord, I am all Thine own;
Oh, may my faith ne'er falter! Lord, keep me Thine alone.
MARY D. JAMES (1810-1883)

Dear God, how I praise Thee today for the marvelous wonder of Thy presence in my life. May I never live a day without this manifest presence. In Jesus' name I pray. Amen.

Then a cloud covered the tent of the congregation, and the glory of the Lord filled the tabernacle. And Moses was not able to enter into the tent of the congregation, because the cloud abode thereon, and the glory of the Lord filled the tabernacle.
EXODUS 40:34-35

Everybody wants a bright day, even when there is no sun. It is as if they deny the sun but still want a bright day, so they invent every kind of light imaginable. They put together all kinds of Roman candles over their head to get a little light. This is called entertainment.

Certainly, entertainment in the theater and all the rest helps people to forget that they are without God. But when the music dies down and the entertainment is finished, they still have an emptiness deep in the soul.

Somebody may say if man's nature is dissimilar to God's, then the remoteness is an everlasting, unbridgeable gulf. God will never change and man cannot change, so how can God and the human race ever come together?

The answer is that the dissimilarities can be reconciled only by One who is both God and man. Man cannot educate himself into the likeness of God, and he cannot cultivate himself into the likeness of God. You can go to art galleries, read Shakespeare, visit the opening nights at the opera, but when it is all over, you will be inwardly what you were before—walking in the vanity of your mind, blinded by the ignorance that is within, cut off from the life of God, without hope and without God in this world.

When a man is willing to turn from the emptiness of the world and embrace Jesus Christ, he will then discover the manifest presence of God in his own heart.

Search me, O God, and know my heart today;
Try me, O Savior, know my thoughts, I pray.
See if there be some wicked way in me;
Cleanse me from every sin and set me free.

J. EDWIN ORR (1912-1987)

Our Father in heaven, I have turned from the emptiness of the world and found in Thee all that I will ever need. Praise the name of Jesus. Amen.

Wherefore in all things it behooved him to be made like unto his brethren,
that he might be a merciful and faithful high priest in things pertaining to God,
to make reconciliation for the sins of the people.
HEBREWS 2:17

Reconciliation between two people usually means each party compromises something in order to come together. If a man and I had four propositions keeping us apart, we might get together and say, "Now, brother, I don't want to be out of friendship with you, and therefore I'll make a concession on this." He will say, "Well, I'll make a concession on that." Therefore, by his moving over this way and my moving that way, we can come to a point of reconciliation.

But, how can God say to the sinner, "I'll move over halfway and then you move over halfway, and we'll come together in the middle and be reconciled"?

To do that, God would have to void the Godhead and cease to be God; I would rather go to hell than go to heaven presided over by a God who would compromise with sin. We want God to be the holy God He is, and remain the holy God He is.

God, through Jesus Christ, made it possible for man to come all the way over on God's side. That is the kind of reconciliation I can believe in. The only way an alienated person can be reconciled to God is through Jesus Christ.

Come, ye sinners, poor and needy, weak and wounded, sick and sore;
Jesus ready stands to save you, full of pity, love, and power:
He is able, He is able, He is willing: doubt no more!
JOSEPH HART (1712-1768)

Oh God, I praise Thee that through Jesus Christ I have found full
reconciliation with Thee. No more bargaining, nothing more
needs to be done. Thank you, Jesus. Amen.

For the wages of sin is death; but the gift of God is eternal life
through Jesus Christ our Lord.
ROMANS 6:23

One of the amazing truths about God is that He will not compromise with sin. I do not think we want God to wink at our iniquity; rather, we want Him to do something about it. What did He do about our iniquity?

He came down, became flesh and became both God and man in order that by His death He might remove everything out of the way so that man could come back into fellowship with God. Before that, man could not come back or would not come back in Christ. Now, because Christ came, died and removed every moral obstacle out of the way, man can come home as the prodigal son did.

Looking at the parable of the prodigal son, it is interesting to note that the father never compromised with the son. The son left but had to come back.

So it is with us. There is only one way back to the Father, and Jesus told us that He was the way—the only way—back. Because He did not compromise with sin, we have the assurance that when we come back to God, we come to a God who never changes, and that is our security.

We come, O Christ, to Thee,
True Son of God and man,
By whom all things consist,
In whom all life began;
In Thee alone we live and move
And have our being in Thy love.
E. MARGARET CLARKSON (1915–2008)

O God, my sin, my sin, oh the thought of it all! Yet, in Jesus Christ my
sin has been dealt with and I have been brought into sweet communion
with Thee. Praise the name of the Lord. Amen.

Whereby are given unto us exceeding great and precious promises:
that by these ye might be partakers of the divine nature, having escaped
the corruption that is in the world through lust.

2 PETER 1:4

The apostle Peter explains this matter of reconciliation in his own way. He says that God has left us with promises of the gospel, that by these promises we might be partakers of the divine nature.

What does that mean?

It means that when the sinner comes home—when he repents and believes on Christ, with saving faith, God implants in the heart of that previous sinner some of His own nature. Then the nature of God in God, and the nature of God in the sinner are no longer dissimilar. They are now one, and the sinner is at home. The dissimilarities are gone, the unlikeness removed and the nature of God in man makes it morally proper that man and God should have fellowship.

Without compromising Himself in any way, God now receives the returning sinner, and puts a deposit of His own nature and life in that sinner.

Standing on the promises
Of Christ my King,
Thro' eternal ages
Let His praises ring;
Glory in the highest
I will shout and sing,
Standing on the promises of God.

R. KELSO CARTER (1849–1928)

Oh, the thought of it, dear God! I can come into blessed fellowship with
Thee. How my heart pants for that fellowship, and how thankful I am
that Thee made it possible through Jesus Christ my Savior. Amen.

Beloved, now are we the sons of God, and it doth not yet appear what we shall be:
but we know that, when he shall appear, we shall be like him;
for we shall see him as he is.

1 JOHN 3:2

I like a certain grotesque illustration that seems to get the idea across. It is simply having an angel and an ape sitting together in a room, staring at each other. There is absolutely no way of getting them together. How could you do it?

If the great God Almighty could take from the angel that glorious and blessed celestial nature that is his, and deposit it in the ape, the ape would leap to his feet, shake hands with the angel and call him by name, because similarity would instantly be there.

As long as the one has the nature of an ape and the other of an angel, there can be nothing but everlasting dissimilarity. Therefore, the world with all of its money and culture and education and science and philosophy is still a moral ape. The holy God cannot compromise Himself to fellowship, and neither can that man understand God, for the natural man cannot understand God, and there can be no fellowship.

God moved in Christ, died on the cross, took the obstacles away and now by the new birth gives some of His own delightful divine nature to the sinner, and the sinner looks up and says, "Abba Father," for the first time in his life.

Standing on the promises I now can see
Perfect, present cleansing in the blood for me;
Standing in the liberty where Christ makes free,
Standing on the promises of God.

R. KELSO CARTER (1849-1928)

Abba Father is so sweet to my lips as I meditate on my relationship with Thee.
I once was nothing more than a moral ape; but Jesus changed all that when He
died on the cross for me. Hallelujah for the Lamb that was slain! Amen.

And, behold, I am with thee, and will keep thee in all places whither thou goest,
and will bring thee again into this land; for I will not leave thee,
until I have done that which I have spoken to thee of.
GENESIS 28:15

In the Old Testament story of Jacob and his ladder, Jacob was converted there and empowered by the Spirit of God. Jacob was a crooked old sinner, running from his twin brother, Esau, from whom he had swindled the birthright. Jacob went out from Beersheba and went toward Haran.

He came to a certain place and tarried there all night because the sun had set. He took some of the stones of that place and put them up for his pillow and lay down to sleep. While he slept, he saw a ladder set up on the earth, and God was above it and the angels ascending and descending upon it. God and Jacob met, and Jacob believed in his God. What a wonderful experience he had!

When he woke from his sleep, he had a new understanding of his relationship with God. His testimony was, *This is the gate of heaven, and I did not know it.* He did not know it when he lay down to sleep that night; but when he awoke in the morning, he knew God's presence was with him. It was there all the time, but for the first time in his life, Jacob experienced the manifest presence of God, and it changed the rest of his life.

We are climbing Jacob's ladder,
We are climbing Jacob's ladder,
We are climbing Jacob's ladder,
Soldiers of the cross.
AFRICAN-AMERICAN SPIRITUAL

O God, as Jacob of old discovered Thy presence, may I do so today.
May I recognize that Thou art with me and Thy presence is the comfort
of my soul. I pray this in Jesus' name. Amen.

For where two or three are gathered together in my name,
there am I in the midst of them.
MATTHEW 18:20

A miraculous work of grace operates in the life of every sinner who is soundly converted and born again. It is the conscious transplantation of the divine nature into his heart through faith in Jesus Christ. It is such an overwhelming experience that he is likely to be explosively happy. He might cry out as Jacob of old did, "God is in this place, and I didn't know it."

What happened? What made the difference? What had been restored to him? It was not the presence of God, but rather the conscious presence of God. What makes heaven what it is? The unhindered and unsullied presence of God. What makes hell what it is? The absence of a consciousness of the presence of God.

That is the difference between a prayer meeting and the dance hall. The unsullied presence of God fills heaven and earth, contains heaven and earth and is present everywhere. In the prayer meeting, some little old lady kneels and says, "O Jesus, where two or three are gathered there Thou art in the midst." God is there. In the dance hall, they would be embarrassed if the presence of God were to be manifest.

My conversion is the implantation of the divine life in this repenting sinner.

O boundless salvation, deep ocean of love!
O fullness of mercy, Christ brought from above,
The whole world redeeming, so rich and so free,
Now flowing for all men, now flowing for all men,
Now flowing for all men come, roll over me!
WILLIAM BOOTH (1829-1912)

Dear heavenly Father, the miracle of grace has so operated in my life to
bring me to appointive communion and fellowship with Thee. How I praise
Thee for my boundless salvation! Through Jesus Christ my Lord, amen.

August 2

The Lord is righteous in all his ways, and holy in all his works.
The Lord is nigh unto all them that call upon him,
to all that call upon him in truth.
PSALM 145:17-18

What I am looking for these days are some old-fashioned conversions. I must confess I do not see too many of that kind today. What we have today, instead, are such milk and water things; such poor, shoddy, ragged things. We convince people they have been converted, but they have not had an implantation of the divine life in them. There is no similarity with them and God, and therefore no fellowship.

We need once more conversions where a man kneels and, in a burst of tears and agony, confesses his sins to God, believes in Jesus Christ and then gets to his feet with light on his face and walks around shaking hands with everybody. The tears would flow, and as best he could, he would try to keep those tears back a little bit.

What did that? Not only the conscious taking away of sin, but the conscious presence of God revealed to his heart. That is the joy of conversion, not bringing God from some distant star, but knowing God by a change of nature, and that He is near "and I knew it not."

Rejoice, ye pure in heart,
Rejoice, give thanks, and sing;
Your glorious banner wave on high,
The cross of Christ your King.
EDWARD H. PLUMPTRE (1821–1891)

O God in heaven, how I long to see people truly converted to Jesus Christ in that radical way we used to see. Use me today to witness to someone who needs that kind of conversion. I pray this in Jesus' name. Amen.

Be glad in the Lord, and rejoice, ye righteous:
and shout for joy, all ye that are upright in heart.
PSALM 32:11

It is my prayer that the evangelical church will discover that salvation is not a lightbulb only, not an insurance policy against hell, but a gateway into God and into His heart.

The cults like to play this little religious game. They like to offer a form of security similar to buying an insurance policy. Unfortunately, what they offer is far less than what the Scripture offers us.

My concern is that the evangelical church has come perilously close to this sort of attitude. For some reason, the whole purpose of conversion has degenerated to this level. It is not so much what a person has been saved from, although thank God for that, but what he has been saved to.

The heaven that has been offered lately is a heaven most people want to go to. It is a place where they will have everything right; a split-level home, two cars, a fountain and swimming pool and golden streets to top it off.

That heaven does not appeal to me at all. Lady Julian, in her book *The Revelations of Divine Love,* says that heaven will be heaven because the Trinity will fill our hearts with joy without end. Here is what we must get into our heads and hearts: Jesus Christ is a full and complete manifestation of the Trinity.

When all my labors and trials are o'er
And I am safe on that beautiful shore,
Just to be near the dear Lord I adore
Will through the ages be glory for me.
CHARLES H. GABRIEL (1856–1932)

Dear God, Thy heaven is a place of Thy blessed abode. Forgive me for trying to put earthly things in heaven. Let me long for that place where Thy presence is manifested continually. This I pray in Jesus' name. Amen.

Thou wilt shew me the path of life: in thy presence is fulness of joy;
at thy right hand there are pleasures for evermore.
PSALM 16:11

Christianity is a gateway into God. When you get into God, with Christ into God, then you are on a journey into infinitude.

The hardest thought for me to grasp is that God is infinite. I must confess I do not understand it fully, and nobody really can grasp it; but reason kneels down and acknowledges that God is infinite. I can make out what is meant by infinite; it means that God knows no limits, no bounds and no end. Whatever God is, He is without boundaries; and all that God is, He is without limits.

My earnest quest and pursuit is to know God. To whatever I know about God and am learning about God, I need to add this element of infinitude. Whatever God is and I am coming to understand, I multiply that by infinity.

That includes God's love, His grace, His mercy and anything else I can learn and know about God. When I come up against this aspect of infinity, I must understand that I am finite. Whatever my problems are, they are nothing in comparison to the infinitude of God.

Days are filled with sorrow and care,
Hearts are lonely and drear
Burdens are lifted at Calvary,
Jesus is very near.

JOHN M. MOORE (1925-)

My heavenly Father, I sometimes feel my problems are so big that I will
never be able to get through them. But one look at Thee and I begin to
understand that in comparison, my problems are as nothing.
As long as I have Thee, I have all that I need. Amen.

Great is the Lord, and greatly to be praised in the city of our God,
in the mountain of his holiness.
PSALM 48:1

Everybody, me included, is guilty of careless speech. We put words together that do not really belong together. For eample, we talk about somebody having boundless energy. We look at our children running around in the backyard and exclaim that they have boundless energy. Nothing like that really exists. They soon run out of energy and are ready for bed.

We also talk about an artist taking infinite pains in his work. He does not take infinite pains, He takes pretty good pains, and does the best he can. Somewhere along the line, he throws up his hands and says, "It isn't right yet, but I'll have to let it go at that." We call that infinite pain, but it is a misuse of the word "infinite."

We misuse the word "boundless" and "unlimited" because the words "boundless," "unlimited" and "infinite" all mean the same thing. They are words used to describe God. In no way, shape or form do they describe man. We have a limit to everything about us. God, on the other hand, has no limits. We are not using words carelessly when we say that God is boundless, limitless and infinite. My grace today rests upon the infinite nature of God.

O Lord my God! When I in awesome wonder
Consider all the works Thy hands have made,
I see the stars, I hear the mighty thunder,
Thy power throughout the universe displayed.
Then sings my soul, my Savior God, to Thee;
How great thou art, how great thou art!
CARL BOBERG (1859–1940),
TRANS. STUART K. HINE (1899–1989)

Our Father in heaven, how awesome art Thou when I consider and
meditate upon Thee. What have I to fear as long as I have Thee.
Praise the name of Jesus! Amen.

August 6

The mighty God, even the Lord, hath spoken,
and called the earth from the rising of the sun unto the going down thereof.
Out of Zion, the perfection of beauty, God hath shined.

PSALM 50:1-2

As created beings, we have devised ways to account for ourselves. Measurement is a way we have of accounting for things, and we are compulsive about this.

You know how much you weigh and wish you did not weigh that much; but it is the gravitational pull associated with how much you weigh. We measure distance by inches, feet, yards and miles. We want to know how far away something is from where we are right now. Then we want to know how long that distance would take in seconds and minutes and hours and days.

We have various other ways of measuring things because everything is relative; it is limited. You can always measure things. We know how big the sun is, how big the moon is, how much the earth weighs, how much the sun weighs and how much many other of the heavenly bodies weigh.

We can weigh all of these things and measure them, because they are finite. When we come to God, there is no way to measure anything of His grace. The grace of God is infinite and beyond our ability to measure. His grace has no beginning and therefore no end.

The mercy of God is an ocean divine,
A boundless and fathomless flood;
Launch out in the deep, cut away the shore line,
And be lost in the mercy of God.

A. B. SIMPSON (1843-1919)

Heavenly Father, I am able to measure everything in my world
and give an account for everything, but I cannot measure Thee.
Your grace in my direction is beyond calculation. And I praise Thee
through Jesus Christ my Lord. Amen.

Be merciful unto me, O God, be merciful unto me:
for my soul trusteth in thee: yea, in the shadow of thy wings
will I make my refuge, until these calamities be overpast.
PSALM 57:1

I once stood at the edge of the Atlantic Ocean and looked out at the seemingly limitless ocean. The water looked like it would never end. If I would begin my journey across the ocean it might take me a long time, but eventually I would end up in Great Britain, if I had my coordinates right.

What looks limitless from our position is only because we are so finite. Anything that is bigger than we are seems to be infinite, boundless and limitless. There is nothing boundless but God; and there is nothing infinite but God. It is not just because God is bigger than we are. It is much more than that.

The reason God is infinite is because God is self-existent and absolute, and everything else is contingent and relative. Everything is relative except God. God knows no degrees. God is never more of Himself one day than He is another day. I can never come to God and find Him to be less than what He was the day before. God does not extend into space; God contains space. Whatever God is, He is without limits, and He never changes.

We praise, we worship Thee, we trust,
And give Thee thanks for ever,
O Father that Thy rule is just,
And wise, and changes never.
Thy boundless power o'er all things reigns,
Done is what ever Thy will ordains.
Blessed are we that Thou reignest!
UNKNOWN

Dear Father, I bow before Thee in humble acknowledgment
of Thy boundless wisdom. Thou knowest all in absolute perfection.
All I know is Thee, and that is more than enough. Amen!

Great is our Lord, and of great power: his understanding is infinite.
PSALM 147:5

C. S. Lewis had the right idea about eternity. He said that if you could think of a sheet of paper infinitely extended in all directions, and if you were to take a pencil and make a line one inch long on that paper, that line would represent time. When you start to push your pencil, that is the beginning of time; and when you lift it off the paper, that is the end of time; and all around that infinity extends.

That is a good illustration.

If there were a point where God stopped, then God would not be perfect. If, for instance, God knew almost everything, but not quite everything, then God would not be perfect in knowledge. His understanding would not be infinite, as David claims.

Wherever my life starts, God was previous. Whenever my life stops, God keeps going. There is no beginning and there is no ending. I cannot understand that, but I can accept it by faith and rest comfortably in the knowledge that God is all that I really need in this life. If I needed anything other than God, then that thing I needed would then be God.

Praise God, He is my all in all.

Once I hoped in Jesus, now I know He's mine;
Once my lamps were dying, now they brightly shine;
Once for death I waited, now His coming hail;
And my hopes are anchored safe within the veil.
A. B. SIMPSON (1843–1919)

O Lord Jesus, all that I am and all that I have rests in Thee.
The only thing that really satisfies my heart these days is Thy presence.
How I praise Thee for that. Amen and amen.

The voice of the Lord is upon the waters: the God of glory thundereth:
the Lord is upon many waters.
PSALM 29:3

What amazes me, and amuses me to a certain extent, is to watch some-body exercise some power. How some people love to exhibit their power! You see it a lot in politicians, and I am afraid it has come into the church to a certain degree.

No matter how much power a person has, there will always be some-body who has more.

The opposite is true about God. If God had all the power except a little bit, and somebody else had a little bit of power that God could not get to, then God would not be all-powerful. We could not say that this God has infinite power, because He would not be an infinite power, just close to it. Falling short of it a little bit would disqualify Him from being all-powerful.

I watch men grab for power, and it is amusing. But when I think of God and His power, it raises within my heart waves of praise and adoration. I bow my knees to the One who is all-powerful, knowing that behind His power is love that knows no limit toward me. God never tries to con me out of power or authority. No matter how much power I need from God, I never exhaust God in the least.

He giveth more grace as our burdens grow greater,
He sendeth more strength as our labors increase;
To added afflictions He addeth His mercy,
To multiplied trials He multiplies peace.
ANNIE J. FLINT (1886–1932)

Dear Father, there are times when I have come to a point of sheer
exhaustion. Then I think of the inexhaustible resources of Thy grace.
How I praise Thee for Thy truth, in the precious name of the
Lord Jesus my Savior. Amen.

They that trust in the Lord shall be as mount Zion, which cannot be removed,
but abideth for ever. As the mountains are round about Jerusalem,
so the Lord is round about his people from henceforth even for ever.
PSALM 125:1-2

Our God is perfect in knowledge, in power and in goodness. If God had goodness, but there was one spot that was not good, then He would not be our God and Father. If God had love but not all the love, just 99.9 percent of the love, God still would not be God.

For God to be God, He must be infinite in all aspects. He must have no bounds, no limits, no stopping place, no point beyond which He cannot go. When you think of God or anything about God, you have to think infinitely about God.

Thinking this way may give you a Charlie horse in your head, but I really believe it is a mighty good choice. This little cheap God that we have around now with modern Fundamentalism, this cheap God you can pal around with—the man upstairs that likes me, the fellow that helps win baseball games and all that; that God, my brother, isn't the God of Abraham, Isaac and Jacob. He is not the God that made the heavens and the earth. He is some other God.

I may get a headache trying to understand this; but what is hard for the head is ointment for the heart.

No matter if the way be sometimes dark,
No matter though the cost be oft-times great,
He knoweth how I best shall reach the mark,
The way that leads to Him must needs be strait.

FREDERICK BROOK (N.D.)

I readily confess, Lord Jesus, Thy grace is beyond my explanation.
I cannot understand it, but I embrace it by faith and allow Thy grace
to dominate my life today. Amen.

But our God is in the heavens: he hath done whatsoever he hath pleased.
Their idols are silver and gold, the work of men's hands.
PSALM 115:3-4

As Christians, we sometimes look aghast at the gods of the heathen. We spend a lot of money trying to reach these heathen and introduce them to the real God and Father of our Lord Jesus Christ.

The sad part is that we as Christians can create gods just the same as the heathen do. We educated Americans are not making gods out of silver or gold or wood or stone. We would rebel at such an idea. However, we can create a god out of our own imagination. The god worshiped in many places today in America is simply a god of the imagination.

Christianity in this generation is decaying, and plunging into the gutter, because the God of modern Christianity is not the God of the Bible. We have fallen short of that altogether.

I do not mean to say that we do not pray to God. I mean to say that we pray to a god short of what He ought to be. We are not praying to the true God—the infinite, perfect, all-knowing, all-wise, all-loving, infinitely boundless God. Instead, we are praying to a God we have created in our imaginations, which falls far short of the real God.

Approach, my soul, the mercy seat,
Where Jesus answers prayer;
There humbly fall before His feet,
For none can perish there.
JOHN NEWTON (1725-1807)

Dear God and Father of our Lord Jesus Christ, forgive me for looking to
"things" instead of looking to Thee. May I keep Thee in my focus today
as I live and serve Thee. In the name of Jesus I pray. Amen.

And God saw every thing that he had made, and, behold, it was very good.
And the evening and the morning were the sixth day.

GENESIS 1:31

Perhaps what I am going to say now will be shocking. We often need a little shock to get us back into the realm of reality, to shake loose the cobwebs in our head. I have prayed, thought about, searched and read the Word too long to ever take this back. I stand on this as solid as any truth in God's Word.

God takes pleasure in Himself and rejoices in His own perfections. The divine Trinity is glad in Himself. God delights in His works. When God created the heaven and the earth, and all things that are upon the earth, He kept saying, "And God saw that it was good."

After He created everything, God created man in His own image. He said the same thing about man that He said about everything else He created. "Behold, it was very good."

God rejoiced in all His works. He was glad in everything He had done; and when we come to redemption, God is totally delighted in the finished work of Jesus Christ on the cross. Even today God looks upon all of His creation, although for a brief time it is under the domination of depravity and sin, and He sees that all things are good.

Praise to the Lord, the Almighty, the King of creation!
O my soul, praise Him, for He is thy health and salvation!
All ye who hear, now to His temple draw near;
Join me in glad adoration!

JOACHIM NEANDER (1650–1680)

O God, today I rejoice in the fact that Thou lookest upon me
as a redeemed man and say, "It is very good." I take great joy in
the joy that Thou takest in me. Amen.

Thou wilt shew me the path of life: in thy presence is fulness of joy;
at thy right hand there are pleasures for evermore.
PSALM 16:11

God made this creation, and He loved what He created. God took pleasure in Himself and took pleasure in His own perfections and in the perfection of His work.

When we come to redemption, this was not a heavy task laid upon God by moral necessity. This was not something that caught God off guard, and he had to stop everything else He was doing and fix a problem. God wanted to do redemption.

Redeeming mankind was not a necessity for God. He did not have to send His Son, Jesus Christ, to die for mankind. Do not imagine the Trinity sitting around a table in heaven trying to figure out what to do next, debating whether it was worth saving mankind or not.

Nothing could be more foreign to the truth. Jesus voluntarily came to die on the cross. Redemption was the happy willingness of God.

A mother does not have to get up and feed her baby at two o'clock in the morning. No law compels her to do such a thing. She does not have to give that baby the loving care that she gives. She wants to give it. She does it because she likes to do it.

Great things He hath taught us, great things He hath done.
And great our rejoicing, through Jesus the Son;
But purer, and higher, and greater will be
Our wonder, our transport when Jesus we see.

FANNY J. CROSBY (1820–1915)

I gaze, O Lord, into the creation around me and almost see the
pleasure Thou must see gazing into my redeemed heart. Thy perfect work
enables Thee to look into my heart and catch a glimpse of Thyself.
To the honor and praise of the Lord Jesus Christ, my Savior. Amen.

The heavens declare the glory of God; and the firmament sheweth his handywork.
PSALM 19:1

Out in western Pennsylvania, certain greedy businessmen bought out the coal rights in certain sections of the state. I grew up in and I loved seeing the beautiful sun-kissed hills, the setting of the sun and the creek that ran out to the rivers and down to the sea.

I went back to my old place a few years ago and found that the coal rights had been sold to certain businesses. They did not dig a hole and go back after the coal. They took bulldozers and dragged the top off the earth, the trees, the grass and everything to get down to the coal and lift the coal out. This resulted in thousands of acres of ground trashed like one vast grave that had not been filled in.

They paid a $300 fine then left the place as it was.

I went back recently, and dear old busy, enthusiastic, fun-loving Mother Nature had been at work drawing a green veil over that ugly trash.

What man had virtually destroyed, God gave Mother Nature the ability to reverse and start the trees growing again. You can now see the glow of God in those valleys man tried to destroy.

> I sing the mighty power of God
> That made the mountains rise;
> That spread the flowing seas abroad
> And built the lofty skies.
> I sing the wisdom that ordained
> The sun to rule the day;
> The moon shines full at His command,
> And all the stars obey.

ISAAC WATTS (1674–1748)

Almighty Creator, what wonders Thou hast put before our adoring eyes. Although the path of man is destruction, Thy redeeming grace can put all things back into Thy pleasure again. Amen.

Where were you . . . when the morning stars sang together,
and all the sons of God shouted for joy?
JOB 38:4,7

I believe that we need to stop thinking like a scientist and start thinking like a Christian. We will get right with God when we stop thinking like a technician or a mechanic.

We need to see that God is enthusiastic over His work. We do not have to try to figure out how God is going to fix anything. God is absolutely happy in His creation.

Scientists try to technically explain creation and the world around us. As soon as they get one thing figured out, they discover something else disqualifying the first thing. I am not sure, but I think God has arranged it that way.

I need to come and view this world of ours not as a technician, mechanic or scientist, but as someone who is a lover of God and appreciates God's enthusiasm in His creation.

Let us stop thinking of God as being heavy-browed and gloomy. When God made the heaven and the earth, the morning stars sang together and joined God in shouting for joy. Personally, I can become so gloomy by looking at the present condition of the world around me. The remedy for that is to look into the smiling face of God who enthusiastically loves what He has created.

This is my Father's world, and to my listening ears
All nature sings, and round me rings the music of the spheres.
This is my Father's world: I rest me in the thought
Of rocks and trees, of skies and seas; His hand the wonders wrought.
MALTBIE D. BABCOCK (1858–1901)

Dear God, what pleasure I get in discovering that which pleases Thee.
All around me are tokens of Thy goodwill and pleasure. May I focus on
those today as I live in the power of the Lord Jesus Christ, my Savior. Amen.

I will declare thy name unto my brethren:
in the midst of the congregation will I praise thee.
PSALM 22:22

I sometimes get irritated at the religious technicians trying to explain Scripture in some technical fashion.

At the annunciation of Christ's birth, the Scriptures tell us that the angels said "Peace on earth, goodwill to men." The technicians point out quite emphatically that these angels were not singing, but according to the Greek, they were "saying." Angels, according to them, do not sing, which we know is not true according to the parallelism of elements in Job 37:7.

I am not sure of the purpose of that kind of technical twisting. I assure you, you cannot read that annunciation without something in you moving. There is a rhythm there, and you get music in your heart: "Peace on earth, goodwill to men," they said. I confess I am not much of the musician, but brother, that was singing.

There was singing at the Incarnation and at the Resurrection. When Jesus rose from the dead, it does not tell us in the New Testament, but it foretells it in the Old Testament in Psalm 22:22 that one of the first things Jesus did was to sing.

One of the last things He did before he went out to dine was to sing a hymn along with His brethren.

I would love to have heard that hymn.

I will sing the wondrous story,
Of the Christ who died for me,
How He left His home in glory,
For the cross of Calvary.

FRANCIS H. ROWLEY (1854–1952)

Dear God, I weary of the experts explaining to me that which rises
above all human explanation. I just want my heart to sing praises unto
Thee for Thy goodness toward me. Amen.

But thou, Lord, art most high for evermore.
PSALM 92:8

I enjoy singing, especially the old hymns of the church that lift up and magnify the God I love.

Recently, I have been exposed to some of the new music gaining momentum, especially in evangelical churches. I have a hard time, personally, joining in on some of these new songs.

I revel in the old hymns of the church. I sing quite comfortably off-key some old hymn every day of my life, as part of my worship. It is part of my connection with the God I serve. My problem is that when you leave the old hymns of Wesley and Montgomery and Watts, and the rest of them that emphasize, "Thou art, Thou art, Thou art, O God, Thou art," you drift off into some other area. The theme of many of the songs today of the modern Fundamentalist is, "I am, I am, I am, I am."

It makes me sick to my stomach, all this "I am-ing."

I know we can testify, and we have a right to; and occasionally a good hymn is a testimony. I believe we have overdone it, as we have overdone almost everything else.

My goal is to get back to, "Thou art, O God, Thou art."

When Christ shall come with shout of acclamation
And take me home, what joy shall fill my heart!
Then I shall bow in humble adoration
And there proclaim, my God how great Thou art!

CARL BOBERG (1859–1940),
TRANS. STUART K. HINE (1899–1989)

Holy Spirit, my heart is challenged each day to lift up the name of the Lord Jesus Christ in praise. All I can say is simply, how great Thou art, O God. Amen.

*And they sung a new song, saying, Thou art worthy to take the book,
and to open the seals thereof: for thou wast slain, and hast redeemed us to God
by thy blood out of every kindred, and tongue, and people, and nation.*

REVELATION 5:9

Every day I celebrate the joy of the Lord. My joy rests upon the fact that I have been ransomed by God and set free from the tyranny of sin and damnation. When we get to heaven, the theme of our singing will be, "Thou art worthy, O God, to take the book."

It is the worthiness of God that causes my heart to sing. It will be my theme throughout all eternity. I am looking forward to walking down the streets of gold in heaven and singing about my Savior who set me free.

I have noticed recently an interest in the second coming of Christ and the Rapture, and our destination in heaven. Some are talking about the book of Revelation again. One of the curious things I have noted in some of the new books coming out is the fascination with angels. Everybody seems to be trying to describe these heavenly creatures. I suppose if you have the luxury of speculation, it would be good to try to figure out who these heavenly creatures are.

Someone recently asked me if I knew anything about these heavenly creatures. I responded simply, "See me five minutes after the Rapture and I'll tell you about it."

Jerusalem, the golden! With milk and honey blest;
Beneath Thy contemplation sink heart and voice oppressed;
I know not, oh, I know not what joy awaits us there;
What radiancy of glory, what bliss beyond compare.

BERNARD OF CLUNY (TWELFTH CENTURY)

*I look forward, O God, to the return of the Lord Jesus Christ.
So much about prophecy I don't know and will never know;
but this one thing I do know: Jesus will soon return for me and
take me to His home. Praise the name of the Lord! Amen.*

And I beheld, and, lo, in the midst of the throne and of the four beasts, and in the midst of the elders, stood a Lamb as it had been slain, having seven horns and seven eyes, which are the seven Spirits of God sent forth into all the earth.
REVELATION 5:6

The infinite Godhead invites us unto Himself to share in all of the intimacies of the Trinity, and Jesus Christ is the way in. No other way can take us into the very heart of the Trinity.

Truth like this causes us to raise our voices in song, singing, "Worthy is the Lamb." He is worthy in more ways than we could ever imagine. The more I contemplate the worthiness of this Lamb, the more I fumble in my ability to express my gratitude. So much about this Lamb I hunger to know; so much about Him that I desire to explore. As I come closer to Him, it is as if my brain stops working and my heart starts beating, and I break out in praise.

I am sure that the major part of heaven will be exploring this Lamb that was slain for our sins. I am not going to give up searching now. My pursuit each day is in this direction.

Although the eternal God is so vast, so infinite, extended out so far into infinity that I cannot hope to know all about God, He has shined down toward us and filled us with rapturous joy.

Mortals, join the mighty chorus, which the morning stars began.
Father love is reigning o'er us, brother love binds man to man.
Ever singing, march we onward, victors in the midst of strife;
Joyful music lifts us sunward, in the triumph song of life.

HENRY VAN DYKE (1852–1933)

O God, I too join the morning stars in singing Thy praise. Who they are, I do not know, but if they love Thee as I love Thee, I will join them through all eternity in praising the wonderful name of the Lord Jesus Christ. Amen.

Even when we were dead in sins, hath quickened us together with Christ,
(by grace ye are saved;) And hath raised us up together,
and made us sit together in heavenly places in Christ Jesus.
EPHESIANS 2:5-6

Years ago, I heard a man sing a song I have never heard before or since. A phrase in that song went to the effect that angels can never know the grace that we as humans know.

Only people who really need a doctor know anything about doctors in the area. If you have a child that is chronically sick, you know more about the doctors in your area than I do. I do not need a doctor, so knowing who the doctors are and what they can do is not pertinent to my life.

But if my health suddenly turns for the worse, I would pursue the knowledge of doctors in the area. I would want to know the best doctors and how they can help me.

Angels do not need grace; and so they know very little about grace. I know a whole lot about the God of grace because every day of my life I am a recipient of God's amazing grace. The more I learn about the sin in my own heart, the more I want to know about God's grace.

God's grace delves into the deepest part of my heart and deals with the crouching sin in the darkness of my soul.

I'll sing of the wonderful promise that Jesus has given to me:
"My strength is made perfect in weakness, My grace is sufficient for thee."
And lest my poor heart should forget it, or ever forgetful should be,
He still keeps repeating the promise "My grace is sufficient for thee."

A. B. SIMPSON (1843-1919)

O God of grace and mercy, how I thrill as I meditate upon
Thy attributes. My sin, O the depth of it, has caused me to seek
that amazing grace Thee promise to those who come to Thee.
I come today, in Jesus' name. Amen.

Unto whom it was revealed, that not unto themselves, but unto us they did minister the things, which are now reported unto you by them that have preached the gospel unto you with the Holy Ghost sent down from heaven; which things the angels desire to look into.

1 PETER 1:12

I have been thinking about angels recently. I have been thinking about the difference between angels and men, particularly Christians. Angels are surrounded by all kinds of mysterious speculations, and I suppose that when we get to heaven we will see a lot of them and understand them a little bit better.

In my thinking of angels, it occurs to me that although the angels wonder at the grace of God, they can never fathom the depth of that grace. No angel can sing with any meaning, "Marvelous grace of our loving God." No angel can sing, "Amazing grace, how sweet the sound."

Yes, they could sing it academically. They could get the right pitch and sing it because it is a theory, but they could not sing it with any meaning, because they have not any occasion for God's grace.

On a Sunday morning, how many people sing these hymns about God's grace and only sing them academically? They get the right words in order and actually sing in harmony. It is, however, only a technical experience in singing.

For those who have had occasion to experience the amazing grace of God, singing about that grace is one of the highlights of our gathering together as believers.

> When we've been there ten thousand years,
> Bright shining as the sun,
> We've no less days to sing God's praise
> Than when we first begun.

JOHN NEWTON (1725–1807)

Dear Father, each day I sing of Thy grace because I have experienced so much of it. I look forward to the day when I will sing it in Thy presence throughout all eternity. Hallelujah for the Lamb! Amen.

Let your conversation be without covetousness;
and be content with such things as ye have:
for he hath said, I will never leave thee, nor forsake thee.
HEBREWS 13:5

My parents loved to tell the story about my first word. Every time we gathered, particularly as I got older, either my father or my mother would share the story.

According to my parents, the first word I uttered as a baby was a curse word. In my defense, I did not invent that word. The simple fact is that I was learning to talk and I heard some scoundrel using vile language. When I opened my baby mouth and uttered my first word, that curse word came out.

As a baby, I had no way to control that. I was just repeating what I heard and not really understanding what I was saying. I could not control the first word I uttered, but I know what my last word is going to be.

The last word I utter is going to be a doxology raised in honor of God's amazing grace. I can control that word. I believe that in God's economy my last word is the word that really defines who I am in Jesus Christ. That first word uttered by me was a result of my surroundings.

The first word was a curse word, but my last word will be praise.

Praise God, from whom all blessings flow;
Praise Him, all creatures here below;
Praise Him above, ye heavenly host;
Praise Father, Son and Holy Ghost.
Amen.
THOMAS KEN (1637–1711)

Dear Father in heaven, I long for my last word on earth to be a word
of praise. To prepare for that event, I plan to praise Thee every day
that I live. In the blessed name of Jesus, amen.

The Lord is not slack concerning his promise, as some men count slackness;
but is longsuffering to us-ward, not willing that any should perish,
but that all should come to repentance.

2 PETER 3:9

In meditating upon the grace of God, I find it to be incomprehensibly delightful and an overwhelming plenitude of goodness and kindness on the part of God.

If every mosquito in all the swamplands of the world were sinners, and every star in the heaven sinners, and every grain of sand on the seashores of the seven oceans were sinners, the grace of God could swallow them all up. I stand on the Word, which says where sin abounded, grace did much more abound. I believe that, my brethren.

Some president of some seminary defined me as a "legalistic santification." I know what the terms mean; I just don't know what that man meant by using them for me. Let me just clear the air and say this: basically, philosophically, theologically, practically and experientially, I am a believer in the grace of God.

How could a man as vile and wicked as me ever hope to have help apart from the grace of God?

Here is the difference. Sin can be measured. That is, there is a beginning and an end to sin. Grace, on the other hand, is limitless, boundless and infinite. My sin, in no way, depletes God's amazing grace.

He was not willing that any should perish;
Jesus enthroned in the glory above,
Saw our poor fallen world, pitied our sorrows,
Poured out His life for us—wonderful love!

LUCY R. MEYER (1849–1922)

Dear Lord Jesus, the precious Lamb of God, how my heart sings of
Thy praise! Thy grace, which led Thee to the cross, was greater than the
sum total of all my sins. I thank Thee for what Thee did for me.
I dedicate my day today to Thee. Amen.

This is a faithful saying, and worthy of all acceptation,
that Christ Jesus came into the world to save sinners; of whom I am chief.
1 TIMOTHY 1:15

In my travels, I've found people that I really love. Like most people, I like to be around people that I love.

What we sometimes overlook is that being nice does not get us into heaven. Some of the nicest people in the world will never get into heaven. I know we forget that. We look at somebody and think he or she is very nice and congenial. But we forget that salvation is not based upon a person's works of righteousness.

You can be as nice as they come and end up in hell. It is the grace of God that saves us, and only the grace of God. There is no other way into heaven; the grace of God never takes into account how nice a person is.

Many people are anything but nice, but the grace of God marvelously changes them. I thank God for His grace, and this grace is bestowed only through the Eternal Son—only through Jesus Christ, the Lord.

God's grace existed before Christ was born in Bethlehem; it existed before He died on the cross; it existed before He rose again; but it could not operate except He die on the cross.

Down from His splendor in glory He came,
Into a world of woe;
Took on Himself all my guilt and my shame,
Why should He loved me so?
ELTON M. ROTH (1891-1951)

Our Father in Heaven, if being nice is a prerequisite for heaven,
I would fall so far short of that goal. I praise Thee that the entrance into
heaven is the grace of the Lord Jesus Christ, my Savior.
To Him be praise. Amen.

For if, when we were enemies, we were reconciled to God by the death of his Son,
much more, being reconciled, we shall be saved by his life.
ROMANS 5:10

Jesus once told a parable about a certain man who had two sons. One day, one of the sons came and said, "Dad, give me the goods that belong to me." The father gave him what was coming to him; and after a few days, the son departed into a far country.

As Jesus tells this parable, this younger son spent all of his inheritance in riotous living. He was having the time of his life, not knowing how much of his life he was destroying. When he had spent everything, a famine came to that land and all the previous friends of this young son deserted him.

Finally, the young boy found himself in that far country working out in the fields to feed swine. For a Jewish boy, this was a terrible degradation. As he fed the swine, the famine became so great that there was nothing for him to eat.

After a while, this young boy came to himself. This was the turning point in this young man's life. Up to this point, he really was not himself, but was living a lie. When the young boy came to himself, he remembered his father and returned to him. Whatever happened after that is a celebration of God's good grace.

In tenderness He sought me,
Weary and sick with sin,
And on His shoulders brought me
Back to His fold again;
While angels in His presence sang
Until the courts of heaven rang.

W. SPENCER WALTON (1850-1906)

Dear Father, I once found myself as the prodigal son, far away from
Thee. I praise Thee that when I did come to myself, I found my way
back to Thy open arms. I rest in Thee today. Amen.

For if ye turn again unto the Lord, your brethren and your children
shall find compassion before them that lead them captive, so that they shall
come again into this land: for the Lord your God is gracious and merciful,
and will not turn away his face from you, if ye return unto him.
2 CHRONICLES 30:9

In meditating on the parable of the prodigal son that Jesus told, I am quite fascinated by the phrase, "when he came to himself." At this point, he said to himself, "What am I doing here?" When he came to himself, he finally realized where he was.

While having the time of his life, he did not have any thoughts of his father. When he came to himself, he remembered his father. Then he put together his strategy for getting back to the father. This is common to man. We put together our strategy of getting back into the good graces of our heavenly Father.

He was going to say to his father, "Father, I am not worthy. I have sinned before heaven and before thee." He was trying to set his own terms for getting back.

The son soon found out that his father was right where he had left him. The son had wandered far, experienced a lot, lost everything and now he was coming home.

When he got near home, his father was waiting for him and ran to him and grabbed him and hugged him to his bosom and hugged life back into him again.

Our heavenly Father is waiting to hug life back into us.

I've wandered far away from God,
Now I'm coming home;
The paths of sin too long I've trod,
Lord, I'm coming home.
WILLIAM J. KIRKPATRICK (1838-1921)

My precious heavenly Father, the word "home" means so much to me.
I remember the days when I was far from home. But I also remember coming
home and being welcomed home by Thee. Praise the name of Jesus. Amen.

August 27

The lofty looks of man shall be humbled, and the haughtiness of men shall be bowed down, and the Lord alone shall be exalted in that day.
ISAIAH 2:11

Unlike the prodigal son, many people have tried to get back and have failed. They have tried and tried and tried, but to no avail.

The path from the Father is so easy and alluring. The devil has made that for certain. The sun shines, the sky is blue and all seems right with the world. It is the path back to the Father that is most difficult. The devil has made that for certain, as well.

How many prodigal sons made it back to the Father's house? How many have given up, or have not yet come to themselves?

They have gone to altars, followed evangelists around, but just cannot somehow seem to make it. They are floundering in the slough of despondency and cannot seem to make it to the other side.

How many have come to themselves and remembered the Father but just can't quite believe that the Father would take them back? This is Satan's lie.

St. Bernard said something to the effect that the blacker the iniquity, the deeper the fall, the sweeter is the mercy of God who pardoned all. No matter how deep and terrible it is, you can always say, "I will arise and go to my father."

> I've wasted many precious years,
> Now I'm coming home;
> I now repent with bitter tears,
> Lord, I'm coming home.

WILLIAM J. KIRKPATRICK (1838-1921)

Dear Lord, many have gone away from the Father's house into the far country and have not yet found their way back home. Use me today in some way to encourage some prodigal to come to himself, or herself, in order that he or she may come home to the Father. Amen.

Thy dead men shall live, together with my dead body shall they arise.
Awake and sing, ye that dwell in dust: for thy dew is as the dew of herbs,
and the earth shall cast out the dead.

ISAIAH 26:19

I find that many people have slipped back a little. At one time, they were always in church helping and busy in the Lord's work. He or she was a good, busy, hard-working brother or sister, and faithful to the church.

Something changed. He got a new position, which forced him to work long nights, evenings, and the first thing to go was the prayer meeting. He begins slipping. He is not where he was a few months ago. He has made a lot of money now and is very successful, but there is a light gone out of his face.

What will it take for this man to "come to himself"?

If you were fine like an archangel, made thousands of dollars, never failed and never fumbled, you would be a saint, and there would be no place in God's grace for you. Because you are the kind of person you are and have fits of slipping back a little, the grace of God operates toward you. This is your hope.

So I say, be cheerful, be hopeful, dare to rise and say, "I'll not sit and be gloomy anymore. I will dare to believe that the grace of God, that vast grace of God, is big enough for me."

I'm pressing on the upward way,
New heights I'm gaining every day;
Still praying as I'm onward bound,
"Lord, plant my feet on higher ground."

JOHNSON OATMAN, JR. (1856–1922)

Dear God, my praise today is because of the vastness of Thy grace in my life.
No problem that I'm going through today could ever exceed Thy grace.
I thank Thee, in Jesus' name. Amen.

August 29

The Lord looked down from heaven upon the children of men,
to see if there were any that did understand, and seek God.
PSALM 14:2

As a youngster, I used to go around ponds and beat on the weeds. Hidden in those weeds were green frogs, and I would beat the weeds and then listen to them all jump into the pond.

That is what I try to do in my ministry. I want to beat the weeds a little bit and see what I can do to encourage some people to make the big plunge, not into a pond, but into the wide ocean of God's grace.

It is easy for us to judge people and say that person got what he deserved. All right, that may be true. It also may be true of each one of us. I often hear people say, "All I want is what I deserve, what's coming to me." I have never been in that camp, and I certainly do not want what is coming to me.

The grace of God is what we need to plunge into. The same grace of God that saved me will save you. Therefore, I recommend if you have slipped a little bit, and all of us have at some point, just take the plunge into the ocean of God's grace.

There's a wideness in God's mercy
Like the wideness of the sea;
There's a kindness in His justice,
Which is more than liberty.
FREDERICK W. FABER (1814–1863)

O Father, I acknowledge those times that I have slipped. I'm not proud
of those times, but I am thankful for the ocean of Thy grace that has
brought me back to where I need to be. Praise the name of Jesus. Amen.

And call upon me in the day of trouble: I will deliver thee,
and thou shalt glorify me.
PSALM 50:15

I once read a testimony of St. Teresa of Avila where she confessed, "I got so discouraged I just quit praying."

She said, "I didn't pray for a long time. I wanted to pray again, but I said to myself, 'Now listen, you haven't prayed for a long time, and you're not worthy to pray.' I felt I wasn't worthy to pray; I wasn't worthy because I hadn't prayed, and I would not pray because I wasn't worthy to pray." How many people are caught in that kind of trap?

She soon caught on and discovered that was Satan talking. "I decided that it wasn't my worth, but it was the goodness of God, and so I went back to my knees and prayed."

Some are not praying today because they do not feel worthy to pray. If the devil tells you that you are unworthy, just smile and say, "Is that so? Well, devil, that just makes me a candidate for the grace of God, because if I were worthy, then the grace of God couldn't reach me; but the fact that I'm unworthy is enough for me."

Then get on your knees and get back into the praying mode.

What a Friend we have in Jesus, all our sins and griefs to bear!
What a privilege to carry everything to God in prayer!
Oh, what peace we often forfeit, oh, what needless pain we bear,
All because we do not carry everything to God in prayer!
JOSEPH M. SCRIVEN (1819-1886)

Our Father which art in heaven, Thou hast bid me come to Thee in the
discipline of prayer. The enemy has tried to hinder me here, but thanks
be to Thy grace that enables me to come into Thy presence,
through Jesus Christ my Lord. Amen.

For sin shall not have dominion over you:
for ye are not under the law, but under grace.
ROMANS 6:14

My old friend Dr. Max Reich, son of a rabbi, was converted in London, England, and graduated from Oxford University. He was a poet, a scholar and a marvelous man of God.

He once visited what we would call a fallen woman. We are all fallen, but she was on her deathbed.

The woman said to him, "Dr. Reich, you're a good man, but you don't know me. I'm a terrible woman, just terrible. I'm not worthy for you to sit here by my bed."

He quietly said to her, "You're dying."

"I know I'm dying," she said, "but I lived a terrible life, a vile life."

"God will save you."

Looking at Max, she said, "Not me, no, no. I'm not good enough. My goodness can't get me in."

Picking up on her attitude, he said, "Sister, if your goodness can't get you in, your badness can't keep you out."

"Is that so, Dr. Reich?" And she began to cry.

"That's right. If goodness can't get you in, badness can't keep you out."

She believed in Jesus Christ and was converted. When the grace of God confronts a moral situation, it pronounces life.

Children of God, oh glorious calling,
Surely His grace will keep us from falling;
Passing from death to life at His call;
Blessed salvation once for all.

DANIEL W. WHITTLE (1840–1901)

My dear Lord and Savior, how I praise Thee today for my salvation!
It is not of me, but it is all of Thee. I praise that grace that has set me free. Amen.

For God, who commanded the light to shine out of darkness,
hath shined in our hearts, to give the light of the knowledge of
the glory of God in the face of Jesus Christ.

2 CORINTHIANS 4:6

I firmly believe that many saints are in heaven that the self-righteous members of the Ladies Aid Society would never have voted into membership. "Not that woman! Never! She's a bad example."

The assessment is probably true, at least on the outside. I am grateful that entrance into heaven is not based on somebody voting me in. I do not particularly like self-righteous people, and I do not believe God is pleased with them. What I am grateful for is that they are not in charge of heaven's membership roll.

Never would they have accepted into their membership Mary, of New Testament fame, that had seven demons.

Let me testify and say that the lowest woman that ever wallowed her way through the vices of the honky-tonks, the grace of God operates to save her, and the blood of Jesus Christ washes her. She is as pure as the purest virgin and as clean as the holiest woman that ever walked.

Goodness cannot get you into heaven, but if you will trust the grace of God, badness cannot keep you out. Put away your discouragement. Rise up and shine for the light of God's grace has fallen upon thee.

There is sunshine in my soul today,
More glorious and bright
Than glows in any earthly sky,
For Jesus is my light.

ELIZA E. HEWITT (1851–1920)

How I praise Thee, O God of my salvation, that your grace
rises above my goodness and my badness! I trust Thee, O Christ,
for all my eternity. Praise be to Thy name. Amen.

And he said, Thou canst not see my face: for there shall no man see me, and live. And the Lord said, Behold, there is a place by me, and thou shalt stand upon a rock: And it shall come to pass, while my glory passeth by, that I will put thee in a clift of the rock, and will cover thee with my hand while I pass by: And I will take away mine hand, and thou shalt see my back parts: but my face shall not be seen.
EXODUS 33:20-23

When Moses wanted to know and see God's glory, the Lord told him that He needed to cover Moses with His hand and He would reveal His glory to him. The Lord descended in the cloud, stood with Moses there and proclaimed the name of the Lord.

I have read that story many times, and each time I always feel that it would be a great privilege to have been with Moses as God revealed Himself there. I am sure that this revelation of God was one of the great turning points in Moses' life. It is one thing to know something technically and theologically, but it is quite another thing to know it experientially.

I refuse to allow my relationship with God to be limited by my understanding of theology. I want my relationship to God to be in His hands and allow Him to lift me up and surround me with the cloud of His presence. Oh, to know God!

On that memorable day, the Lord passed by Moses and proclaimed, "The Lord, the Lord God, merciful and gracious, long-suffering and abundant in goodness and truth."

I surrender everything and everybody, and so position myself as to experience the glory of God in my life. Nothing else really matters.

All to Jesus I surrender, all to Him I freely give;
I will ever love and trust Him, in His presence daily live.
JUDSON VAN DE VENTER (1855-1939)

Heavenly Father, I want to know Thee in the fullness of Thy revelation. Nothing in my life is more important than knowing Thee. Fill me with Thyself. I pray this in Jesus' name. Amen.

Have I any pleasure at all that the wicked should die? saith the Lord God:
and not that he should return from his ways, and live?
EZEKIEL 18:23

God's people revel in His mercy.

Things were bad, but Jeremiah believed that if it had not been for the mercy of God, God would have consumed them like dry leaves on fire.

Ezekiel says, "As I live, says the Lord God, I have no pleasure in the death of the wicked."

Human speech cannot describe the depths of the heinousness of the iniquity of man. History has recorded for us the dastardly deeds of wicked men who have all but destroyed society. And the evil continues. I lived through the horror of Adolf Hitler and the terrible things he did to the nations around him, and even to his own people.

I could go on recounting men who were so evil that the thought of them is despicable. When these men died, the world sighed a sigh of relief. Not so with God. God has no pleasure in the death of the wicked, no matter how much the wicked deserve it; God takes no pleasure in any man's dying, particularly when he is wicked.

All of God's work is toward man's redemption. Everything He does has a redemptive element to it. God delights in wooing man back to where he belongs, in fellowship with God. He is the Father of mercies and the God of all comfort.

Jesus, Lover of my soul, let me to Thy bosom fly,
While the nearer waters roll, while the tempest still is high!
Hide me O my Savior hide, till the storm of life is past.
Safe into the haven guide; oh, receive my soul at last!

CHARLES WESLEY (1707-1788)

O God, I know how bad things can become. I know the wretchedness
of my own sin. Because of that I come to Thee as my haven of rest.
In Jesus' name I pray. Amen.

Behold, we count them happy which endure. Ye have heard of the patience of Job,
and have seen the end of the Lord; that the Lord is very pitiful, and of tender mercy.
JAMES 5:11

If James had said that the Lord is pretty full of pity, we would have set-
tled for that. Because it's the Lord who is pitiful, He has to be infinitely
pitiful. In his rash of feeling about it, James puts the word "very" before
the word "pity" and says God is "very pitiful."

Peter explains why wicked men are not destroyed. He says that God
is not slack concerning His promises, as some men count slackness, but
is longsuffering to us, not willing that any should perish but that all
should come to repentance.

These few verses tell us that God is a merciful God. Mercy is an attribute of God. It is something God is, not something God has.

If mercy was something God has, God might lose it; it might diminish
or cease to be. But it is a facet of God's unitary being, much like a diamond
with many shining facets all around. It is one diamond, but there are a
thousand facets catching the rays of the sun and flashing them in 100,000
directions. Therefore, God is one, and all one; and one facet of God's character is His mercy.

Oh, let us launch out on this ocean so broad,
Where floods of salvation o'erflow;
Oh, let us be lost in the mercy of God,
Till the depth of His fullness we know.
A. B. SIMPSON (1843–1919)

Our Heavenly Father, I am thrilled by the endlessness of Thy pity
toward such a one as me. My sin and wretchedness is no match
for Thy mercy. In Jesus' name I pray. Amen.

September 5

I will extol thee, O Lord; for thou hast lifted me up, and hast not made my foes to rejoice over me. O Lord my God, I cried unto thee, and thou hast healed me.
PSALM 30:1-2

God's infinite goodness is that within God that desires His creature's happiness, and it is an irresistible urge to bestow blessedness. God takes no pleasure in the death of the wicked but takes pleasure in the pleasure of His people. It is that in God which suffers along with His friends and grieves over His foes.

It is that in God that we call mercy, which looks with compassion upon men who are in need of judgment.

Mercy, according to the Old Testament, means to stoop in kindness to an inferior. It is to have pity upon and to be actively compassionate. The mercy of God is not a passive thing; it is an active thing. God is compassionate, but He is actively compassionate.

God is more anxious to be compassionate toward us than we are to receive His compassion. Actually, our idea of God puts a great gulf between God and us. I would agree there is that separation, but God is anxious to bridge the gap and has done everything necessary to do away with that separation. God has made it possible that His compassion can flow into our lives through Jesus Christ.

O the deep, deep love of Jesus, love of ev'ry love the best!
'Tis an ocean full of blessing, 'tis a haven giving rest!
O the deep, deep love of Jesus, 'tis a heav'n of heav'ns to me;
And it lifts me up to glory, for it lifts me up to Thee!
SAMUEL TREVOR FRANCIS (1834–1925)

Dear Lord Jesus, I'm a happy recipient of Thy love.
I earnestly believe that Thee has my best interests for the longest
period of time. Blessed be Thy name. Amen.

It is of the Lord's mercies that we are not consumed, because his compassions fail not. They are new every morning: great is thy faithfulness.
LAMENTATIONS 3:22-23

Allow me to give some facts about the mercy of God as revealed in the Scripture. The mercy of God never had a starting point.

The Mississippi River, for example, has its beginning way up north in Minnesota, and goes all the way down into the Gulf of Mexico. It begins somewhere and ends somewhere, and everything in between is affected by its beginning and end.

We must never think of God's mercy as originating somewhere and flowing out. It never began to be, because it is an attribute of the uncreated God, and therefore always was. It has never been any more than it is now.

If you ever think there was ever a time in the past that God was more merciful than today, you are absolutely wrong. God's mercy does not change. Although it flows from the heart of God, it has no beginning and no end. It is absolutely pure in every regard. As God was merciful to Moses, Abraham and all the rest of those Old Testament characters, God is merciful to you and me today. It is the mercy of God that makes my life the joy that it is today.

Great is Thy faithfulness, O God my Father!
There is no shadow of turning with Thee;
Thou changest not, Thy compassions, they fail not;
As Thou hast been Thou forever wilt be.
THOMAS O. CHISHOLM (1866–1960)

O God of mercy never failing, my life is what it is today, and I enjoy Thy joy in my life, because of the mercy Thee has showered on me. Praise the name of Jesus. Amen.

September 7

Blessed be God, even the Father of our Lord Jesus Christ, the Father of mercies,
and the God of all comfort; Who comforteth us in all our tribulation,
that we may be able to comfort them which are in any trouble,
by the comfort wherewith we ourselves are comforted of God.
2 CORINTHIANS 1:3-4

Many preachers and evangelists tell tearjerker stories. They want the stream of mercy to flow out of the human eye and think that if we cry enough the Lord will have mercy upon us.

God will have mercy upon you if your heart is as hard as a stone. If you never weep over your iniquity, God is still a merciful God; He cannot be anything else. If everybody in the world suddenly turned atheist, and the entire world turned into devils, it would not change the mercy of God in the slightest. God would still be as merciful as He is now.

If Christ were to die 100 times on the cross, it would not make God any more merciful than He is now, and He will never be less merciful than He is now. Nothing that occurs can increase, diminish or alter the quality of God's mercy. The cross did not increase the mercy of God. Remember, God's mercy did not begin at Calvary, the mercy of God led to Calvary. It was because God is merciful that Christ died on the cross.

On a hill far away stood an old rugged cross,
the emblem of suffering and shame;
and I love that old cross where the dearest and best
for a world of lost sinners was slain.

GEORGE BENNARD (1873-1958)

Dear Father, Your mercy led Jesus to Calvary and to die for me.
I thank Thee for the boundless mercy that has brought me into Thy favor.
In Jesus' name, amen.

For all have sinned, and come short of the glory of God; Being justified freely
by his grace through the redemption that is in Christ Jesus.
ROMANS 3:23-24

Mercy is God's goodness confronting human guilt and suffering, and all men are recipients of this mercy. There is not an atheist on the continent that is not the recipient of God's mercy.

If God should let His justice loose without mercy, God could justly rain fire on the North American continent. We are so proud of ourselves here in the United States. We are proud that we live lives such as we do in comparison to the rest of the world. If justice had its way—unrestrained and without mercy, God would rain fire from the Rio Grande to the Hudson Bay. All men are recipients of the mercy of God. For all have sinned and come short of the glory of God, and mercy postpones that execution.

Justice and judgment are God's way of confronting iniquity; but God's mercy spares us and postpones the execution. Even those who shake their fists in God's face are recipients of God's mercy or else they would be destroyed right on the spot. God's mercy gives people a chance to back away from their life and repent and put their trust in Jesus as Savior. Without that mercy, no man would stand.

Wonderful grace of Jesus,
Reaching to all the lost.
By it I have been pardoned,
Saved to the uttermost;
Chains have been torn asunder,
Giving me liberty.
For the wonderful grace
Of Jesus reaches me.

HALDOR LILLENAS (1885–1959)

Our Father which art in heaven, how I praise Thee for Thy mercy that has
rescued me from the just penalty I deserve! This I pray in Jesus' name. Amen.

Knowing that a man is not justified by the works of the law,
but by the faith of Jesus Christ, even we have believed in Jesus Christ,
that we might be justified by the faith of Christ, and not by the works of the law:
for by the works of the law shall no flesh be justified.
GALATIANS 2:16

I thank God for the mercy He extends toward us. Mercy brought Jesus Christ to the cross and established blood atonement for us. Those who have embraced Jesus Christ are different from all other people in the world or in the universe. Now, justice and mercy see righteousness instead of iniquity and a just God looks down upon a sinner who has been covered by the atoning merits of Jesus' blood—not a sinner anymore, but a justified man.

Justification by faith is the great cornerstone of the church and of the epistles of St. Paul. But when we see it like this, we then wonder about the perfections of God and the unitary nature of His being—the oneness of all His attributes, and His infinity and perfection. How can such a God look upon such a sinner?

One of the deep mysteries to me and, I would suppose, to any Christian thinker is how God who is perfect and self-contained and self-sufficient can suffer. God sent His Son to suffer on my behalf, and I can only paraphrase the language of Frederick W. Faber and say, "How Thou can suffer, Oh my God, and be the God thou art? It is darkness to my intellect, but sunshine to my heart."

There is gladness in my soul today, and hope and praise and love,
For blessings which He gives me now, for joys "laid up" above.
ELIZA E. HEWITT (1851-1920)

Dear God, my heart breaks as I think that I have caused
any suffering on Thy behalf. I do not understand it and cannot
fathom the depth of that suffering. But this I do know, Jesus Christ
has made the difference in my life. Amen.

But to him that worketh not, but believeth on him that justifieth
the ungodly, his faith is counted for righteousness.
ROMANS 4:5

I do not mean to offend anybody, but let me just say that the least important thing about you (and me, for that matter) is your head. God gave you a head and wants you to use your head. I have used mine quite a little in my time, and some think I overuse it. But I would like to say that the least important thing about you is your head.

Your head may be important to put your hat on and keep your glasses in place, and other useful items. Let me just say that which is darkness to your intellect can be sunshine to your heart. Your head may lead you astray, but your heart will lead you into the sunshine of God's grace and mercy.

Each day, I struggle to try to figure God out. I exhaust my brain trying to understand and reason my way to God. It is useless. The knowledge of God is contrary to human reason; it is, however, above and beyond human reasoning and intellect. I take by faith that which I cannot understand intellectually.

My relationship to Jesus Christ goes beyond theology and rests quite nicely in the area of doxology.

I'll praise my Maker while I've breath,
And when my voice is lost in death,
Praise shall employ my nobler powers;
My days of praise shall ne'er be past,
While life, and thought, and being last,
Or immortality endures.

ISAAC WATTS (1674–1748)

Dear God, by faith I claim all that I cannot understand intellectually.
Thy mercy is so awesome that it fills me with uncontrollable doxology.
In Jesus' name, amen.

September 11

Unto thee, O God, do we give thanks, unto thee do we give thanks:
for that thy name is near thy wondrous works declare.

PSALM 75:1

I do not know what Jesus did on the cross, and I am afraid of the man who is too smart about the atonement, who can explain it too well. For surely it was the mystery of godliness. Surely, what He did can never enter the mind of a man. Surely, what He did that dark morning, when it became as dark as 1,000 midnights, Jesus Christ our Lord did in that awful hour something that can never be explained.

After Christ had risen from the dead, Peter said something rather odd—that angels desire to look into these things. I do not know about the atonement. I do not know what Jesus did on the cross; but I know whatever He did satisfied the heart of God forever. I know that whatever He did turned my iniquity into righteousness; it turned my inequity into equity and terminated the sentence of death on me into a judgment of life. I know He did that.

Therefore, I can only stand before Him and say, "O my God, O my God, Thou art." Darkness to my intellect but, praise God, sunshine to my heart.

> All praise to Him who reigns above
> In majesty supreme
> Who gave His Son for man to die,
> That He might man redeem!

WILLIAM H. CLARK (NINETEENTH CENTURY)

O God, I stand before Thee today in wonder and amazement.
My life has been changed, but how Thou hast changed my life is beyond
my intellect. Praise the name of Jesus. Amen.

September 12

I have preached righteousness in the great congregation:
lo, I have not refrained my lips, O Lord, thou knowest.
PSALM 40:9

So many things I do not understand, and so I find myself getting on my knees before God and crying from the depths of my heart, "Thou knowest, O my Lord and my God, Thou knowest."

I take refuge in the fact that I may not know everything, but I know and have confidence in Someone who does know everything. Maybe someday in that bright tomorrow, when we know as we are known, these poor befuddled heads of ours will suddenly be glorified and made like His. Maybe with clearer and brighter vision, we will look upon the wonder of atonement and know what it all meant. Not all of the brilliant minds in Christendom, down through the years, are able to put together an adequate explanation of the atonement that occurred on Calvary's cross.

I do not understand the mystery of it, but I know the joy and the sunshine that affects me, and my friends, and those who truly know God. Our joy is not in understanding but rather in believing. On my knees before this merciful God, I lift my voice in praise, adoration and worship. It is not my brain God really wants, but my heart—a heart that rests fully in Jesus Christ.

Forever here my rest shall be,
Close to Thy bleeding side;
This all my hope, and all my plea,
For me the Savior died!
CHARLES WESLEY (1707–1788)

My God and Father, my head aches because of what I do not know.
Maybe someday I will know all things, but now I rest most peacefully
in the fact that I know Thee. I praise Thee through
Jesus Christ, my Lord. Amen.

September 13

*Like as a father pitieth his children, so the Lord pitieth them that fear him.
For he knoweth our frame; he remembereth that we are dust.*
PSALM 103:13-14

During the Second World War, I traveled across the continent on a train. On board was a police officer whose business was to keep order on the train. He was the meanest-looking fellow I think I've ever seen. He looked over the crowded train with a stern and tough-as-nails demeanor.

When someone tried to step off the platform when the train stopped, this officer barked, "Back on the train. You're not in uniform." Everybody on the train sat up very stiffly as this officer walked back through the center aisle.

Out from one of the seats came a little baby girl, curly hair and shining eyes. Everybody thought this old tough officer would growl at her, sending her back to her seat crying. She skipped up the aisle.

When he came to this little girl, he reached over, patted her curly head three or four times and then went on his way.

A woman in front of me burst out in laughter and said, "I knew he was a phony."

Many have been taught that it is just not manly to be tender, but God who knows people said, "As a father pities his children, so the Lord pities them that fear him."

Though He giveth or He taketh,
God His children ne'er forsaketh;
His the loving purpose solely
To preserve them pure and holy.
CAROLINA V. SANDELL BERG (1832-1903)

Dear Father in heaven, as a recipient of Thy pity, I rejoice with unceasing joy. I approach Thee in trembling fear only to discover the graciousness of Thy nature. Blessed be the name of Jesus. Amen.

For a day in thy courts is better than a thousand. I had rather be a doorkeeper in the house of my God, than to dwell in the tents of wickedness.
PSALM 84:10

The mercy of God is my life and my breath. I breathe it daily. Oh, the mercy of God, that God is compassionate, that He stoops to pity and have mercy upon His people!

The mercy of God is more than a theological doctrine to me. It is more than something I believe in; it is something that I experience every day of my life. What I am today is because of His mercy.

The thing I most delight in with God is the fact that He sympathizes with my grief. He knows the absolute depths of my sorrow, my agony and pain. I do not know how badly off I am because I cannot fully understand my grief or my sorrow. I feel the agony of my pain, however, when I come to God. I know He knows my pain in depth more than I will ever know.

As much as I know myself, I do not deserve anything from God. All I deserve is hell. That is why when I come to the mercy of God as a deer panting after the cool water brooks, nothing slakes my spiritual thirst like a fresh dose of God's mercy.

> Why restless, why cast down, my soul?
> Hope still, and thou shalt sing
> The praise of Him who is thy God,
> Thy health's eternal spring. Amen.

NAHUM TATE (1652–1715) AND NICHOLAS BRADY (1659–1726)

O God of mercy and compassion, how I delight in Thee today!
I know what I deserve, but Thy grace has given me Thy pleasure.
All this through Jesus Christ my Savior. Amen.

Go ye therefore, and teach all nations,
baptizing them in the name of the Father, and of the Son,
and of the Holy Ghost: Teaching them to observe all things
whatsoever I have commanded you: and, lo, I am with you always,
even unto the end of the world. Amen.
MATTHEW 28:19-20

We have a message and a witness to give to the world. We are sent to tell the world that which they never would hear if we did not tell them. We are sent to tell the world that God is merciful and gracious and slow to anger and full of loving-kindness. This God sent His Son to die so that there is a door of mercy open wide for us. We are to tell the world this, and keep telling the world until some here and some there, one here and one there, hear it and come home, and the bells of heaven ring. That is our message.

We do not go out into the world and ask their permission, "What would you like to hear?" I suppose many do that and try to give what the world wants to hear. We are to go out into the world and say, "Thus saith the Lord."

Whether we live in an age of rockets and space travel or in the day of the horse and buggy, this is the way our God is. We are to go out into the world and tell them to come home, because God is waiting to receive them.

To the regions beyond I must go, I must go
Where the story has never been told;
To the millions that never have heard of His love,
I must tell the sweet story of old.

A. B. SIMPSON (1843–1919)

Dear Lord Jesus, Thy commission is to go into all the world and preach
the gospel. May this day be a day I diligently pursue that commission.
Let me tell the world of Thy amazing grace. Amen.

Behold, I stand at the door, and knock: if any man hear my voice, and open the door, I will come in to him, and will sup with him, and he with me.
REVELATION 3:20

I hear many people talking about being backslidden. Personally, I do not like the word, but I must acknowledge that people do backslide. People who turn their back lose their first love and their joy and find themselves in a terrible predicament. What they once were they no longer are and cannot find their way back home.

I have a message for such a person: God still remembers you. God's heart goes out to you, and He pities you and wants you back home. Once you turn around, you will find the doors are open—they have never been closed. Those doors will never be closed as long as Jesus Christ is at the right hand of God the Father.

Here is what hurts me. You can never get people to make a decision along this line when you talk about God's mercy and grace and love. For some reason, you have to preach judgment and hell to get people to move in the right direction. Whether anybody moves or not, I will discharge my obligation and give my witness from the Scriptures that God is merciful and full of pity and desires to welcome you back. Why not come home today?

Behold, the loving Savior stands outside your bolted door,
There knocking with His nail-pierced hands as oftentimes before.
Don't turn Him away, don't turn Him away,
He has come back to your heart again although you've gone astray;
Oh, how you need Him to plead your cause on that eternal day!
Don't turn the Savior away from your heart, don't turn Him away.

HALDOR LILLENAS (1885-1959)

O Savior of all mankind, what a privilege it is for me to share the good news of Thy grace to those who need it today! Empower me to share Thy grace to everyone I meet today. Amen.

By terrible things in righteousness wilt thou answer us,
O God of our salvation; who art the confidence of all the ends of the earth,
and of them that are afar off upon the sea.

PSALM 65:5

I believe it is tremendously important that we know what God is like. It is tremendously important that we know what kind of being we are serving.

German theologian Gerhard Tersteegen (1697–1769) said, "Oh God, thou art far other than men have dreamed and taught, unspoken in all language, unpictured in all thought."

Certainly, I agree that it is impossible to know everything there is to know about God. But it is the worshiping heart that seeks after God. It is the heart aflame with divine love that searches into the knowledge of the holy.

I do not allow that which is impossible to hinder me in my search after God. The one thing I can know about God is that He is a just God. It may not be so pleasant to contemplate, but we certainly can put this down as one of God's attributes.

In the Scriptures when the word "righteousness" occurs, the word "justice" also occurs, because the two words are indistinguishable. The word means uprightness and moral rectitude, and they are so near to being the same that eventually translators used one instead of the other interchangeably.

What my head cannot comprehend my heart can adore.

Earth from afar has heard Thy fame,
And worms have learned to lisp Thy name:
But, O! the glories of Thy mind
Leave all our soaring thoughts behind.

ISAAC WATTS (1674–1748)

O God, my head aches when I try to comprehend Thee, but my heart beats
in adoring wonder and worship. Praise be the name of Jesus. Amen.

The Lord shall judge the people: judge me, O Lord, according to my righteousness,
and according to mine integrity that is in me.
PSALM 7:8

Whenever justice is applied to a moral situation, you have a judgment. A man is called into the courtroom as the defendant; another man as the plaintiff. He is accusing the defendant of something. You have these two men, and there is a legally moral situation before them, and justice has to decide who is right.

When a judge pronounces a judgment, he is pronouncing on a moral situation—if it is a criminal offense or simply a common judicial affair. Therefore, it may be favorable or unfavorable. Every time we use the word "judgment," we imagine that it is unfavorable judgment, but it is not always so. Sometimes a court will bring in a favorable judgment.

The verdict is not always guilty, and sometimes they bring in an opposite verdict depending upon what justice says about the moral condition. If the one has been inequitable in his conduct, he is judged guilty. If he has been equitable, he is judged not guilty. That is what justice is. It is moral equity, the balance of scales balanced evenly so there is not too much here and too little there, nor too little and too much there, but just right.

Open my eyes that I may see
Glimpses of truth Thou hast for me;
Place in my hands the wonderful key
That shall unclasp and set me free.
Silently now I wait for Thee,
Ready my God Thy will to see.
Open my eyes. Illumine me, Spirit divine!
CLARA H. SCOTT (1841–1897)

Dear God, Thy justice is beyond challenging.
I praise Thee today for the justice Thou hast laid upon me.
May my life bring glory and praise unto Thee. Amen.

Doth God pervert judgment? or doth the Almighty pervert justice?
JOB 8:3

Preachers sometimes talk very foolishly. I think we ought to watch what we say, because the Scripture says we shall give an account on the last day for even our idle words. I have been guilty of this myself, but I try to watch myself from foolish talk.

Sometimes preachers will say, "Justice requires God."

We say that when you accept Jesus, justice requires God to save you. Justice requires God to take you to heaven.

This is a great error of thinking as well as speaking. Justice does not require God to do anything. If we say justice requires God to do this or that, we postulate a principle of justice somewhere to which God has to conform.

We put justice out there as a great perpendicular pillar, and we say, "There it is, that tall shining pillar of justice, and even God is compelled to obey it."

Justice is not outside of God; let us remember that. Justice is what God is, and nobody can manipulate God into doing things no matter how little they may be.

I am thankful that justice is in the hands of God, because man would abuse it like he abuses everything else.

Frail children of dust, and feeble as frail,
In Thee do we trust, nor find Thee to fail;
Thy mercies how tender! How firm to the end!
Our Maker, Defender, Redeemer and Friend!
ROBERT GRANT (1779-1838)

Dear God, forgive me for careless and foolish talk. Help me today to be mindful of the heavenly audience for not only my speaking but my thinking. May Jesus be praised today. Amen.

Who is like unto thee, O Lord, among the gods?
who is like thee, glorious in holiness, fearful in praises, doing wonders?
EXODUS 15:11

When somebody says that justice requires God to do something, it must mean there is a principle in existence somewhere that God must bow to. What I want to know is simply this, who enforces that?

If there is something that God must do, who is going to make God do it, and who is going to enforce it? If God should refuse to bow to a principle of justice, who would arrest God and bring Him before the bar of judgment? Who would put handcuffs on the Almighty and lead Him before a court of inquiry to see if He had been just or not, whether He had conformed to that external principle we called justice?

That kind of business is completely foolish, because if there were anybody superior to God, then that person would be God.

It all sounds very silly to me. Nothing outside of God can require Him or force Him to do anything, for that very thing would then be God. I refuse to worship a God who can be manipulated and controlled from something outside of Himself.

Keep in mind, there is nothing outside of God. God contains all things, and everything that is, is within the confines of God.

Immortal, invisible, God only wise,
In light inaccessible hid from our eyes;
Most blessed, most glorious, the Ancient of Days;
Almighty, victorious, Thy great name we praise.
WALTER CHALMERS SMITH (1824-1908)

My heavenly Father, nothing is higher than the Highest.
I honor Thee today as that One in my life that deserves all of my worship.
I give it to Thee through my Lord and Savior, Jesus Christ. Amen.

Clouds and darkness are round about him:
righteousness and judgment are the habitation of his throne.
PSALM 97:2

The tenor of scriptural teaching is that there is not anything outside of God that can move him. There are many things outside of you and me that can move us, all right. All created beings are vulnerable to outside forces manipulating us one way or the other.

Nothing outside of God can move Him in the least. Nothing has been added to God from eternity and nothing has been taken away. God is incapable of gain or loss. God acts justly from within, not in obedience to an abstract principle of justice; He acts like Himself toward all creation. When God is just, He is not putting on an act, but simply acting like Himself.

When God is just, He is not bowing to some pillar of justice somewhere. A judge sitting on a court bench bows to justice; but when God acts justly, He is just acting like God acts. He is acting the way God acts, and God will yet balance the scales.

I like that. It is possible for a judge to be corrupt and misuse his position of authority. Not so with God. God will always act justly; He will always act like Himself. I can rest in that wonderful truth.

Jesus, I am resting, resting in the joy of what Thou art;
I am finding out the greatness of Thy loving heart.
Thou hast bid me gaze upon Thee, and Thy beauty fills my soul;
For by Thy transforming power Thou hast made me whole.
JEAN S. PIGOTT (1845–1882)

Dear Judge of all the earth, I praise Thee because Thou art always
just in Thy dealings with mankind. Today I revel in the absolute Justice
I find in Thee. In Jesus' name, amen.

For there is one God; and there is none other but he.
MARK 12:32

I believe with everything inside of me that God will yet balance the scales; He will condemn the unequal and vindicate the just. Remember, judgment not only condemns the unequal and iniquitous, it also vindicates the just.

Anselm of Canterbury (c. 1033–1109) said: "But how dost thou spare the wicked, if thou art all just and supremely just? For how, being all just and supremely just, dost thou aught that is not just?" Then he comforts himself a little bit and says, "We see where the river flows, but the spring whence it arises, we see not. We see the river of God's mercy flowing down the centuries but where it arises we know not."

How is it possible for God to justify an iniquitous sinner? How does God turn us around and pronounce us just?

God has no parts that come together harmoniously. There are no wheels in the infinite being of God that mesh into each other with perfect precision, because that would mean God was composed of parts. If God had parts, somebody had to put them together. If somebody put God together, then that somebody would be God. Therefore, nothing that the justice of God does forbids Him to exercise His mercy, because it is the same God. God is merciful and just.

> All glory be to God on high,
> Who hath our race befriended.
> To us no harm shalt e'er come nigh;
> The strife at last has ended.
> God showeth His goodwill to men,
> And peace shall reign on earth again;
> O thank Him for His goodness!
>
> NIKOLAUS DECIUS (C. 1485–1541),
> TRANS. CATHERINE WINKWORTH (1827–1878)

Dear God, who is merciful and just, I yield this day to Thee, confident that Thou hast my best interests in mind for all my life. In Jesus' name, amen.

For there are three that bear record in heaven, the Father,
the Word, and the Holy Ghost: and these three are one.
1 JOHN 5:7

Sometimes we picture God presiding over a court of law and administering laws that He dislikes and disagrees with. We have Him sentencing a man with tears and apologies to a hell he does not believe in. We picture the Father angry and full of justice, and the Son tender and full of mercy; and the two do not agree.

We have the Father rushing forward with an upraised sword to destroy humanity, and the Son comes in between, takes the blow and dies on the cross. God offers repentance because His Son died; and He forgives us for His Son's sake.

The truth is, the Father and the Son have never, and can never disagree, because they are one. The Father and the Son together believe the same thing and have the same will. Christ laid down His life because He wanted to, and He laid it down because the Father wanted Him to. The Father and the Son and the Holy Ghost work harmoniously, because they are of one nature, have one thought, one will and one desire.

Glory be to Him Who loved us,
Washed us from each spot and stain!
Glory be to Him Who bought us,
Made us kings with Him to reign!
Glory, glory, glory, glory,
To the Lamb that once was slain!
HORATIUS BONAR (1808-1889)

O holy Trinity, sometimes I fail to give Thee, the Three in One,
Thy just due in all things. Today I celebrate Thy blessed unity.
I rest peacefully in Thee. Amen and amen!

That be far from thee to do after this manner, to slay the righteous with the wicked: and that the righteous should be as the wicked, that be far from thee: Shall not the Judge of all the earth do right?
GENESIS 18:25

A judge sits on the bench, sentencing people under the law that he may not want to, but he did not establish the law; he is merely the servant of the law.

In contrast to this, God is the servant of none. He is not making decisions based on any exterior criteria apart from Himself. If God has to abrogate justice to take you to heaven, then God will not take you to heaven. If God has to abrogate His holiness to save the man, He will never save that man.

How, then, can it be that God can be just and yet spare the wicked?

Simply because the attributes of God do not clash with each other. When God punishes the wicked, it is just, because it is consistent with the man's wickedness. When God spares the wicked, that also is just because it is consistent with God's goodness. God is never unjust to save any man. God's unitary being, being Himself, one God—Father, Son and Holy Ghost, coequal and coeternal—permits God to exercise His attributes as He chooses, as He wills. So when God wills to show mercy to a man, it never contradicts His justice.

We rest on Thee, our Shield and our Defender!
We go not forth alone against the foe;
Strong in Thy strength, safe in Thy keeping tender,
We rest on Thee, and in Thy name we go,
Strong in Thy strength, safe in Thy keeping tender,
We rest on Thee, and in Thy name we go.
EDITH G. CHERRY (1872–1897)

O God of justice and mercy, I celebrate Thy faithfulness in being to us what we absolutely need. You never fail, and I praise Thee today! In Jesus' name, amen.

And the peace of God, which passeth all understanding,
shall keep your hearts and minds through Christ Jesus.
PHILIPPIANS 4:7

I can believe in my salvation, not because I think I deserve it, but because I believe the passion, the death and the sufferings of Christ for me were infinite. His passion overflowed into infinity; and if every drop of blood in my body was of gross sin, there still would be enough in the infinite atonement to make up for all my sins and cancel them out.

If every human being that has ever or shall ever live, should breathe in and out sin continually from the moment of birth until the moment of death, and all should live to be 1,000 years old, they still would be finite. They could be counted if you had time to count them.

My finite sins compared to His infinite mercy get lost in a shoreless ocean of God's grace.

Every time I am bogged down in the immensity of my sin and my sin nature, and I become discouraged almost to the point of defeat, I look up into the infinite mercy of God and realize how small I really am. The devil may want me to be an accountant, but God desires me to be a worshiper and leave the numbers with Him.

My sin, O the bliss of this glorious tho't,
My sin, not in part, but the whole,
Is nailed to the cross, and I bear it no more.
Praise the Lord, praise the Lord, O my soul!
HORATIO G. SPAFFORD (1828-1888)

O, the glory of my salvation in Jesus! How I praise Thee, O God,
for the vastness of my salvation. Although my sin weighs me down
tremendously, it is not too much or too great for Thy infinite grace.
Praise the name of Jesus. Amen.

September 26

And in the midst of the seven candlesticks one like unto the Son of man, clothed with a garment down to the foot, and girt about the paps with a golden girdle.
REVELATION 1:13

I have noticed many Pollyanna types in the pulpit today, so unreasonable and illogically optimistic about everything. Everything is positive. The trouble with this is, without a negative, you have no positive. Because of this, some people think of God as being highly perfumed and beautiful, but rather sadly smiling; He would like to be good to us but does not know how.

That kind of God and that kind of Savior and that kind of Christ—the Christ of the pale, weak face—is not the Christ of the Bible. In the book of Revelation, we see a different portrait of Christ. We are serving the Christ of Revelation, not the Christ of some Pollyanna preacher who does not want to offend anybody and believes everything is going to turn out just nice.

I try being optimistic, but after reading my Bible and then reading the newspaper and listening to world news, I just do not find any foundation for optimism in this world. The only optimism is in the Christ of Revelation. The One who will soundly defeat the enemy and exercise perfect justice and perfect mercy and perfect unity. That is who I am serving today.

I serve a risen Savior,
He's in the world today.
I know that He is living,
Whatever men may say.
I see His hand of mercy,
I hear His voice of cheer;
And just the time I need Him
He's always near.

ALFRED H. ACKLEY (1887–1960)

Dear heavenly Father, all around me are those who are putting their trust and confidence in the exterior things of this world. Today my faith and trust is completely in the Lord Jesus Christ my Savior. Amen.

By so much was Jesus made a surety of a better testament.
HEBREWS 7:22

Somebody once asked me how the death of Jesus could make a mantle and a covering for me and undo my moral state and change it.

I always appreciate questions, even questions I cannot answer. As for this question, I do not know; all I know is that it does. I know that the iniquitous man who all his life has tried, and hopped along on two immorally unequal legs, comes before the bar of God's justice with all the evidence against him and with a verdict a foregone conclusions—guilty. Jesus Christ did something to change that moral situation.

He did it there on the cross. So now, when God looks at me, He sees a moral situation changed. Theologians call that justification. When God justifies me, He acts toward me just as if I had never sinned, and all that because of the wonder of Christ's atonement.

I do not claim to understand all of that. I have read and studied theological books on the atonement, and men do not all agree.

I do not build my life on things that I do not know, but rather on a surety that I have that Jesus Christ is my Savior.

Arise, my soul, arise; shake off thy guilty fears.
The bleeding Sacrifice in my behalf appears.
Before the throne my Surety stands,
Before the throne my Surety stands;
My name is written on His hands.

CHARLES WESLEY (1707–1788)

Dear God, there are so many things I do not know in this world. So much about Thee I cannot fully comprehend. My only surety is Jesus Christ. Amen and amen.

Therefore, brethren, we are debtors, not to the flesh, to live after the flesh.
ROMANS 8:12

I wonder if we will ever know the proper theory of atonement? It seems that everybody has an exclusive view of atonement, which rules everybody else out. I wonder if we ought not to repent before God for this kind of arrogant attitude.

Quite simply, I owed a debt; Jesus came, slapped down some "money" and said, "Here, I paid it all." Therefore, I slip that which Jesus gives me across the counter, and God unwillingly gives a verdict of not guilty, and I sing about it.

No, the truth is that when the atonement of Jesus was made, justice was on my side, not against me. We confess our sins and He is faithful and just to forgive us our sins and cleanse us from all unrighteousness. I am glad He did not say "merciful" and "gracious" to forgive our sins. Always remember that justice has to be satisfied, and God never raises His hand and says, "Here, slide under there. I'll sweep you under the rug until the Judgment Day is over, and hope nobody will see you."

Never does God treat anybody like that. Heaven would be completely empty and hell crammed if in order to get anybody to heaven and save them from hell God had to violate justice.

When this passing world is done,
When has sunk yon glaring sun,
When we stand with Christ in glory,
Looking o'er life's finished story
Then, Lord, shall I fully know—
Not till then—how much I owe.

ROBERT M. McCHEYNE (1813–1843)

I praise Thee, O God, for the faithfulness of Thy mercy and justice.
I do not have it all figured out now, but I know I shall then,
and I am willing to wait. In Jesus' name, amen.

*How much more shall the blood of Christ, who through the
eternal Spirit offered himself without spot to God, purge your conscience
from dead works to serve the living God?*
HEBREWS 9:14

Personally, I think we ought to think more about the blood of the Lamb
than we do, and less about Calvary; more about the blood and less about
the place where He died; more about the wonder of what happened there
in the darkness.

It is not so much the place, but rather what happened at that place.
People can become enamored with the symbol of the cross and forget what
really happened on the cross. It is not the cross that saves us, but what Jesus
Christ did on that cross.

No wonder the heavens became dark as He hung there for several hours.
In the darkness, God was doing the work that man can't explain and can
never know. He did that wonderful, awful work of atonement.

The holy God, without violating His holiness, arranged it so that He
could look upon our moral situation, smile and say, "You're justified."

If we go to heaven that is the way we will go.

Some people think they can get to heaven by works. One tries it this way,
another tries it that way; but they will never get there. If you have the covering
of the blood, God will see a moral situation that was just, and then you can
go to heaven.

> Alas! and did my Savior bleed?
> And did my Sovereign die?
> Would He devote that sacred head,
> For such a worm as I?
>
> ISAAC WATTS (1674-1748)

*Our heavenly Father, with what joy we come into Thy presence, not
because of anything we have done to deserve it, but because of the precious
blood Jesus shed on the cross. Hallelujah for the Lamb of God! Amen.*

For if, when we were enemies, we were reconciled to God by the death of his Son, much more, being reconciled, we shall be saved by his life. And not only so, but we also joy in God through our Lord Jesus Christ, by whom we have now received the atonement.

ROMANS 5:10-11

Remember, we are all sinners, and our lives have been wrong. Every moral inequity will be a judgment of mercy, but covered by sufficient atonement. Every active iniquity may be an act we call commission or an act we call omission. It may be a word or it may be a thought. The iniquitous thoughts that go through our heads and the iniquitous words that come out of our mouths, and the acts that we should do and do not do, and the acts that we do and should not do—all are part of our moral inequity.

This is our awful black record. No one can make sufficient atonement, except Jesus Christ our Lord. Every moral being must face up to his sins; every moral being in the day of the great judgment, the great white throne judgment, they will be dealt with by all the attributes of God.

All of God will concur in everything God does; but because justice is part of the nature of God, when it confronts injustice, it must condemn it. God will condemn and send off to hell those who have not been taking coverage in the atonement. I must have a sufficient atonement because my sins have been many. Thank God, Christ's atonement is sufficient.

My sins, they are many, their stains are so deep,
And bitter the tears of remorse that I weep;
But weeping is useless; thou great crimson sea,
Thy waters can cleanse me, Thy waters can cleanse me,
Thy waters can cleanse me, Come, roll over me!

WILLIAM BOOTH (1829-1912)

O God, when I think of Thy mercy and grace, the word "boundless" comes to mind. How I rejoice in my boundless salvation provided through Jesus Christ. Amen.

*And the blood shall be to you for a token upon the houses where ye are:
and when I see the blood, I will pass over you, and the plague shall not be upon
you to destroy you, when I smite the land of Egypt.*

EXODUS 12:13

No one can make sufficient atonement but one—that is, Jesus Christ—and He did make it. And He did not repeat it; He made it once. Some believe in what they call a perpetual sacrifice. That is not what the Bible teaches. The Bible teaches one sacrifice with perpetual efficacy. Jesus died only once, not a dozen times, not 100 times. Think how many times Christ would have to die, every day, every Sunday, around the world every time a mass was held and the bread was blessed and became the body of Christ.

No, He is not dying in heaven; He is living in heaven the life forevermore. He is our Lord; and because He is our Lord, He can dispense mercy that satisfies justice and righteousness, and He can save us because He is God.

Because this is true, we take refuge in the blood of the Lord Jesus Christ that was shed only once, back at Calvary. We do not take things for granted. We must be careful that we do not have a casual attitude about our Christianity. Rather, we rejoice in the sufficiency of God's atonement for us and look forward to seeing Him face-to-face.

Christ our Redeemer died on the cross,
Died for the sinner, paid all his due;
All who receive Him need never fear,
Yes He will pass, will pass over you.

JOHN G. FOOTE (NINETEENTH CENTURY)

*Dear Father in heaven, I praise Thee today for the sufficiency of
Christ's sacrifice on the cross. I rejoice in an act once done but
perpetually enjoyed. In Jesus' name, amen.*

But God forbid that I should glory, save in the cross of our Lord Jesus Christ,
by whom the world is crucified unto me, and I unto the world.
GALATIANS 6:14

I am concerned about the casual attitudes I see in much of Christianity today. I do not think we should be casual about anything that neither Satan nor God are casual about. I want to see seriousness and gravity here.

I do not mind humor. However, when I am talking about my soul and its relationship to God, I want gravity and seriousness.

Time is a relative thing, but it is passing swiftly away and never coming back. Tragedies and troubles are everywhere, and we cannot take things for granted.

God does not need you, but oh, how you need Him! For when the holy eyes of God look upon your life, and those eyes see moral inequity, God pronounces iniquity. But when you cover yourself with the atoning blood by faith; when you believe in the Lord Jesus Christ who is risen, those same righteous, just eyes of God see you justified because Somebody cared enough to interpose, and His precious blood covers you.

Thanks be unto God for the blood of the atonement that is sufficient to cover our iniquity.

The cross, it standeth fast,
Hallelujah! Hallelujah!
Defying every blast,
Hallelujah! Hallelujah!
The winds of hell have blown,
The world its hate hath shown,
Yet it is not over-thrown.
Hallelujah for the cross!

HORATIUS BONAR (1808–1889)

O God and Father of our Lord Jesus Christ, I thank Thee for the provision
Thou made for my iniquity. Under the blood of the Lord Jesus Christ,
I can come guiltless into Thy presence. Praise the name of Jesus. Amen.

October 3

Follow peace with all men, and holiness, without which no man shall see the Lord.
HEBREWS 12:14

The Bible teaches quite plainly that God is infinite. This above all other things that may be said about God makes the greatest demand on our intelligence and imagination. It requires us to picture a mode of being that we are not familiar with, unlike anything we have ever known.

We are familiar with matter and space and time and motion and energy. We are familiar with creatures composed of matter living in space, and that have some energy and make motions. I am asking you to receive into your mind ideas of something that is not matter, and does not dwell in space; it overflows. The heaven of heavens cannot contain it; it is not subject to time, and it is not a creature. It is the uncreated One, and it is an energy through all that has energy in the world.

To think about God is almost impossible, because our thoughts must rise above everything else we might think about. Faith is involved here. We look beyond what we can actually see and experience a vision of God that cannot be explained in human language.

Oh, how wonderful it is to meditate on God!

Take time to be holy,
Speak oft with thy Lord;
Abide in Him always
And feed on His Word.
Make friends of God's children,
Help those who are weak,
Forgetting in nothing
His blessing to seek.
WILLIAM D. LONGSTAFF (1822-1894)

Today is a glorious day, O God, as I take the time to meditate upon Thee and Thy nature. How wonderful it is to nourish my soul on those high thoughts of Thee. In the blessed name of Jesus I pray. Amen.

And this is life eternal, that they might know thee the only true God,
and Jesus Christ, whom thou hast sent.
JOHN 17:3

Theology at its finest moment can do no more than tell us about God. To know about God and to know God are two different things. This may explain why there are so many icicles hanging around on the eaves of some theological seminaries even in July. There is a lot of death there— the reason being that our brethren, who ought to know better, confuse knowing about God with knowing God.

If you are ever to know God, you are going to have to enter by the new birth, by the illumination of the Holy Spirit and by the revelation of the Spirit. If theologians were to tell it, they would say there has to be revelation and illumination. Until there is an illumination of that truth, it does not do you any good at all.

Only the Holy Spirit can make us know God. That is why, when we speak of the Holy Spirit, we do not want to speak apologetically or be ashamed or be afraid to talk about Him, for only He can make us know God. Theology can teach us about God, but that is only the beginning.

I know that my Redeemer lives!
What joy this blest assurance gives!
He lives, He lives, who once was dead;
He lives, my ever-living Head.

SAMUEL MEDLEY (1738-1799)

Our heavenly Father, for long I have sought knowledge about Thee;
now I desire to know Thee as only the Holy Spirit can show me.
Amen and amen!

And God said unto Moses, I AM THAT I AM: and he said, Thus shalt thou say unto the children of Israel, I AM hath sent me unto you.

EXODUS 3:14

From Scripture we know that God has declared certain things about Himself to be true. We can know what God is like by nature and by Scripture; the two go hand in hand.

I believe we threw out the baby with the bath water when we threw out so much of the old traditional ways of the church. Evangelicals went overboard and threw out everything, and even some very wonderful treasures. Our Puritan fathers, the old Presbyterians, Congregationalists and Baptists used to preach about what they called natural theology, and they did not hesitate. They were not liberals or modernists; they were the church fathers, and they talked about a theology that could be built up just by looking round about you. We all know that is true, but we are afraid to say that nowadays.

We are afraid that somebody will come along and accuse us of being liberals.

I hope I am liberal; I am not liberal in theology, and I am not a modernist, but I believe that through His creation God has declared certain things true of Himself. The psalmist says so and the prophets, and even the apostle Paul.

The God of Abraham praise,
Who reigns enthroned above;
Ancient of everlasting days,
And God of love.
Jehovah, great I AM,
By earth and heaven confessed;
I bow and bless the sacred Name,
Forevermore blest.

DANIEL BEN JUDAH (FOURTEENTH CENTURY)

Thou, O God, hast declared Thyself in both the Scriptures and in nature; and in my thirst for Thee, I have discovered Thee in both. Praise the name of Jesus. Amen.

October 6

That which was from the beginning, which we have heard, which we have seen with our eyes, which we have looked upon, and our hands have handled, of the Word of life; (For the life was manifested, and we have seen it, and bear witness, and shew unto you).

1 JOHN 1:1-2

We say that a human mind can go a long way, but it cannot go all the way to limitlessness. But God is limitless, boundless and has no end.

The ocean has a boundary, but God has none. God knows no limit, I say, and whatever God is, He is without limit or measure.

Here is where we begin to get in trouble by using words carelessly. We say about a certain man that he has unlimited wealth. No matter how much he has, it can be counted.

We look up into the starry sky at night and say the universe is unlimited. Well, from our standpoint it sure does look unlimited. The universe is much larger than we could ever fathom. However, there is a beginning to it and there is an end. Nothing with a beginning can be infinite.

God has no beginning, and therefore He has no end. It simply means that our means of measurement is useless when it comes to God. He is much more than we could ever think or fathom.

> Of the Father's love begotten,
> Ere the world began to be;
> He is Alpha and Omega,
> He the source, the ending He.
> Of the things that are, that have been
> And that future years shall see;
> Evermore and evermore!

MARCUS AURELIUS CLEMENS PRUDENTIUS (FOURTH CENTURY), TRANS. JOHN M. NEALE (1818–1886)

Dear God, the magnitude of Thy divine nature overwhelms me and creates within my soul adoration that sparks into worship and praise. How I love and adore Thee. Amen and amen!

Trust ye in the LORD for ever:
for in the LORD JEHOVAH is everlasting strength.
ISAIAH 26:4

I remember reading about a 25-year-old professional athlete. He had a little son about four years of age and decided one morning that right after breakfast he was going to follow his son all day long and do exactly what he did. If his little boy lay down on the floor, he would lie down on the floor. If he sat down flat, he would sit down flat. If he turned a somersault, he turned a somersault.

All day, well, not quite all day, but as long as he could keep up, this big strapping athlete followed his little boy. Along about noon, he was lying down with his tongue hanging out while the little boy was still going strong.

You can easily see who had the energy, but neither of them had boundless energy. The little boy's energy had a bound to it, but along about supper time, a little head began to go down over his plate and needed to be woken up, "Eat your dinner, Junior. You can go to bed right after you eat."

He did not have boundless energy, although he had so much of it that we carelessly say it was boundless.

When we talk about anything unlimited, boundless, either we are using words carelessly or we are talking about God.

And now, hallelujah! the rest of my days
Shall gladly be spent in promoting His praise
Who opened His bosom to pour out this sea
Of boundless salvation, of boundless salvation,
Of boundless salvation for you and for me.
WILLIAM BOOTH (1829-1912)

Dear God, Thy boundless salvation is my portion today.
I rejoice in the fullness of Thy mercy in my life.
May my life today honor the Christ of my salvation. Amen.

I bring near my righteousness; it shall not be far off, and my salvation shall not tarry: and I will place salvation in Zion for Israel my glory.
ISAIAH 46:13

I remember reading of Admiral Byrd who went to the South Pole, up over the ice barrier, and had all of those experiences and adventures. When he returned home, everybody was interviewing him. He was all over the newspapers and media at the time. Everyone was interested in all of those experiences they wished they could experience.

We live in a thrill-seeking culture. Nobody seems to be happy with the life they are living, and they try to find some kind of a thrill outlet to make their life worth living.

One reporter asked a very interesting question: "Was it a thrill, Admiral?"

It was an appropriate question, I believe. Everybody was thinking about all of those great adventures and going to places where nobody else had been before.

The admiral looked at the reporter and said with a straight face, "Thrill is a word that I never use."

Everybody was talking about the thrill, but the man who experienced it never used the word.

We need to be careful about carelessly using words, especially when we are talking about God. What is appropriate for us is highly inappropriate for God.

"Worthy is the Lamb," the hosts of heaven sing,
As before the throne they make His praises ring;
"Worthy is the Lamb the book to open wide,
Worthy is the Lamb who once was crucified."
JOHNSON OATMAN, JR. (1856–1922)

O Father, I am always seeking some thrill to satisfy some inner yearning. Only Thee can truly satisfy that inner yearning. May I rest today in the joy of Thy presence. In Jesus' name, amen.

The LORD will give strength unto his people;
the LORD will bless his people with peace.
PSALM 29:11

Gustave Flaubert, the great French writer, used to walk the floor for hours to select one word. Flaubert said, "There's no such thing as a synonym. Get the right word." So he would search all night for the French word that fit what he wanted to say.

That is taking pains, all right, but it is not infinite pains because there was an end to it. If it had been infinite pains, there would never have been an end. When we say "infinite," we are referring to God.

When we use the word "measureless," it can only be used of God. Measurement is the way created beings have of giving account of something. You reach into your pocket to see how much change you have, and you count it. Or you get on the scales and weigh yourself or stand up to see how high you are. Measurement is giving an account to yourself.

Everything that we describe by limitations is contingent and relative; whereas God is self-existent and absolute and boundless. He is a boundless ocean; no one can describe how far out He goes in infinite distances in every direction.

We bless Thee for Thy peace, O God,
Deep as th'unfathomed sea,
Which falls like sunshine on the road
Of those who trust in Thee.
ANONYMOUS

Eternal God and Father of our Lord Jesus Christ,
how I praise Thee that I can count my sin;
and even though they are many, Thy grace to forgive can
never be numbered. Praise the name of Jesus. Amen.

Cast thy burden upon the LORD, and he shall sustain thee:
he shall never suffer the righteous to be moved.
PSALM 55:22

Have you ever noticed what gravity does to you? It never bothers a two-year-old unless he falls out of his high chair; but gravity pulls the old fellow down. It pulls him slowly down and down, and pretty soon he is bent over. Gravity, the tug of the earth, has done that.

The more you weigh, the more gravity seems to pull at you. It has to do with measurement. Measurement is the distance between objects in space; length is the extension of objects in space; and we have all kinds of ways of measuring. We have liquid measurements, and measurements of energy and sound. We also can measure intelligence.

The list goes on and on. We have a need to measure things and find out how much they weigh or how big they are. We can never bring this over into God. God does not fit into our petulance for measuring. Somebody will say that we have a big God. The word "big" is a relative word. It is a word that should not be associated with God.

I come to God, lay aside all elements of curiosity and lift my heart in simple adoration of the God and Father of our Lord Jesus Christ.

Troubled soul, the Saviour can see,
Ev'ry heartache and tear;
Burdens are lifted at Calvary
Jesus is very near.
JOHN M. MOORE (1925-)

Dear God, I often am guilty of saying that Thou art a big God.
But I know that Thou art much more than our human measurements can
measure. Thy glory fills all of creation and beyond. Amen and amen.

Great is the LORD, and greatly to be praised in the city of our God,
in the mountain of his holiness.
PSALM 48:1

Most people have a desire to describe God. The frustration comes when we have nothing to compare God with. All of our words of description are imperfect and inadequate. We cannot put God into our little measurements. Look out on the work of God's hands and you see it. You see a mountain or a man and you have size there. Size is a relative thing.

When I step on the scales and come in at 150 pounds wringing wet, I am referred to as a small man. A man who weighs 210 pounds is supposed to be big. But when you put that 210-pound man over against the mountain, he is pretty small potatoes.

When a baby is born into the world and weighs 10 pounds, people say, "My, isn't he a big one!" Or, how many tons does a whale weigh?

Trying to compare God with anything that is familiar to us leaves us far short of understanding God. With God, there is no size, no degree, no measurement, no plurality, no weight, because God is just God.

When through the woods, the forest glades I wander
And hear the birds sing sweetly in the trees,
When I look down from lofty mountain grandeur
And hear the brook and feel the gentle breeze . . .

CARL BOBERG (1859–1940),
TRANS. STUART K. HINE (1899–1989)

O God, I am so glad Thou art who and what Thou art.
Nothing in the created universe in any way compares to Thee.
I do not understand that, but my worship does not come from my head,
but from my heart—a heart panting after Thee. Amen.

Thine, O LORD, is the greatness, and the power,
and the glory, and the victory, and the majesty:
for all that is in the heaven and in the earth is thine;
thine is the kingdom, O LORD,
and thou art exalted as head above all.
1 CHRONICLES 29:11

I often hear people, especially preachers say, "Brethren, we have a big God." They may mean well, but I really do not like that expression because I do not think we ought to pull God down as if we were selling dry goods over the counter. I think God is too holy, too infinite, too high, too wonderful, too glorious for us even to think of Him like that.

If God were simply a big God, He would be so big He would scare us; but He would be too little for us to worship. I could not worship a God who is just a little bit bigger than man is. God cannot be compared to man in any regard. If God were simply big, we might then run the chance of somebody coming along bigger than God. To use the word "big" means that you have been measured. And, oh, brethren! God cannot be measured.

Frederick William Faber wrote a hymn about the infinity of God. Few churches sing it, but Faber got it out of his system, and I read it and am blessed by it.

O majesty unspeakable and dread!
Wert thou less mighty than Thou art,
Thou wert, O Lord, too great for our belief,
Too little for our heart.

FREDERICK WILLIAM FABER (1814–1863)

O God in heaven, how much I think of Thee; but my fault is trying to
bring Thee down to my level. Instead, lift me up into Thy
high and holy level. In the name of Jesus I pray. Amen.

October 13

And when Abram was ninety years old and nine,
the LORD appeared to Abram, and said unto him,
I am the Almighty God; walk before me,
and be thou perfect.

GENESIS 17:1

I've attended an art gallery whenever I was in close proximity to one.
Often I walk very fast through the gallery and come away discouraged.
I remember seeing a painting of Michelangelo's God, "The Creator." There
was a great, monstrous old baldheaded man lying outstretched on a cloud.
He is doing something with his finger. It is supposed to represent God
and His Almighty power in creation.

I really do not like to think of God in those terms. In some regard,
it is offensive to me. I could not worship that God at all. I do not know
how Michelangelo ever got down on his knees to a baldheaded old man.
I could not do it; I would want him at least to have a decent head of hair,
even if I do not. This baldheaded old man was Michelangelo's concept of
God the Father Almighty, God of heaven and earth, dwelling in eternity,
and no man can approach unto.

I think it tragic and terrible. If God were just a big God like that, He
would be too great for our belief, but He would be too little for our worship.

When Christ shall come with shout of acclamation
And take me home, what joy shall fill my heart!
Then I shall bow in humble adoration
And there proclaim, my God how great Thou art!

CARL BOBERG (1859-1940),
TRANS. STUART K. HINE (1899-1989)

Dear God Almighty, forgive us for trying to bring Thee down to
our level and understanding. Lead me today to lift my heart up
in absolute worship of that which I really cannot understand.
In the blessed name of Jesus I pray. Amen.

For ye have not received the spirit of bondage again to fear;
but ye have received the Spirit of adoption, whereby we cry, Abba, Father.
ROMANS 8:15

An American Indian chief went to Washington DC to represent his tribe before the president. Everybody expected him to come cringing in before the great white father, but he walked in and stood straight up, leaned back, folded his arms over his breast and said, "You are a man, I am another."

I would have been proud of that Indian. He was not going to be looked down on even though he might have been a chief of a tribe of a few hundred, and the president was chief over millions.

If God were simply a big and great God, I would have a greatness, and He another greatness. His greatness would be bigger than mine, but I could say, "I'm not as big as you, but I'm coming."

Our God is infinite, and so I have no greatness apart from Him. Greatness, which is infinite, makes room for all things finite. Because He is infinite, He makes room for all things, and we should be crashed by magnificence short of infinity.

Just as a little boy is brave when his dad is around, so we can be brave children of God because He is all around.

Our Father, who in Heaven Art,
Holy art thou with voice and heart
Thou bid'st us call upon Thy name
Forever blest, for aye the same!
Oh, may Thy kingdom soon appear,
Thy will be done, Thy reign be here!
MARTIN LUTHER (1483-1546)

Abba Father, I rest in Thy grace today.
What I cannot comprehend about Thee,
I take by faith and lift my heart in wondrous praise.
Amen and amen!

October 15

Canst thou by searching find out God?
canst thou find out the Almighty unto perfection?
JOB 11:7

Nobody is quite as bold as a four- or five-year-old boy when his big, strapping father is around. Nobody can beat his father. He does not quite know his father yet, but he loves his father and worships him.

So it is with us. Our confidence comes from abiding in the shadow of the Almighty. How could I endure the passing of my years if I did not know that I had been baptized into the heart of One who knows no years, who is the Ancient of Days, who had no beginning and can have no end? How could I endure my weakness if I did not know that I had been baptized into the heart of One who has infinite strength?

So this is our God, and this is the God we adore.

Regardless of the path we are currently walking, we know that it is not our strength that is going to get us through. Like that brave little boy with his hand in his father's hand, so we walk down the pathway with our hand in our heavenly Father's hand, unconscious of the dangers all around us. After all, our Father is taking care of us day by day.

> Father of Heaven, whose love profound
> A ransom for our souls hath found,
> Before Thy throne we sinners bend;
> To us Thy pardoning love extend.
>
> EDWARD COOPER (1770–1833)

O Ancient of Days, when I am conscious of Thy presence in my life,
I am unconscious of the weakness of the world around me.
My strength is weak, but I am living by Thy strength today.
In Jesus' name, amen.

Who shall separate us from the love of Christ?
shall tribulation, or distress, or persecution,
or famine, or nakedness, or peril, or sword?
ROMANS 8:35

If God is infinite—all theologians believe it, the Bible teaches it and the hymnists have written about it—what does it mean to us now? Are we just having a lesson in theology upon which we're going to have an exam one of these days?

Absolutely not! If this is true, and it is true, then God's love is infinite.

I heard a man preach years ago from the text where Jesus said "He that loveth me, the same is my brother, my sister and my mother." The preacher said, "Now that's the way it works. Your brother, his love is pretty good, but it is not too strong. He could desert you, but your sister will stick to you after your brother has dumped you over. After your sister cannot stand you anymore, you still have your mother. But there is a love that is closer than the love of a mother, and that is the love of God."

A mother's love can be outraged and die, or a mother can die, and her love dies with her; but God cannot die; and because He cannot die, His love is forever.

Could we with ink the ocean fill,
And were the skies of parchment made,
Were every stalk on earth a quill,
And every man a scribe by trade;
To write the love of God above
Would drain the ocean dry;
Nor could the scroll contain the whole,
Though stretched from sky to sky.

FREDERICK M. LEHMAN (1868-1953)

Thy love, O God, is my stay for today. I praise Thee that Thy love never fails. Everybody else has failed me; I have even failed myself. But Thy love is my rock and foundation. Amen and amen!

October 17

So Christ was once offered to bear the sins of many;
and unto them that look for him shall he appear the
second time without sin unto salvation.

HEBREWS 9:28

Søren Kierkegaard, the great Danish writer, wrote a little sermon on the text, love covers a multitude of sins. He said, "How did Jesus deal with our sins? How did He do it? He covered them. What did He cover them with? His life? If He had covered them with His life, they could have taken His life away and exposed our sins again; but He covered them with His death."

When Jesus died, He covered our sins with His death. By His death on the cross He covered our sins and hid them forever and ever, as a fog hides the landscape, from the eyes of angels and demons and God.

Because Jesus covered our sins so thoroughly, no devil in hell and no angel in heaven will be able to uncover them. When God does something, He does it thoroughly and in such a way that it can never be undone. My sins are permanently covered, hallelujah!

I know the devil tries to discourage me with my past, reminding me of my sin. When he does that, I simply point him to Jesus and His death on the cross.

Living, He loved me,
Dying He saved me,
Buried, He carried
My sins far away;
Rising, He justified
Freely, forever;
One day He's coming
O glorious day!

J. WILBUR CHAPMAN (1859–1918)

Dear Lord Jesus, how I praise Thee for covering my sins so thoroughly.
Today I live my life, not from the past, but from Thy grace
that cleanses me of all sin. Praise Thy name. Amen.

*Now before the feast of the passover, when Jesus knew that his hour
was come that he should depart out of this world unto the Father, having loved
his own which were in the world, he loved them unto the end.*
JOHN 13:1

I think it is an awful thing to fall in love and then fall out of love. How shocking it is when you read of divorce cases where a person will say, "I no longer love him." She once loved him, but no longer. Her love did not last.

Sometimes we hear about mothers who forsake their children so that even the finest love of a mother has a limit. The love of a father, a mother, a sister, a wife has limits; but the love of God is infinite, as is everything pertaining to God. One thing you can be sure of, God's love knows no limit, and He will never "fall out of love" with you.

Some days the enemy tries to taunt me with the idea that God does not really care about me. God is way up there, and I am way down here; and the twain shall never meet. That is what the devil thinks. It does not matter what I think either. God has demonstrated His love, and His love cannot change; for if His love would ever change, He would not be God anymore. I am not worried about that.

Love divine, all loves excelling,
Joy of heaven, to earth come down;
Fix in us Thy humble dwelling,
All Thy faithful mercies crown.
Jesus, Thou art all compassion,
Pure, unbounded love Thou art;
Visit us with Thy salvation,
Enter every trembling heart.
CHARLES WESLEY (1707–1788)

*Thy love O God, is simply amazing to me. All of the facts to
the contrary, Thy love comes shining down, filling my life with
unspeakable joy and praise. Hallelujah for the Lamb! Amen.*

The LORD hath appeared of old unto me, saying,
Yea, I have loved thee with an everlasting love:
therefore with lovingkindness have I drawn thee.
JEREMIAH 31:3

I was praying the other day and thinking to myself about how vast the grace of God is compared with our human sin. If I only look at my sin, I can become rather discouraged. But when I look at my sin and compare it to the grace of God, my discouragement turns into joy unspeakable and full of glory.

If you do not think your sin is big, the Lord cannot save you. If you think your sin is bigger than God, He cannot save you. You must realize that though your sin is big, God is infinite and, therefore, bigger than all your sin. Where sin abounded, the grace of God does much more abound.

When God says "more," referring to Himself, we ought to extend our imagination into borderline unto infinity. When God said "much more" about grace, what can you do but kneel and say, "My Lord and my God, how Thy grace did much more abound."

Just remember, sin is man's doing. Because it is man's doing, it has a limit to it. Grace is God's doing; and because it is God's doing, it has no limit to it whatsoever.

O love that wilt not let me go,
I rest my weary soul in Thee;
I give Thee back the life I owe,
That in Thine ocean depths its flow,
May richer, fuller be.

GEORGE MATHESON (1842-1906)

Dear God, I sometimes become overwhelmed with my own sin.
Sometimes I feel it is bigger than what Thou canst handle.
One glimpse of Thy love and I am convinced that
Thy grace is more than sufficient. Amen.

*Yet Michael the archangel, when contending with the devil
he disputed about the body of Moses, durst not bring against him
a railing accusation, but said, The Lord rebuke thee.*
JUDE 1:9

Grace is God's doing; and because its God's doing, it has no limit to it.

When the infinite, limitless grace of God attacks the finite, limited sin of a man, that sin has no chance. If we only repent and turn from it, God will pulverize it and whirl it into eternity where it can never be known again while eternity rolls on.

That is what happened to my sin and the sin of everybody that believes.

I have a very high respect for the devil; I do not like him, and I know he is the personification of evil and everything sinful; but I also know that even the archangel Michael refused to rebuke him.

I would like just in a sneaking way to have the devil know about this. I would like the devil to know that Jesus Christ our Lord is infinite; His blood is infinite and the purchase of His blood is infinite. If every man had sinned as bad as Judas, still the grace of God could cure it, because God has no limit, but sin does.

Have you been to Jesus for the cleansing power?
Are you washed in the blood of the Lamb?
Are you fully trusting in His grace this hour?
Are you washed in the blood of the Lamb?
ELISHA A. HOFFMAN (1839–1929)

*I praise Thee, O God and Father of our Lord Jesus Christ,
for the power of the blood of Jesus to cleanse me of all my sin.
Glory be to the Lamb of God! Amen.*

Neither is there salvation in any other:
for there is none other name under heaven given among men,
whereby we must be saved.

ACTS 4:12

In my life, the big sins have never been the ones that bothered me; It's the sneaking little mousy sins, the sins I am ashamed of, the sins I do not even want to think about. They are the ones that bother my conscience. Even though you have sinned all those little rascally sins, they have a limit to them.

God could set 8 or 10 angels counting, and in 10 years or so, they could all be counted. They could find my sins, add them up and say, "Here's the total," and the number would string clear across the room.

Some angel would say, "I guess he's doomed."

God would say, "No, look at My grace. It extends not across the room but from eternity past to eternity to come."

When Jesus died, it was enough. I am glad to have enough of something. All those little mousy sins weigh me down, and the devil wants me to concentrate on them. God, on the other hand, wants me to concentrate on His unlimited grace in Jesus Christ.

Marvelous, infinite, matchless grace,
Freely bestowed on all who believe!
You that are longing to see His face,
Will you this moment His grace receive?

JULIA H. JOHNSTON (1849-1919)

Dear God, how wonderful and marvelous Thy grace is.
I cannot fathom the extent of that grace in my direction.
All I can do is rejoice in that grace. Amen and amen.

*I will greatly rejoice in the LORD, my soul shall be joyful in my God;
for he hath clothed me with the garments of salvation, he hath covered me with
the robe of righteousness, as a bridegroom decketh himself with ornaments,
and as a bride adorneth herself with her jewels.*

ISAIAH 61:10

I believe that Jesus died for everybody. I believe that when Jesus died on the cross, He died for every human being that was ever born or will ever be born into the world. I believe He died for every baby that died at birth and for every man who lived to be 150. I believe He died for all.

Some of my good friends say, "He died for the elect; and when you go preaching the gospel, God finds His elect."

If I were preaching the gospel to a hundred people, and only 10 of them were the elect, and the other 90 were not, I would be lying to 90 of them. If He only died for the 10 who are the elect, when I say, "Whosoever will, let him come," I would be lying to the 90, because they were not ones that should come.

I think Christ died for all of us. When He was out there on the cross, I was in His heart; Hitler was in His heart; Khrushchev was in His heart; and every person was in the heart of Christ as He died out there on the cross. Jesus paid the ransom for all.

Lord, I believe were sinners more
Than sands upon the ocean shore,
Thou hast for all a ransom paid,
For all a full atonement made.

NIKOLAUS LUDWIG VON ZINZENDORF (1700-1759),
TRANS. BY JOHN WESLEY (1703-1791)

*Dear Lord Jesus, Savior of mankind, I praise Thee today that I was in
Thy heart when Thee died on the cross. Praise Thy name! Amen.*

The same came for a witness, to bear witness of the Light,
that all men through him might believe.
JOHN 1:7

Do not imagine that because Abraham Lincoln was a good man and Adolf Hitler was a bad man that Christ died for Lincoln and not for Hitler. We categorize man as good and bad, but as far as God is concerned "all have sinned and come short." Therefore, He died for all men, good and bad, vicious and wicked, around the world.

He died for the homosexual, the dope fiend, the alcoholic, the prostitute; He died for all. Ah, the infinite patience of Jesus and the patience of God with the power to save. He has infinite power to save and breaks the power of canceled sin.

Paul Rader used to say, "You name it and God will break it." He was so right. If you can name it, God can break it for His honor and glory.

God's being infinite is not a theological bit of lumber to put up inside of somebody's attic labeled "This is the infinitude of God."

If this is your last hour, and you expect to face that awful judgment hour, look to the infinite protection of the atoning Lamb who died from the foundation of the world. Glory be to the Lamb that was slain!

He breaks the power of canceled sin;
He sets the prisoner free.
His blood can make the foulest clean;
His blood availed for me.
CHARLES WESLEY (1707–1788)

Dear Lamb of God, Thy precious blood shed on the cross
cleanses me from all my sin; and not me only, but it can avail every
person that has ever been born and ever will be born.
I thank Thee for this marvelous provision. Amen and amen.

October 24

Then spake Jesus again unto them, saying, I am the light of the world:
he that followeth me shall not walk in darkness, but shall have the light of life.
JOHN 8:12

I once knew a man, a Southerner, who never quite made the English language hang together. He was a dear saint of God and was converted down in the southern part of Ohio. His conversion was so real and so marvelous, and he knew when and where it all happened.

Every year he would go back to the little church where he was converted, walk down the isle, kneel at the old-fashioned wooden altar and have an hour of Thanksgiving to thank God Almighty that He saw fit to save him.

One summer, he went back to find that the church had been sold and turned into a garage with a concrete floor. It was the same building, only it had been gutted out, and now they were using it for a garage. He stepped off to the approximate place where the old altar had been and knelt down in the oil and grease with all the fellows around him working and drilling while he praised and thanked God that he was ever converted.

Dare to believe in the infinite love and grace of God, and let His power bring you out of darkness and into His marvelous light.

The whole world was lost
In the darkness of sin;
The Light of the world is Jesus;
Like sunshine at noon-day
His glory shone in,
The Light of the world is Jesus.

PHILIP P. BLISS (1838–1876)

Dear God, I remember when Thee met my soul and Thy infinite grace
rolled over me with cleansing power. I praise Thee today that
Thee saw fit to save me. Amen.

October 25

For I have said, Mercy shall be built up for ever:
thy faithfulness shalt thou establish in the very heavens.

PSALMS 89:2

Faithfulness is that in God which guarantees He will never be and will never act inconsistent with Himself. God will never cease to be what He is, and who He is; everything God says or does must accord with His faithfulness. He will always be true to Himself and to His works, and to His creation.

God is His own standard; He imitates nobody and is influenced by nobody.

I know that is hard to take, because in this day, when the church is tragically degenerate, we have introduced the idea of the VIP and the man with influence. Today we say, "It isn't what you know, it's who you know." And if you know the right people, you can influence the whole congregation to act in conflict with the plain teachings of the Bible.

Remember this: God is influenced by nobody. No one can force God to act otherwise than to be faithful to Himself and to us.

Tell of His wondrous faithfulness
And sound His pow'r abroad;
Sing the sweet promise of His grace,
The love and truth of God.

ISAAC WATTS (1674-1748)

Dear God, how I praise Thee that Thou art all that Thou art.
The more I meditate on Thee, the more I am amazed at Thy
faithfulness. Today I want to tell everybody about Thy faithfulness.
In the precious name of Jesus Christ, my Lord, amen.

October 26

Hast thou not known? hast thou not heard, that the everlasting God,
the LORD, the Creator of the ends of the earth, fainteth not, neither is weary?
there is no searching of his understanding.

ISAIAH 40:28

If you can imagine something to influence God strongly enough to change His mind or compel Him to do anything He had not planned to do, or be anything He is not, then you are thinking of someone greater than God, which is utter nonsense. Who can be greater than the Greatest? Who can be higher than the Highest? Who can be mightier than the Mightiest?

The faithfulness of God guarantees that God will never cease to be who and what He is. If God changed in any way, that change would be in one of three directions.

He would have to change from better to worse, from worse to better, from one kind of being to another kind of being. God, being absolutely and perfectly holy could not be anything less than holy, so he could not change from better to worse. God, being absolutely and perfectly holy, could not get any holier than He is, so He could not change from worse to better. And God, being God and not a creature, He could not change the kind of being that He is.

God's perfection and faithfulness secure that God can never cease to be who He is and what He is.

O Jesus! by that matchless name,
Thy grace shall fail us never;
Today as yesterday the same,
Thou art the same forever!

GEORGE W. BETHUNE (1805–1862)

Eternal God, Thou who art the same yesterday, today and forever.
Today I rest in Thy unchanging nature and character.
Praise Thy name. Amen.

*The LORD is longsuffering, and of great mercy, forgiving iniquity and
transgression, and by no means clearing the guilty, visiting the iniquity of the
fathers upon the children unto the third and fourth generation.*
NUMBERS 14:18

You can live on froth, bubbles and little wisps of badly understood theology
until the pressure is on. When the pressure is on, you will want to know
what kind of God you are serving.

All that God says or does must accord with all of His attributes.
Every thought God thinks and every act of God must accord with His
faithfulness, wisdom, goodness, justice, holiness, love, truth and all the other
attributes of the deity. To magnify one phase of God's unitary character
to diminish another is always wrong. This is the danger the man of God
faces who stands in the pulpit.

He ought to see to it that we see God fully rounded in all of His perfection and glory. If we magnify one attribute to the diminishing of another,
we have not a symmetrical concept of God. We have a lopsided God. You
can look at a tree standing straight and then look at it through the wrong
kind of lens and you will see it crooked. Just so you can look toward God
and see God crooked, but the crookedness is in your eye and not in God.

The spacious firmament on high,
With all the blue ethereal sky,
And spangled heav'ns a shining frame
Their great Original proclaim.
Th'unwearied sun from day to day,
Does his Creator's pow'r display,
And publishes to every land,
The work of an Almighty hand.

JOSEPH ADDISON (1672-1719)

*I want to know Thee, O God, in the fullness of knowledge. My heart yearns
to know all concerning Thee. Help me, through Jesus Christ my Lord. Amen.*

And whosoever shall not receive you, nor hear you, when ye depart thence, shake off the dust under your feet for a testimony against them. Verily I say unto you, It shall be more tolerable for Sodom and Gomorrha in the day of judgment, than for that city.
MARK 6:11

There was a time when the church swung over to hell, judgment and sin. All she talked about was the justice of God. Consequently, God was looked upon as a tyrant, and the universe was a kind of totalitarian state, with God at the top, ruling with a rod of iron. That is the concept we will have if we think only of the justice of God.

Over on the other side is defining God solely as a God of love. God is love is our main text now; and so we have not a God of justice, but a sentimental, spineless God. God is love and love is God, and God is all in all. Pretty soon we have not a thing left but theological cotton candy—nothing but sweetness—because we have magnified the love of God without remembering that God is just.

If we make God all good, we then have the weak sentimentalist of the modernists and the liberals.

Let us not separate God from Himself—from everything that He is—but take God in the perfectness of His holiness.

Glory be to Him who loved us,
Washed us from each sinful stain;
Glory be to Him who made us
Priests and Kings with Him to reign;
Glory, worship, laud and blessing
To the Lamb who once was slain.

HORATIUS BONAR (1808-1889)

I sing of Thy glory, Almighty God, for Thou hast revealed to me the truth of Thee. I will worship and honor Thee this day with a heart that has been cleansed by the blood of the Lord Jesus Christ. In His name I pray. Amen.

And I will bring them, and they shall dwell in the midst of Jerusalem: and they
shall be my people, and I will be their God, in truth and in righteousness.
ZECHARIAH 8:8

The Christian church in America, over the last several generations, has made God almost a God of grace and nothing else. So we have a God who cannot see moral distinctions; and because He cannot see moral distinctions, His church has been unable to see moral distinctions. Instead of a separated, holy church, we have a church that is so geared into the world that you cannot tell one from the other. The reason is that grace has been preached to the exclusion of everything else.

It was said of a certain English preacher that he preached grace in such a manner as to lower the moral standards of England. It is entirely possible to preach grace in the church until we become arrogant and brazen, forgetting that grace is one of the attributes of God, but not all. God is a God of grace, but He is also a God of justice, holiness and truth.

God, being who He is, will always be true to His creatures because He is a faithful God. Faithlessness is one of the greatest sources of heartache and misery in the world, and God is the only One who will never be faithless. He cannot be. He will always be true to His nature.

Great is Thy faithfulness, O God my Father!
There is no shadow of turning with Thee;
Thou changest not, Thy compassions, they fail not;
As Thou hast been Thou forever wilt be.
THOMAS O. CHISHOLM (1866-1960)

Our heavenly Father, I bow in humble recognition of Thy great
faithfulness. I praise Thee for all that Thou art to me.
Thy faithfulness is my strength today. Amen.

While the earth remaineth, seedtime and harvest, and cold and heat,
and summer and winter, and day and night shall not cease.
GENESIS 8:22

Rumors are going around that the world is going to be swept away with an atom bomb or a hydrogen bomb. The human race is going to be annihilated. I've got news for you. Pay no attention to that.

God's word to Noah was given long before any bombs were made. Long before modern science was developed, God said what was going to happen. He made a covenant with Noah, and I am perfectly restful in that covenant. I rest in His Word, "shall not cease." Because God said it, I believe it.

I must say that reading the newspapers can give someone the idea that we are headed for a terrific catastrophe. I know that times can get bad. However, we who know who is really in charge have our faith in the Word of God. If God said it, it will happen regardless of what man tries to do.

That is what I like about God. He always says what He means and means exactly what He says. And if I can tune into the Word of the Lord, my heart will be at rest despite what my circumstances may look like. God's promises "shall not cease."

Soon the conflict shall be done,
Soon the battle shall be won,
Soon shall wave the victor's palm,
Soon shall sing th' eternal psalm.
Then our joyful song shall be,
"I have overcome for thee."

A. B. SIMPSON (1843-1919)

Our heavenly Father, my surroundings sometimes depress me,
but one look in Thy direction and my heart delights in joyful anticipation.
I stand upon Thy Word. Amen.

For this is as the waters of Noah unto me:
for as I have sworn that the waters of Noah should no more go over the earth;
so have I sworn that I would not be wroth with thee, nor rebuke thee.

ISAIAH 54:9

I do not expect my children, grandchildren, great-grandchildren and great-great grandchildren to cease to be; nor do I expect them to turn into hairy apes or green men with one eye in the middle of their foreheads as a result of radiation or some other thing. Generation will follow generation until the Lord's time has been fulfilled and Jesus returns to earth, contrary to certain forlorn predictions.

I expect God to fulfill His promise, because God cannot help but do it. God must be true to Himself; and when God makes a promise, He must keep that promise. When God makes an unconditional promise, that promise stands, and God will see to it that it stands. God said it, and I believe it.

It is essential that we get to know the promises of God. He will never do anything He has not promised. The more we get to know the promises of God, the more we begin to understand who God really is. For me, the promises of God are a window into His character and nature.

'Tis so sweet to trust in Jesus,
Just to take Him at His word;
Just to rest upon His promise,
Just to know, "Thus saith the Lord."

LOUISA STEAD (1850-1917)

Blessed heavenly Father, I am counting on Thee for all the days
of my life. Rumors notwithstanding, my hope is in Thee and
Thy unfailing Word. Hallelujah for the Lamb! Amen.

Rest in the Lord, and wait patiently for him: fret not thyself because of him who prospereth in his way, because of the man who bringeth wicked devices to pass.
PSALM 37:7

God is faithful and will be faithful because He cannot change and is perfectly faithful because God never does anything in part.

This faithful God who never broke a promise, never violated His covenant, never said one thing and meant another, and never overlooked anything or forgot anything, this is the God of our Lord Jesus Christ. This is the God we adore and preach.

God has declared that He will banish from His presence all who love sin and reject His Son.

He has declared, warned, threatened and said it will be so. Let no one trust in desperate hope, for every such desperate hope is based upon the belief that God threatens but does not fulfill.

God waits that He may be gracious and give us opportunity to make up our mind. However, just as sure as the mills of God grind, they grind exceedingly small, and the souls of men fall into them. God moves slowly, and God is patient; but God has promised that He will banish from His presence all who love sin, reject His Son and refuse to believe.

Engage the faithfulness of God today.

"Almost persuaded," harvest is past!
"Almost persuaded," doom comes at last!
"Almost" cannot avail;
"Almost" is but to fail!
Sad, sad, that bitter wail—
"Almost," but lost!

PHILIP P. BLISS (1838–1876)

Lord, we know and trust in Thy faithfulness and patience.
I am so glad Thou wast patient enough with me to give me opportunity
to trust in Jesus. In His blessed name I pray. Amen.

*Likewise, I say unto you, there is joy in the presence of
the angels of God over one sinner that repenteth.*
LUKE 15:10

Sinners come in all kinds of varieties. There is a sinner who does not intend to come; he will not come because he loves his sin too much. No matter what you say, he loves his sin and will not repent.

Then there is that sinner the old Puritan writers used to call "the returning sinner." I like that old phrase. He is a sinner all right; he is up to his chin in sin, and the marks of sin are all about him. No question that he is a sinner, but he is on his way back.

The prodigal son said, "Father, give me the portion of the goods that fall unto me." He wanted his part of the will before the old man had died. The father gave it to him and he took it and left. When he came down to nothing, he started back. That is the returning sinner.

He still is a sinner, because he still has his rags on and smells of the swine pen, but he is a returning sinner. Jesus says, "Come unto me," and the promises and the invitations of the Lord are as valid as the character of God.

No matter how far you go, there is always a path called forgiveness back to God.

There for me the Savior stands,
Shows His wounds and spreads His hands;
God is love! I know, I feel;
Jesus weeps, and loves me still.
CHARLES WESLEY (1707-1788)

*How I praise Thee, O God, for the wonders of Thy love!
A love so deep that it reached into the deepest part of my repentant heart.
Through Jesus Christ my Lord, I pray. Amen.*

And the LORD thy God will make thee plenteous in every work of thine hand, in the fruit of thy body, and in the fruit of thy cattle, and in the fruit of thy land, for good: for the LORD will again rejoice over thee for good, as he rejoiced over thy fathers.
DEUTERONOMY 30:9

When God promises anything, you may be sure God expects to do exactly that. I am afraid the church has come to the place where we scarcely expect anything at all from God. New Testament Martha, for example, believed her brother, Lazarus, would rise again at the Great Day, but she did not believe the Lord would raise him right then.

We have a tendency to put off everything into the future. That is called eschatology, a big word for unbelief. "Eschatology" is the theological word for future things, the end times. I have noticed that eschatology has become a dustbin into which we sweep everything we do not want to believe.

We believe in miracles, but eschatologically, they will come way out there in the future. We believe the Lord will heal the sick, but way out there. We believe the Lord will manifest Himself to men, but He will do it in the next millennium. So we sweep it under the rug and go off about our own business. That is eschatology. We believe God will bless Abraham, and we believe He will bless the Jews in the days to come. But we have a nice little excuse for not expecting God to bless us in the now.

Are you longing for the fullness
Of the blessing of the Lord
In your heart and life today?
Claim the promise of your Father;
Come according to His Word,
In the blessed old-time way.

LELIA N. MORRIS (1862–1929)

My heavenly Father, too often I have pushed into the future that which Thou longs to give me today. May this day be the day I claim Thy promise for me. In Jesus' name, amen.

We then, as workers together with him, beseech you also that ye receive not the grace of God in vain. (For he saith, I have heard thee in a time accepted, and in the day of salvation have I succoured thee: behold, now is the accepted time; behold, now is the day of salvation.)

2 CORINTHIANS 6:1-2

I once preached a sermon and later on heard another fellow preach that same sermon. I think he forgot where he heard it, but it is all right. I sat and listened to him preach the whole sermon, and all he did was add one point. He is welcome to it; and if the Lord blessed it, it is all right. That is what I preach them for.

I believe God will use anyone who does not care who gets the glory.

I said in that sermon that unbelief is one of the slickest things in the world. Unbelief always says that somewhere else, but not here; some other time, but not now; some other people, but not us. That is unbelief.

Unbelief says some other time. We will fight for the miracles of the Old Testament, but we will not believe in them now. We believe in miracles for tomorrow or yesterday, but we stand in the gap between two miracles. If we had faith, we would see miracles now. I do not believe we ought to celebrate miracles, go out, put up big tents and advertise that we are going to have a miracle.

True belief says God works now,

Others saw the giants, Caleb saw the Lord;
They were sore disheartened, he believed God's Word;
And that Word he fully, fearlessly, obeyed;
Was it not sufficient that the Lord hath said?

ANNA E. RICHARDS (N. D.)

Dear God, I want to fearlessly obey Thy Word regardless of what I understand. Thy Word does not come under the scrutiny of my understanding. By faith I take Thy Word, in Jesus' name. Amen.

*If we confess our sins, he is faithful and just to forgive us our sins,
and to cleanse us from all unrighteousness.*
1 JOHN 1:9

Francis R. Havergal came to a point in her life when she believed the Lord meant exactly what He said. When He said that "if we confess our sins He is faithful and just to forgive our sins and to cleanse us from all unrighteousness," He meant it. That was a turning point in her life.

I was scheduled to preach at a certain camp meeting one time, and when I arrived they announced a night of miracles. The only thing that happened that night was that a man drowned in the lake. People tried to revive him and keep him alive, but he never did come to. There was no miracle around that place, at least that night.

I do not believe in advertising miracles, because God is not going to allow Himself to be the focus of some advertisement. The Lord never gives cheap miracles in order to expose His glorious, mysterious will to please carnal saints. The Lord is willing to do the impossible when His people dare to believe that He is a faithful God and means exactly what he says.

Thou art coming, O my Savior,
Thou art coming, O my King,
In Thy beauty all resplendent,
In Thy glory all transcendent;
Well may we rejoice and sing;
Coming! In the opening east,
Herald brightness slowly swells:
Coming! O my glorious Priest,
Hear we not Thy golden bells?

FRANCES RIDLEY HAVERGAL (1836–1879)

*Dear Father in heaven, I believe Thy Word. I believe Thou meanest
exactly what Thou sayest and Thou will fulfill every promise in Thy Word.
My trust is in the Lord Jesus Christ. Amen.*

*Thy word have I hid in mine heart,
that I might not sin against thee.*
PSALM 119:11

With so many Bible translations now, I meet myself coming back around two or three times. They all add up to about the same thing; it is one of the biggest fallacies and delusions possible to imagine that if you get it said another way it will mean more.

Suppose I met you and said, "Hi" or "Good morning" or "How do you do?" or "How are you?" It would all mean the same. I would be greeting a friend.

People imagine that a new Bible translation will tell them a little better what God means—it will be wonderful. It will not be wonderful but will simply be a big disappointment. I am the prime sucker for a new translation. Every time one comes out, I run out and get it. A new translation is all right, but it does not give me any more faith; it does not make God any more real; it does not bring heaven any closer; and it does not bless me any more. The only difference is a little change in the language.

Let us start reading our Bibles with the thought that God means exactly what He says.

Thy Word is like a garden, Lord, with flowers bright and fair;
And everyone who seeks may pluck a lovely cluster there.
Thy Word is like a deep, deep mine, and jewels rich and rare
Are hidden in its mighty depths for every searcher there.
EDWIN HODDER (1837–1904)

*O Christ, who art the Living Word, how I delight in Thee;
how I search the depths of Thy beauty.
I believe everything Thou sayest in Thy Word.
Amen and amen.*

But if we walk in the light, as he is in the light, we have fellowship one with another, and the blood of Jesus Christ his Son cleanseth us from all sin.

1 JOHN 1:7

Someone said to me, "I don't believe in sinning Christians." I don't either, but I meet a lot of them. I do not think sin is funny, and I do not think we ought to make light of it.

I think that when a Christian sins he or she is doing a deadly, dangerous, terrible thing. We may not think lightly about sin, especially our own sin. In prayer, I often ask God to allow me to think about my sin as He thinks about it.

It is amazing how sanctimonious we can become when we are talking about other people. It is so easy to point at somebody else's sin. When I do that, what I am really doing is drawing people's attention away from my sin. Sin is a terrible thing, and either we deal with our sin or our sin will deal with us.

Instead of shaking a sanctimonious finger at a Christian who has fallen into sin, put yourself in that Christian's place and extend a helping hand. We must come to the Bible and believe that if God wrote this, and God is faithful, then God cannot lie.

Our sin is at the disposal of God's forgiveness.

My sin, O the bliss of this glorious tho't,
My sin, not in part, but the whole,
Is nailed to the cross, and I bear it no more;
Praise the Lord, praise the Lord, O my soul!

HORATIO G. SPAFFORD (1828–1888)

Dear God, I feel the weight of my sin. I grieve because of my weakness that shows itself in sinful acts. How I praise Thee that Thou art never intimidated by my sin. Glory be to Jesus Christ my Savior. Amen and amen.

Against thee, thee only, have I sinned, and done this evil in thy sight:
that thou mightest be justified when thou speakest,
and be clear when thou judgest.

PSALM 51:4

God is faithful and just to forgive us our sins and to cleanse us from all unrighteousness. We like that word "faithful." And somebody will say, "Well, that's good. God promised He would forgive, and so He will forgive," and He does forgive.

The thing we must not forget is that He is faithful *and* just to forgive. Justice is on our side now. Instead of justice being against us, and grace being for us, the blood of Jesus Christ has brought justice over on the side of the returning sinner.

When the sinner comes home, there is not a thing standing between him and the very heart of God. It has all been swept away by the blood of the Lamb, and there is not anything preventing him from coming, not even justice. It is an amazing wonder before the throne of God and before the presence of man. Justice is on our side.

If, in the back of your mind, the devil tells you that justice is against you, just say, "The Scripture says He's faithful and just to forgive." Justice has come over on the side of the Christian because Jesus Christ is on the side of the Christian.

I lay my sins on Jesus, the spotless Lamb of God;
He bears them all, and frees us from the accused load.
I bring my guilt to Jesus to wash my crimson stains
White in his blood most precious, till not a spot remains.

HORATIUS BONAR (1808–1889)

Dear God of faithfulness and justice, my sin can no longer keep me
out of Thy presence. Through the blood of the Lamb, I stand before Thee
completely justified. Hallelujah for the Lamb! Amen.

There hath no temptation taken you but such as is common to man:
but God is faithful, who will not suffer you to be tempted above that ye are able;
but will with the temptation also make a way to escape, that ye may be able to bear it.
1 CORINTHIANS 10:13

Sometimes I hear a suffering Christian say, "I feel all boxed in. I feel as if there's a wall all around me."

The Scriptures instruct us that when we cannot get away to the right or to the left; neither forward nor backward, we can always get up. There is always a way up. God's faithfulness is the way out, because it is the way up. You can be sure of that.

Your temptation is common to everybody. Right now, somebody is on the borderline. Sure, that person is a Christian, but he is on the borderline of the victorious life. He says, "I simply am living under circumstances, and I just can't make it. That's all, I can't make it."

God said your temptation was common to all. Every time someone gets a headache he thinks it's a unique headache; there's never been a headache like that since the beginning of the world. Everybody gets a headache sometimes.

Remember, there have been saints who crossed that briary patch where you are now, and they got out all right. Some have gone through tougher situations. If you believe God, you will make it. You will get out all right too.

Yield not to temptation, for yielding is sin;
Each vict'ry will help you some other to win;
Fight manfully onward, dark passions subdue;
Look ever to Jesus, He'll carry you through.

HORATIO R. PALMER (1834-1907)

I sometimes feel, Lord Jesus, that I am about to sink into despondency.
Then I look unto Thee and realize Thou hast made a way up for me.
Keep me looking up, I pray. Amen.

And we know that all things work together for good to them that love God,
to them who are the called according to his purpose.
ROMANS 8:28

Some men have wives that are wildcats. John Wesley was married to one, and she did not even have her claws trimmed. But God got Wesley through that all right.

Wesley used to kneel down on his knees and pray in Latin so his wife would not know what he was saying. While he was praying in Latin, she was throwing old shoes at his head. What a nice family affair; but that is the way they got on.

The time came when he had to preach, so he said goodbye to her and went off preaching. They never did get together much after that. He looked after her so that she was taken care of, but she did not want him to preach. John wanted to preach, so he went on preaching, and she went on grumbling. She stayed home and grumbled while John went out everywhere preaching the gospel and transforming England.

One day, while riding along on a horse—he usually read, wrote, meditated, prayed or did all four—someone rode up alongside him and said, "Mr. Wesley, your wife is dead."

Wesley looked up and said, "Oh, she died, did she?" And then he went on with his work. No matter what our circumstances, God will get us through.

O Love that gave itself for me,
Help me to love and live like Thee,
And kindle in this heart of mine
The passion fire of love divine.

A. B. SIMPSON (1843-1919)

Dear heavenly Father, I sometimes feel my burden is so heavy.
But through it all, Thy provisions are enough to carry me on.
Praise the name of Jesus! Amen and amen.

The righteous also shall hold on his way,
and he that hath clean hands shall be stronger and stronger.
JOB 17:9

A woman I knew in Chicago recently died. She was a saint if ever there was one. But she wasn't married to a saint. He was a drunkard, and she prayed for him constantly.

He would come home after an evening of drinking, with his clothes dirty clear to his feet. She cleaned him off, got him into clean clothes and put him to bed. He woke up the next morning with a hangover and promised to change everything, but that night he would go out again with the boys and come down the street singing "Sweet Adeline," swaying from side to side and covered with that same filth.

She prayed for years and years for that man. I do not know how that poor woman ever endured it, but she prayed on and on.

I can imagine her saying, "God, how do you expect me to hang on?" But something would whisper in her heart, "This is common to all. Believe me, I'm faithful, I won't let you down."

The result was that not only was he converted, but many members of the family were converted as well.

When God says He is faithful, He means it beyond what we are able to bear ourselves.

When I cannot understand my Father's leading,
And it seems to be but hard and cruel fate,
Still I hear that gentle whisper ever pleading,
God is working, God is faithful, only wait!

A. B. SIMPSON (1843–1919)

I am grateful, Father, for Thy faithfulness in all things.
I grow weary so easily, but Thy grace is so sufficient and available.
In Jesus' name, amen.

November 12

Faithful is he that calleth you, who also will do it.
1 THESSALONIANS 5:24

After serving God for quite a while, instead of feeling that I was getting better, I felt that I was getting worse. What was happening was, I was getting to know myself better.

Once, when I did not know who I was, I thought I was pretty fine. I had a high opinion of myself. Then, by the good grace of God, I saw myself as He sees me. What a shock and disappointment! I barely recognized myself and became a little discouraged. I need not succumb to discouragement, because faithful is He that called me who will also do it. God is going to finish the job.

Whenever God begins something, we have the assurance that He will finish it. Nothing will stand in the way of Him accomplishing His purpose in this world and in our lives. What God starts, He finishes, and nobody can hinder Him.

Sure, delays will happen. Just remember, God is in charge of the delays as well as the progress.

If the Lord is not making you feel as you want to be now, continue to believe and trust in the faithfulness of God. It is coming around. God is faithful.

When peace like a river, attendeth my way,
When sorrows, like sea billows roll;
Whatever my lot, Thou hast taught me to say,
"It is well, it is well, with my soul."
HORATIO G. SPAFFORD (1828-1888)

Precious Father, I get weary sometimes resting upon my own strength. Hallelujah, Thou art the One that truly is in charge of my life and the progress in my life. I praise Thy name today. Amen.

And therefore will the LORD wait, that he may be gracious unto you,
and therefore will he be exalted, that he may have mercy upon you:
for the LORD is a God of judgment: blessed are all they that wait for him.
ISAIAH 30:18

I often wondered how a hen must feel about the twentieth day. She has been sitting nearly 3 weeks on 13 eggs; my mother always set 13 eggs and had me set them. She said if I set them, they hatched. I do not know what I had to do with it, but she set 13 eggs under the hen, and the old hen would sit right there, and only take a little coffee break once in a while to jump up and run off the nest and then get back and sit on the nest again.

You might endure two weeks, but that last week must have been torture—sitting there, listening, and nothing happening. Twenty days go by, nothing has happened. Twenty-one days, nothing has happened. Then about noon of the twenty-first day, the first little feet is heard down there somewhere under her wings, and she smiles, if a hen can smile, and says, "Thank God, they're here." After that, it is just a question of time.

Waiting is not something I am good at. I want something done, and I want it done now. Waiting, however, is one of the disciplines in the spiritual life. Waiting is simply transferring the responsibility to someone else.

When the promise seems to linger, long delaying,
And I tremble lest perhaps it come too late,
Still I hear that sweet-voiced angel ever saying,
"Though it tarry, it is coming, only wait."
A. B. SIMPSON (1843-1919)

How I praise Thee, O God that Thou art always on time. Consequently,
I want to transfer all the responsibility over to Thy broad shoulders.
I gladly wait for Thee. Amen.

Blessed is that man that maketh the LORD his trust,
and respecteth not the proud, nor such as turn aside to lies.
PSALM 40:4

God sometimes makes us wait. Search the Scriptures and you will find many examples of God making people wait. In spite of that, we need to keep in mind that God is faithful and will do what He says he will do.

In light of this, I would recommend that you withdraw your vote from the changing world, a treacherous false world, and put your trust in Jesus Christ who is faithful. Believe now that what He has promised, He will fulfill. Believe now that He meant what He said. You are dealing with a faithful God who cannot lie, or change His mind or be anything but what He is.

It is very tempting at times to take things into our own hands. Every time we do that we mess it up. The reason we mess it up is because we do not have at our disposal what God has at His disposal. When God promises something, that promise is based on the foundation that God knows all things from the beginning to the end. Waiting on the Lord is simply my way of trusting God for a particular situation.

When we walk with the Lord
In the light of His Word,
What a glory He sheds on our way!
While we do His good will,
He abides with us still,
And with all who will
Trust and obey.

JOHN H. SAMMIS (1846-1919)

Father, we pray, help us to believe; forgive us for doubting.
Take away our unbelief and our diffidence and our slowness to believe
and help us now to put our trust in Thee and throw ourselves
upon Thee completely. Amen.

Oh that men would praise the LORD for his goodness,
and for his wonderful works to the children of men!
PSALM 107:8

The goodness of God is something that God, by revelation, has declared to be true. It is an attribute of His and can be unequivocally asserted concerning God: God is good.

When I say that God is good, I do not mean to say that God is righteous or holy. God is both righteous and holy, but that is not what I am talking about here. Moreover, to say that God is good, and that good does not mean righteous and holy, should not be interpreted as coming down lightly on the righteousness and holiness of God. When we talk about the goodness of God, we have in mind something else altogether.

God is kind, favorable, merciful, good-hearted and of good will. Keep in mind that none of God's attributes conflict with any other attribute. There is a oneness and unity about God and His attributes that transcends our ability to comprehend fully.

What God declares to be true about Himself is what I accept and build my life upon.

I thank God every day that He is bigger than my ability to comprehend.

O love, how deep, how broad, how high,
It fills the heart with ecstasy,
That God, the Son of God, should take
Our mortal form for mortals' sake.

FOURTEENTH CENTURY, TRANSLATED
BY BENJAMIN WEBB (1819–1885)

O God, Thou art good and doest good. Thy goodness is not in
competition with any of Thy other attributes. I thank Thee for the
goodness Thou hast showed to me even today. Amen and amen.

But thou, O Lord, art a God full of compassion, and gracious,
longsuffering, and plenteous in mercy and truth.
PSALM 86:15

God is a God of goodwill, and there is no cynicism in Him. That is, God is not sensitive or resentful or sulky.

I have met a few sulky saints in my lifetime. If they do not get their way, they sulk. Then there are cynical people of God. I have been accused of being a cynic in my time. Someone heard me preach, and on leaving the building, said, "A clinic conducted by a cynic." I do not know whether he was just being a poet or whether he was right.

I guess we all have occasion to be a little cynical. However, there is no cynicism in God. God is goodhearted and friendly all the time. I have tried in my ministry to show something of the greatness, magnitude, altitude, transcendence and ineffability of the great God Almighty. He is infinitely greater than we could ever imagine. I believe that until we see how infinitely elevated God is in His being, we will not be the kind of Christians we should be. We will certainly not have the kind of conviction for sin there ought to be on sinners.

There's a wideness in God's mercy
Like the wideness of the sea;
There's a kindness in His justice,
Which is more than liberty.
FREDERICK W. FABER (1814–1863)

Dear Father, we pray in the name of the Lord Jesus Christ that our
hearts would be open to receive the magnitude of Thy presence.
Oh, that we might know Thee in the beauty of Thy revelation! Amen.

He hath builded against me, and compassed me with gall and travail.
LAMENTATIONS 3:5

I honestly believe that God is open, frank and candid. When saying these things, I am only saying what every Hebrew scholar knows is within the framework of the Hebrew words translated as "good."

I wonder whether I ought to say that God is benevolent? I am only saying and using a Latin word to say what I said before when using an Anglo-Saxon word. The dictionary is like that. Go to the dictionary for one word, "benevolent," and it will say "goodhearted." Then go to the word "goodhearted" and it will say "benevolent." It is just giving you a different way of saying the same thing. I can say that God is cordial.

I had a dear friend write a very severe letter to me because I signed one of my letters "Cordially yours." He said, "Cordiality ought not to exist between Christians. We have something finer than cordiality."

I wrote back, "When I sign my letter, 'Cordially yours,' it's just a way for me to stop. Don't pay any attention to it."

God is cordial and gracious and good. It is God's nature to wish and to will for you every good thing in time and eternity. That is the way God is.

When years of time shall pass away
And earthly thrones and kingdoms fall,
When men, who here refuse to pray,
On rocks and hills and mountains call;
God's love so sure shall still endure,
All measureless and strong;
Redeeming grace to Adam's race
The saints' and angels' song.

FREDERICK M. LEHMAN (1868–1953)

Dear God, Thou art gracious and cordial and have set the standard for these qualities. I give Thee praise that Thou hast my best interests in mind for time and eternity. In Jesus' name, amen.

The LORD is nigh unto all them that call upon him,
to all that call upon him in truth.
PSALM 145:18

God does not look upon our tears except with tears of His own heart.

One of my favorite poets is William Blake. He put it correctly when he wrote,

Think not thou canst sigh a sigh,
And thy Maker is not by:
Think not thou canst weep a tear,
And thy Maker is not near.

God is so patient with us. One of the Old Testament writers alluded to the fact that God makes all our bed in our sickness (see Ps. 41:3). He cares for us that much.

I have heard about saints that got sanctified when they were sick. Some got up out of their sick bed with a new revelation of God. Not so with me. When I get sick I just get bored. I can't pray. I can't think. I can't write. I can't do anything. I just lie there and suffer. Sickness has never done me any good up to now.

In spite of that, I know that my Maker feels my pain, sorrow and sickness as acutely as I do.

There are depths of love that I cannot know
Till I cross the narrow sea;
There are heights of joy that I may not reach
Till I rest in peace with Thee.

FANNY J. CROSBY (1820-1915)

I am thine, O Lord, and I long to be with Thee come sickness or health.
Thy strength is my portion today. Amen and amen.

The LORD will strengthen him upon the bed of languishing:
thou wilt make all his bed in his sickness.
PSALM 41:3

I find it interesting that some people, when they are in their sick bed, have a great experience with God. I may be just a little envious of them. My experience in the sickbed is just that; I am in it because I am sick.

On one occasion, David indicated that before he was sick, he went astray; but now, after his sickness, he has returned unto the Lord. He had the kind of sickness that allowed him to pray.

I never get that kind of sickness. I get the kind that all the wheels come to a stop until I get out of bed. I just lie there waiting it out. Not a thing to do but wait it out. I never got anywhere with God that way.

In spite of it all, God meets us wherever we are. My sickbed experiences are nothing to write home about. But some people have really found God in a sickbed. Regardless of where you meet God, you will find Him to be a good God.

At even, ere the sun was set,
The sick, O Lord, around Thee lay.
Oh, in what divers pains they met!
Oh, with what joy they went away!

HENRY TWELLS (1823–1900)

Dear God, whether it be in the sickbed, behind my desk or in the
marketplace, I know that Thy goodwill will be my portion.
I thank Thee for it today. Amen.

Therefore thus saith the Lord GOD, Behold,
I lay in Zion for a foundation a stone, a tried stone,
a precious corner stone, a sure foundation:
he that believeth shall not make haste.
ISAIAH 28:16

When we weave the attributes of God together, we can see what a mighty foundation is laid there. If God is good now, and also immutable, then God will always be good, and you never need to worry about God having a change of mind. God does not blow hot and then cold

Being who he is, God is perfect goodness. God has no imperfection, but a perfect goodness. Henceforth, there can be no improvement. In other words, God could not feel any kinder toward you than He does; and He never has felt any kinder toward anyone than He feels toward you now. He never will feel any kinder toward anybody than He feels toward you now. God's perfection is constant throughout all eternity.

Someone may say, "You don't know me." No, I don't know you, but I know God, and I know what the Scripture says about Him. Since God is eternal, immutable and perfect, there can be no improvement in the kindness of God.

I pray that God will not allow me to live to become a sour old man. I want my life to reflect the perfect goodness of God in every level of my life.

Christ is made the sure foundation,
Christ the head and cornerstone.
Chosen of the Lord and precious,
Binding all the Church in one.
Holy Zion's help forever
And her confidence alone.

JOHN MASON NEALE (1818–1866)

Our heavenly Father, what a joy it is to know that when I come to Thee,
I will come to Thee as Thou hast been for all eternity.
I praise Thee through Jesus Christ my Lord. Amen.

The statutes of the Lord are right, rejoicing the heart:
the commandment of the Lord is pure, enlightening the eyes.
PSALM 19:8

I remember when Dr. H. M. Shuman was resting one afternoon in my home, I posed a question to him. I said, "Dr. Shuman, I'm bothered about something. I have noticed that so many old Christians, when they get old, ought to be sweet and ripe and fruity and gracious, but they get bitter and sour and critical. Why?"

Dr. Shuman had always had answers for questions I posed before, but he did not have an answer for this one.

Usually, when people get old, they either get tart-tongued, critical and harsh or else they get tender, loving and kind. I have met some of the sweetest old Christians that ever lived in this world. I know some Christians that if you could just take all the rest of us and wipe the slate of the world clean and populate the world with them, there would be no reason to have any heaven above, because there would be one down here just full of loving-kindness.

The world would be all right, because it would be populated with men of good will. These are the kind of people that reflect the glory and grace of our Father in heaven.

We praise, we worship Thee, we trust and give Thee thanks forever,
O father, that Thy rule is just and wise, and changes never;
Thy boundless grace o'er all things reigns,
Thou dost whate'er Thy will ordains;
'Tis well Thou art our Ruler!

NIKOLAUS DECIUS (C. 1485–1541),
TRANS. CATHERINE WINKWORTH (1827–1878)

Dear God and Father, I am trusting Thee each day to grow sweeter
and not become a grouchy old man who is bitter on the world.
My joy, my peace is in Thee. I pray this in Jesus' name. Amen.

For thou hast said in thine heart, I will ascend into heaven,
I will exalt my throne above the stars of God:
I will sit also upon the mount of the congregation,
in the sides of the north.
ISAIAH 14:13-14

Some secular universities blame Christians for what they call anthropo-morphism. Well, I have been called worse names than that, not bigger ones, just worse ones. Anthropomorphism simply means making God in our own image. All you need to do is take the best qualities in a man, project them upward, and you've made God in man's image. How far off can you actually be?

If, for example, you see a kind man, you say, "All right, then, that God up there must be kind." We project that kindness out of the heart of the man up to God and say that God is kind, and then we add that He is infinitely kind.

Whatever man is, especially the best qualities of a man, is our idea of God. That idea is completely backwards. God is not made after man's image. That would mean God is no bigger than or better than the biggest and best man we can find here on earth.

That was what Lucifer invented. He projected himself into the high and holy throne of God and desired to be "like the most high." It just was not high enough, however, to reach the cross on Calvary.

When Christ shall come with shout of acclamation
And take me home, what joy shall fill my heart!
Then I shall bow in humble adoration
And there proclaim, my God how great Thou art!

CARL BOBERG (1859-1940),
TRANS. STUART K. HINE (1899-1989)

O blessed Savior, how I praise Thee that Thou art not the best that
man has to offer, but the best that God has to offer. Amen.

Not that any man hath seen the Father,
save he which is of God, he hath seen the Father.
JOHN 6:46

Because you are a Christian, somebody may hurl at you the charge of anthropomorphism and say that you are anthropomorphic. What they are saying is simply that you are making God in your own image and that your concept of the heavenly Father is only a manufactured one.

When someone hurls this accusation against me, I simply respond, "All right, how did you find it out? You could only find this out by discovery or revelation.

"When did you discover God, so that you can tell us what kind of God He is? If you did not discover Him, then you had a revelation. Please tell us where that Revelation is. What is the revelation?"

This idea presumes the critic knows something about God that we Christians do not know. They know something the Bible does not know; the prophets and apostles did not know; that even our Lord Jesus Christ did not know. How did they come to this kind of information that nobody else, including the church fathers, the martyrs and the revivalists did not know?

God is not the way we say He is, God is the way the Bible says He is.

I'd sing the characters He bears,
And all the forms of love He wears,
Exalted on His throne:
In loftiest songs of sweetest praise,
I would to everlasting days
Make all his glories known,
Make all his glories known.

SAMUEL MEDLEY (1738–1799)

Dear heavenly Father, I know Thee because I have discovered
Thee in the Book of books, even the Word of God. May Jesus,
the Living Word be praised. Amen.

For ye were sometimes darkness,
but now are ye light in the Lord:
walk as children of light.
EPHESIANS 5:8

The opposition often accuse us of being anthropomorphic obscurantists. An obscurantist is one who covers things up and keeps them obscure. That is what Christians are supposed to do, according to our critics. But we believe that sinners are covering things up and keeping them obscure.

The obscurantist draws up a crooked contract to cheat a widow out of her property. He hides in the darkness; but the children of light come into the light. They are the illuminati, if I might use that word; they are the ones walking in the light.

When I say, "God is love," the obscurantist responds by saying, "That's what you would like God to be like; you like to see love in people, and you like to see love in God."

The whole thing is nonsense to me. If God made man in His image, isn't it reasonable to believe that the best things in a man would be the nearest to what God is? I believe in God, and I believe God made me in His image; and I believe that every good there is in humanity came from God.

O Hope of every contrite heart,
O Joy of all the meek,
To those who fall how kind Thou art!
How good to those who seek!

BERNARD OF CLAIRVAUX (1091–1153),
TRANS. EDWARD CASWALL (1814–1878)

Dear God, how I praise Thee that I was made in Thy image.
The redeeming blood of the Lord Jesus Christ has enabled Thee to shine
through me into the world around me. Amen and amen.

But God commendeth his love toward us, in that,
while we were yet sinners, Christ died for us.
ROMANS 5:8

When we come to God, there is a basic datum of truth that God is good. Regardless of which generation, place or people, this truth never changes.

You can go down where men cheat each other, lie, misuse figures for their own selfish purposes and make 2×2=7 so they can fill their own pockets. That doesn't change the fact that 2×2=4.

Go out into the world and see the cruelties and murders and all the horrific acts of wicked men; and when it is all finished, nothing changes the fact that God is good. You can see everywhere among men their evil ways and their cruelty, and the darkness of wickedness, but it does not change the fact that God is good.

That is the datum of truth. It is a foundation stone of believing God. It is necessary to human sanity to believe that God is good, that the God who is in the heavens above is not some unkind, malicious God who seeks out evil, but a God who seeks out good. To allow God to be any other kind of God would be to upset and completely change all of the moral values of mankind.

My faith has found a resting place
Not in device nor creed;
I trust the Everliving One,
His wounds for me shall plead.

LIDIE H. EDMUNDS (NINETEENTH CENTURY)

Our Father which art in heaven,
I stand firm on the solid rock of truth.
There are many tests to my faith,
but I rest completely in Jesus Christ.
In His name I pray. Amen.

Even as the Son of man came not to be ministered unto,
but to minister, and to give his life a ransom for many.
MATTHEW 20:28

There is only goodness in the heart of God; therefore, I do not need to worry. God is kind.

What do I mean that God is kind? I mean that God is gracious and filled with loving-kindness. He is full of goodwill toward His creation. Christ came because He was a man of goodwill, and He walked among men as a man of goodwill.

O, what contrast between the Christ who walked among men and the evil men among whom He walked! The malicious, beard-pulling, whispering men over against the calm, quiet, loving Jesus, with a tender look on His face for every harlot at his feet and every babe on the lawn and every sick child, and every pain and sorrow in the world.

Christ walked among men with goodwill; and the men among whom He walked finally nailed Him to a cross. When they nailed Him on that cross, they did not change His goodness. He did not turn on them and curse them. He said, "Father, forgive them, for they know not what they do."

In all of this, we need to understand that God's goodness is the grounds for our expectation.

O the love that drew salvation's plan!
O the grace that brought it down to man!
O the mighty gulf that God did span
At Calvary!
WILLIAM R. NEWELL (1868–1956)

Thy goodness, O God, is the grounds for expecting good things from
Thee. I give Thee thanks for not treating me as I deserve,
but for treating me as reflecting Thy kindness. Amen.

But go ye and learn what that meaneth, I will have mercy, and not sacrifice:
for I am not come to call the righteous, but sinners to repentance.
MATTHEW 9:13

The basis of our hope is the goodness of God. Many things we might think would be are not the basis of our hope and expectation.

Repentance, for one, is not the basis for our expectation. Repentance is not meritorious, but a condition God lays down. He says we are to repent and believe in His Son; that is necessary because God has established that as a condition.

If a man has been a thief for 50 years, there is no merit if the fifty-first year he stops being a thief. You do not give him a crown. Nobody pins a medal on his chest and says, "For service rendered. This noble hero used to steal everything that wasn't nailed down, and now he's quit it." Everybody applauds and the band plays. No, you do not do things like that. A man ought to stop stealing because it is right to stop; but there is no merit in it. It was wrong to do it in the first place.

Repentance is not a meritorious act, and though necessary, it carries no virtue with it at all. Our hope is based upon the goodness of God.

Let not conscience make you linger,
Nor of fitness fondly dream;
All the fitness He requireth
Is to feel your need of Him;
This He gives you;
'Tis the Spirit's rising beam.

JOSEPH HART (1712–1768)

How I praise Thee, O God, for Thy goodness enabling me to come
before Thee in repentance. I thank Thee for making this pathway
available to me. Amen and amen.

Remember not the sins of my youth, nor my transgressions:
according to thy mercy remember thou me for thy goodness' sake, O LORD.
PSALM 25:7

There is a grave danger in the church that we shall make faith meritorious.

German pastor and theologian Dietrich Bonhoeffer, although loyal to the Lutheran church, wrote in his book *The Cost of Discipleship* that his church, in their great emphasis upon justification by faith, had made an idol out of faith.

There is no merit in faith. You have faith in God because God is good and has demonstrated His goodness in a variety of ways.

Suppose in a great hour of temptation and weakness you wronged a man. After coming to yourself, like the prodigal son, you said, "I'm going to my friend, and I'm going to confess and make that right." Your wife says, "But do you think he'll forgive you?" And you say, "Yes, I know he'll forgive me because I know what kind of man he is. I know he's a kind, good-natured gentleman, and he'll pardon me and forget the whole thing and never mention it again. That's the kind of man he is."

Where does the merit lie here? Does it lie in the request for forgiveness or does it lie in the nature of the man who forgives?

It lies in the man who forgives. And so it is with God.

How firm a foundation, ye saints of the Lord,
Is laid for your faith in His excellent Word!
What more can He say than to you He hath said,
To you, who for refuge to Jesus have fled?

ATTRIB. TO GEORGE KEITH (EIGHTEENTH CENTURY)

Now Lord, I come to Thee not in any expectation of
merit on my part, but solely upon Thy goodness. I thank Thee for the
goodness of Thy heart for accepting me in the Beloved. Amen.

For he is our God; and we are the people of his pasture,
and the sheep of his hand. Today if ye will hear his voice.
PSALM 95:7

When I go to God, to confess my sin and trust Him to forgive me, by faith I take forgiveness. Now, does the merit lie in my faith?

Never. It lies in the good God who forgives me, because He is that kind of God. He is gracious and kind and ready to forgive, and glad and merry and cheerful. All those words are found in the original Hebrew text about God.

What does all this mean to me? So many texts blossom and flower out when we think of the goodness of God.

David did not say in Psalm 23:6, "Surely goodness and mercy will follow me" as though it were a hope in his heart, but he wasn't quite sure. That is not the meaning of the text. David said, "Surely goodness and mercy shall follow me all the days of my life." Why would goodness and mercy follow a man all the days of his life? Simply because, the God of goodness and mercy followed him all the days of his life. God was the source.

The merit is never in us or in our coming, but absolutely in the character of God.

Jesus, and shall it ever be
A mortal man ashamed of Thee?
Ashamed of Thee, whom angels praise,
Whose glory shine through endless days?

JOSEPH GRIGG (1720-1768)

Dear God, Thou hast bid me come and accepts me, not because
I deserve it, but because of Thy goodness. How I praise Thee today!
Amen and amen.

But after thy hardness and impenitent heart treasurest up unto thyself wrath against the day of wrath and revelation of the righteous judgment of God; Who will render to every man according to his deeds.
ROMANS 2:5-6

I believe in the Judgment Day, and I believe that every man shall receive according to the deeds done in the body. I believe there will be a resurrection of the just and the unjust, and a resurrection of men unto eternal life and of men unto damnation. I believe all that. Yet, I also believe that God takes no pleasure in judgment.

When I was a boy, I used to hear a little song, "In the shadow of His wings there is rest, sweet rest." If we realize that God is that kind of God, then we will never go around with a hangdog look or a feeling of inferiority in our heart; never. You never need to go away with a deep sense of inferiority. There is quite a difference between real repentance and a feeling of inferiority.

That inferiority feeling makes you say, "Oh, I'm no good, I'm just no good."

Well, of course you are no good. But He is good; and because He is good, His doors are wide open for any sinner to come in and taste and see that the Lord is good. Today you can learn how good God is.

In the shadow of His wings
There is rest, sweet rest;
There is rest from care and labor,
There is rest for friend and neighbor;
In the shadow of His wings
There is rest, sweet rest,
In the shadow of His wings
There is rest (sweet rest).

E. O. EXCELL (1851-1921)

Dear God, the enemy of my soul would have me dwell upon the fact that I am no good. Today, I choose to dwell upon Thy goodness and how that has changed my life through Jesus Christ my Lord. Amen.

In the multitude of my thoughts within me thy comforts delight my soul.
PSALM 94:19

I have been spending a little time with the Lord each day and have been overwhelmed at how kind God has been to me—how utterly good and kind He has been. Thinking about His kindness and blessings in my life has brought me to a real spirit of thanksgiving.

Someone might look at me and see a partly bald gentleman that looks as if he might be a saint. But brother, you do not know me. You do not know my past; you do not know my nature; and you do not know my temptations. You just do not know me. Do not get any false ideas about any angel wings mounted on my back. I am just not that kind of a man.

If it were not for the grace of God, I would be roasting in hell or languishing in jail. If God's goodness had not found me, surrounded me, pardoned me and forgiven me, the United States government would have had me somewhere behind bars long before this.

I must give testimony that God and His loving-kindness has made my life reasonably decent, and not because I am good, but because He is good.

O safe to the Rock
That is higher than I,
My soul in its conflicts
And sorrows would fly;
So sinful, so weary, Thine,
Thine would I be.
Thou blest Rock of Ages,
I'm hiding in Thee.

WILLIAM O. CUSHING (1823-1902)

*Praise your wonderful name, O Christ! I rejoice not in my
accomplishments but in Thy kindness that has enabled me to do
something with my life for Thy honor and glory. Amen and amen.*

I thank my God upon every remembrance of you, Always in every prayer of mine for you all making request with joy, For your fellowship in the gospel from the first day until now; Being confident of this very thing, that he which hath begun a good work in you will perform it until the day of Jesus Christ.

PHILIPPIANS 1:3-6

The fellowship of the brethren is the sweetest thing short of heaven. We do not need each other; that is, we do not need each other in that ultimate final sense, though as a church we need each other. Nothing is more wonderful than that sweet fellowship among the brethren.

I was preaching over in Pennsylvania, at Mahaffey campground, and afterward a couple came up and the wife looked down at my feet. I wear size 10 ½ shoes, but that was not what she was looking at.

Finally, she said, "I was just wondering if they were feet of clay. I have never had an idol yet that didn't turn out to have clay feet."

"Lady," I replied, "I've got clay feet!" We had a good laugh over that.

Because someone gets help out of a preacher's preaching there is a tendency to put him on a pedestal. Never make that mistake.

To my congregation, I've said, never love me so much that I become necessary to you. No man is necessary to me, but only God. When a man becomes necessary to me, I lose my perspective of God's grace.

Oh how sweet to walk in this pilgrim way,
Leaning on the everlasting arms!
Oh how bright the path grows from day to day,
Leaning on the everlasting arms.

ELISHA A. HOFFMAN (1839-1929)

O dear God, Thou art so necessary to me that I need nobody else. That alone makes fellowship with other believers so very sweet. In Jesus' name, amen.

*Let the priests, the ministers of the LORD, weep between the porch
and the altar, and let them say, Spare thy people, O LORD, and give not thine
heritage to reproach, that the heathen should rule over them:
wherefore should they say among the people, Where is their God?*

JOEL 2:17

I have a little book that I have never gone anywhere without for years. It is a prayer book, but not one that you would buy in a bookstore. I write my prayers. I guess I have had this book for maybe 18 years, and I go over these prayers very seriously before God.

This little prayer book is important to me because I have a little understanding with God. I do not try to con God into believing I am better than what I know I am. By nature and conduct, I am the worst man that has ever lived. Because of that, I want God to do more for me than for any man that ever lived. I believe I have a right to ask, because the Bible says that where sin abounds grace did much more abound.

If the goodness of God specializes in hard cases, and can shine the brighter against the dark sky, I can provide that dark sky.

No matter what your past has been, you can start with God right now. No matter how you have failed God, you can come home now.

Sweet hour of prayer, sweet hour of prayer,
That calls me from a world of care
And bids me at my Father's throne
Make all my wants and wishes known.
In seasons of distress and grief
My soul has often found relief,
And oft escaped the tempter's snare,
By Thy return, sweet hour of prayer.

WILLIAM W. WALFORD (1772–1850)

Blessed be Thy name, O Lord and Savior. My sin, though the worst of all, cannot exhaust Thy grace. I thank Thee for bringing me into fellowship with Thee. Amen.

December 4

Have mercy upon me, O God, according to thy lovingkindness:
according unto the multitude of thy tender mercies blot out my transgressions.
PSALM 51:1

A young man was converted in our church and afterwards came to me and said, "I'm in a real jam. I'm saved now, but I'm in trouble with the law. I've got to go to the police and confess. When I go and confess, I'm in the clink for sure."

"Well," I said, "better to go to the clink than to go to hell. You'll get out of the clink, but you never get out of hell."

The man went to the police the next day, and I never expected to see him back. I thought I would be preaching to one less man. The next Sunday he was back down near the front, and his face was shining. Afterwards, I went to him and said, "You look great. What happened?"

"I went down and confessed and told them what I'd done. Then I told them I was converted and wanted to make things right." He told me they went over the books and could not find any charge against him. They could have found something, all right, but they did not want to find it, so they just turned him loose. God is very, very good.

Though your sins be as scarlet, they shall be as white as snow;
Though your sins be as scarlet, they shall be as white as snow;
Though they be red like crimson, they shall be as wool.
Though your sins be as scarlet, though your sins be as scarlet,
They shall be as white as snow, they shall be as white as snow.

FANNY J. CROSBY (1820–1915)

Father, I give Thee thanks for the way in which Thou dealest with our sin.
I thank Thee for the Lord Jesus Christ, the Lamb slain before the foundation
of the world. Hallelujah for the Lamb! Amen.

Come now, and let us reason together, saith the LORD: though your sins be as scarlet, they shall be as white as snow; though they be red like crimson, they shall be as wool.
ISAIAH 1:18

As a young chap, I used to sneak onto one of the boxcars and ride from one town to another. I often would get under, on the possum belly of an old steel car, and ride.

When I was converted, what I had done bothered me. So I wrote to the traffic manager: "Dear Sir, I have been converted to Jesus Christ and I'm a Christian now and want to straighten up my life. A little while back, I rode possum belly from here to there, and now I would like you to send me a bill. I want to pay up."

I received a letter from an official that read:

Dear Sir, your letter has been received. We note that you have been converted and want to live a Christian life. We want to compliment you on becoming a Christian. Now, about what you owe us. We rather suppose you did not get very good service on our line when you traveled, and therefore we are going to just forget the whole thing.

Sincerely yours, Traffic Manager.

Actually, I did not have enough money to pay all I owed the railroad line. But God is good, and my conscience was clean and free.

I hear the Savior say, "Thy strength indeed is small;
Child of weakness watch and pray, find in Me thine all in all."
ELVINA M. HALL (1820–1889)

Father of all mercies, praise goes to Thee for the power of forgiveness in my life. I could not pay the debt I owed, but praise the Lord Jesus, my debt was wiped clean. Praise Thy name! Amen.

*Ho, every one that thirsteth, come ye to the waters,
and he that hath no money; come ye, buy, and eat; yea, come,
buy wine and milk without money and without price.*

ISAIAH 55:1

Although God is a just and holy God, He is severe with unbelief and sin. Because of the vastness of His grace, He does not ignore this. His judgment against sin is more than severe; it is final.

If there is any kink in your life, any crooked thing or any failure, you need not despair. If you are not a Christian, or if you became a Christian and have cooled off and slipped away, God is good and infinitely kind, and He calls you back to Himself. God never wearies in inviting people to come and experience His goodness and taste His wonderful grace.

When you come to Jesus Christ, remember that God's goodness is channeled through His Son, Jesus Christ. Jesus said, "No man cometh unto the Father but by me" (John 14:6).

What makes the Father rejoice with unspeakable joy is when a sinner returns home. He is expecting you to come just as you are. He expects you to come without trying to spruce up or make yourself better. Come just as you are and allow Him to forgive you and cleanse you and make you the way He wants you to be.

Come and experience the goodness of God.

Just as I am, without one plea
But that Thy blood was shed for me,
And that Thou biddest me come to Thee,
O Lamb of God, I come! I come!

CHARLOTTE ELLIOTT (1789-1871)

*Our Father which art in heaven, how thankful and grateful I am that
Thou hast invited me to come as I am. The change, the transformation
is in Thy hands. I long to be everything Thee wants me to be.
Through Jesus Christ my Lord I pray. Amen.*

Every good gift and every perfect gift is from above, and cometh down from the
Father of lights, with whom is no variableness, neither shadow of turning.
JAMES 1:17

The word "immutable" is a negative of "mutable," from the Latin word meaning subject to change. "Mutation" is a word we often use, meaning a change in a former nature or substance. Mutability, then, is subject to change; immutability means that it is not subject to change.

Many school children remember Percy Bysshe Shelley's little poem that starts out with the cloud talking.

> I am the daughter of Earth and Water,
> And the nursling of the Sky;
> I pass through the pores of the ocean and shores;
> I change, but I cannot die.

It's a cloud now, but the next day it may vaporize; and then the next day become a cloud again. It is constantly changing and passing through the pores of the ocean and shores, and it changes because it is mutable.

There is in God no mutation possible. James makes it very clear that there is no variableness when it comes to God. In the Old Testament, God says, "I am Jehovah, I change not." He is the only One who can say that, in all of the universe. God never changes, and He never differs from Himself.

> Great Father of glory, pure Father of light;
> Thine angels adore Thee all veiling their sight.
> All praise we would render, O help us to see
> 'Tis only the splendor of light hideth Thee. Amen.
> WALTER CHALMERS SMITH (1824–1908)

Eternal God, I rest in Thy immutability today. My life is always
changing, for the better or for the worst, but there is no change
whatsoever in Thee. It is Thy great name that I praise today. Amen.

For I am the LORD, I change not;
therefore ye sons of Jacob are not consumed.
MALACHI 3:6

Our anchor in the storm of life is that there is no possibility of change in God, and God never differs from Himself.

One of the sickest pains we know in life is how people change. A friend to whom you used to write once a week, you now have not written to in five years now. A change has taken place, or that person has changed or you have changed or circumstances have changed.

Little babies are tiny soft things you can pick up; but give them a little while and they will change. That tendency to cling to mama will disappear, and the little guy will put his hands on his hips and back off. He is somebody now, and that is a change.

My wife and I take pleasure in occasionally looking at our family picture album. Our kids were such little fellows, and so delightful; but they are great, long, lean men now, lanky and tall. They are not the way they used to be; but give them 40 more years and they will not be as they are now. Change is what life is all about.

In a world of constant change, there is One who never changes.

O Thou, the great eternal One,
Whose goodness every age has stood,
Thou art exalted over all,
For Thou art great and Thou art good.
ELSIE BYLER (1883–1957)

Dear God, all around me is change, which sometimes is uncomfortable.
My anchor today is the truth of Thy immutability.
Praise God, Thou art the same yesterday, today and forever. Amen.

December 9

Now unto the King eternal, immortal, invisible,
the only wise God, be honour and glory for ever and ever. Amen.
1 TIMOTHY 1:17

Change and decay are all around us. And like Frederick Faber wrote, "my heart is sick." Regardless of where you look these days, change is inevitable. Things are not what they once were. I am not one who bemoans the past for the simple reason that the past was not as good as we remember.

When I was a youngster, I remember sitting around listening to some of the older men long for what they called the "good old days." When I am thinking of change in this regard, this is not what I have in mind.

I'm not one who puts a positive spin on things. By nature I am rather negative.

One good thing about change is that as everything changes it proclaims that the Lord is eternally the same and never changes. There is not a "shadow of turning" with God. That is a theological fact. It is something you can build on.

I do not reason or think that I might believe; I reason because I believe. I think, not that I might have faith, but because I have faith. All of my reasoning and thinking brings me to the wonderful truth that God never changes.

O Lord! my heart is sick,
Sick of this everlasting change;
And life runs tediously quick
Through its unresting race and varied range.
Change finds no likeness to itself in Thee,
And wakes no echo in Thy mute eternity.

FREDERICK W. FABER (1814–1863)

O Lord, my heart is sick as I witness the change and decay around me.
When I focus upon Thee, I rejoice that change finds no likeness to itself
in Thee. Praise the name of Jesus! Amen.

*[The Lord Jesus Christ] shall change our vile body, that it may be
fashioned like unto his glorious body, according to the working whereby
he is able even to subdue all things unto himself.*
PHILIPPIANS 3:21

An apple hanging on the tree changes from green to ripe—from worse to better. Let that apple hang there long enough and it will change from better to worse and then rot and fall away. Change is important in everything created. "Created" is the key word.

When we come into the area of God, we are coming into the area of the uncreated. God cannot alter or change. In order for God to be different from Himself or change in any manner whatsoever, one of three things has to take place. He must go from better to worse, from worse to better, or He must change from one kind of being to another. I can accept change in every area of life but not in God. Our problem is that we think God is like us in every aspect. This is a concept difficult to understand as we think of the character and nature of God.

God, being eternal, can never be any less than He is now; and He can never be any more than He is now. God is perfect, has always been perfect and always will be perfect. That is why we can trust Him.

In heavenly love abiding,
No change my heart shall fear;
And safe in such confiding,
For nothing changes here.
The storm may roar without me,
My heart may low be laid,
But God is round about me,
And can I be dismayed?

ANNA L. WARING (1823-1910)

*Dear God, I thank Thee for the changes Thou hast wrought in my own
life to make me more like Thee. Praise the name of Jesus. Amen.*

But we all, with open face beholding as in a glass the glory of the Lord, are changed into the same image from glory to glory, even as by the Spirit of the Lord.
2 CORINTHIANS 3:18

Changes are necessary in all things—people and creatures; but no change is necessary in God. God, being the eternally holy God, does not go from better to worse or worse to better. He is always the same.

You cannot think of God being any less holy than He is right now, any less righteous, any less merciful. Whatever God is He is fixed forever throughout all eternity.

This is good for God, but not for us. We need to change. Often we see people go from good to bad, and occasionally somebody goes from bad to good. All of creation is in a constant flux. Thank God, He who is unchangeable has become the foundation of all our change.

Because God cannot change, He can reach out to those who are constantly changing and bring us into harmony with His nature. The greatest change comes at conversion. That is only the beginning; throughout our life God is affecting some marvelous changes in us, from glory to glory. The criterium for our change is none other than the Lord Jesus Christ.

Holy, holy, holy!
Though the darkness hide Thee,
Though the eye of sinful man
Thy glory may not see.
Only Thou art holy;
There is none beside Thee,
Perfect in power,
In love and purity.

REGINALD HEBER (1783–1826)

I rejoice, O Father, in that changeless foundation which is Thyself.
I look unto Christ and rejoice in the changes Thou art making in my life
to become more like Him. Hallelujah for the Lamb!

For now we see through a glass, darkly; but then face to face:
now I know in part; but then shall I know even as also I am known.
1 CORINTHIANS 13:12

For every good man you can find there will always be someone better. No matter how bad a person may be, someone always turns up worse. That is the way with mankind.

This cannot be said about God. God is the apex. God is the fountain. God is the top. With God, there are no degrees.

I believe we can say that with angels there are degrees; and certainly there are degrees in people; but there are no degrees in God. Therefore, certain words do not apply to God. Words like "greater" or "better" cannot be applied to God. You cannot say that God is greater, because that would put God in a position where He was in competition with someone else who is great.

God does not live according to the tick of the clock or the revolution of the earth around the sun. God does not observe seasons or days, although He allows us to because we are caught in the stream of time. We follow the sun that goes down at night and rises in the morning, and the year as it goes around the sun, which always tells us we are in time. But God remains eternally the same.

> What rejoicing in His presence
> When are banished grief and pain;
> When the crooked ways are straightened
> And the dark things shall be plain.
> CARRIE E. BRECK (1855–1934)

Eternal God, You stand unchallenged in all the universe.
What Thou art Thou hast always been, which brings comfort and
stability to my life that seems to change continuously.
Praise the name of the Lord Jesus Christ my Savior! Amen and amen.

Unto thee it was shewed,
that thou mightest know that the LORD he is God;
there is none else beside him.
DEUTERONOMY 4:35

Next week I am going to get on an airplane and fly down to Chicago, get on another airplane and fly down to Wichita, and then get in an automobile and go to Newton, Kansas. where I will preach in a Bible conference. I will be going somewhere. I will be, and then I will be moving toward somewhere else. That seems to be the way it is with mankind; always on the move.

This is never true of God. God is not in one place moving toward another place, because God fills all places. It does not matter whether you are in India or Australia or South America or California, or wherever you are around the world or out in stellar spaces, God is already there.

We can go backward and forward and upward and downward, but these directions do not apply to God. God is omnipresent. God is already everywhere, and the heaven of heavens cannot contain Him.

God, the eternal God, remains unchanged, that is, He is immutable.

Lord of all being, throned afar,
Thy glory flames from sun and star;
Center and soul of every sphere,
Yet to each loving heart how near!
OLIVER WENDELL HOLMES, SR. (1809–1894)

Dear God, what a joy it is to know that wherever I am, Thou art there.
Thy presence is the joy and strength of my day.
In the blessed name of Jesus I pray. Amen.

Behold, I shew you a mystery; We shall not all sleep, but we shall all be changed,
In a moment, in the twinkling of an eye, at the last trump: for the trumpet shall
sound, and the dead shall be raised incorruptible, and we shall be changed.
1 CORINTHIANS 15:51-52

Change can be a rather mysterious thing. Part of being a creature is that we change from one thing to another, from one kind of being to another kind.

That butterfly in the springtime is so lovely, and even breathtaking, but it starts out as a little worm and then changes into that beautiful thing—a different kind of creature altogether.

This has happened in our home a few times. I never knew how they got in, but occasionally a moth, one of those great broad moths as wide as my hand, just appeared. It began as a cocoon, which is simply a worm all wrapped up in winter clothes. You rarely notice them when they are worms; but when they hatch into beautiful moths, you say, "Whoo, isn't that lovely? Isn't that a beautiful thing?" You pick it up and tenderly let it fly away.

Just a little while ago, it was a miserable, hairy worm crawling across the road. You would not have touched him; but now you say, "Isn't it beautiful?"

When we become a Christian, we change; we go from one kind of creature to another. It is the moral changes made in a man through the power of Jesus Christ.

What a wonderful change
In my life has been wrought
Since Jesus came into my heart!
I have light in my soul,
For which long I have sought,
Since Jesus came into my heart.

RUFUS H. MCDANIEL (1850–1940)

Father, I praise Thee today for the Lord Jesus Christ who has brought such
wonderful changes into my life. I look forward to that last great change
when I shall be like Him, for I shall see Him as He truly is. Amen.

Then we which are alive and remain shall be caught up together with them in the clouds, to meet the Lord in the air: and so shall we ever be with the Lord. Wherefore comfort one another with these words.

1 THESSALONIANS 4:17-18

I enjoy singing the hymns of John Newton. He was a great preacher and, in my opinion, a greater hymn writer. Did you know that before his conversion he was one of the vilest men that ever lived? Read his testimony some time. Men did not come more wicked than John Newton.

John Bunyan, the author of *Pilgrim's Progress*, was a vile man, too, before his conversion to Jesus Christ.

We can even go back to the New Testament and read about a man by the name of Saul, who later became the apostle Paul. He considered himself the "chief of sinners."

All of these men became saints of God. Thank God, a bad man can change by the grace of God and become a good man. These men were not immutable; otherwise, there would be no hope for them. Thank God, you and I are not immutable. We are able to change by the grace of God.

God cannot change, He is immutable; He cannot change, But He can effectively and eternally change our lives. The change rests completely in the hands of the One who cannot change.

On that bright and cloudless morning when the dead in Christ shall rise,
And the glory of His resurrection share;
When His chosen ones shall gather to their home beyond the skies,
And the roll is called up yonder, I'll be there.

JAMES M. BLACK (1856–1938)

O God, because of the changes Thou hast wrought in me, I look forward to a life abounding in Thy grace. Amen and amen.

December 16

Go ye therefore, and teach all nations,
baptizing them in the name of the Father, and of the Son,
and of the Holy Ghost.
MATTHEW 28:19

When I say that God is always the same, I am referring to the three persons of the Trinity. Whatever is true of one person of the Trinity is true of all persons of the Trinity. If one is incomprehensible, all three are incomprehensible. Run through the gamut of the attributes of God and what you say about the Father you can say about the Son without modification. What you say about the Father and the Son you can say about the Holy Spirit without modification. They are of one substance, and together are to be worshiped and glorified. When we say that God is the same, we say that Jesus Christ is the same and we say that the Holy Ghost is the same.

All God ever was, God still is; and all God was and is, God will ever be.

This is something we need to remember. I believe it will help you in the hour of trial, help you in death and in the resurrection and the world to come to know that all God ever was God still is, and all that God was and is, God will ever be. His nature and His attributes are eternally unchanging.

Thine own Self forever filling
With self-kindled flame,
In Thyself Thou art distilling
Unctions without name!
Without worshipping of creatures,
Without veiling of Thy features,
God always the same!

FREDERICK W. FABER (1814–1863)

I worship Thee, blessed Trinity. The essence of Thy nature overwhelms
me, but my heart is open to praise Thee. Hallelujah for the cross that
brought me to Thee—Father, Son and Holy Spirit. Amen.

Therefore, my beloved brethren, be ye stedfast, unmoveable,
always abounding in the work of the Lord, forasmuch as ye know that
your labour is not in vain in the Lord.
1 CORINTHIANS 15:58

Around this time of the year, I spend some time going back over old sermons and some articles I have written throughout the year. Looking at them, I often wonder why I wrote them or why I preached that sermon.

Reviewing them from my vantage point of the present, I can see where I could make some big improvements and changes. The sad thing is, I cannot improve any of those. What is written is written, and it is beyond my power to change or edit them.

If I bring this over to God and review the things God has done, and the things He has revealed, I find no room for improvement anywhere. When God does something, He does it with the benefit of absolute and perfect wisdom. He does it with a sense of knowing the end from the beginning. Nothing He says can be improved on and nothing He does needs to be changed.

Thank God, He does not have a review board to fact-check and make corrections on His work. What this does for me now is give me confidence in what God is doing in my life today. When God makes a decision it is absolutely final and perfect.

Come, labor on! Who dares stand idle on the harvest plain,
While all around him waves the golden grain,
And every servant hears the Master say,
"Go, work today"?
JANE L. BORTHWICK (1813–1897)

O Lord, my obedience today is based upon my confidence in Thy Word.
Whatever Thou sayest today will be true and appropriate tomorrow.
I follow Thee all the way home. Amen.

For ye know the grace of our Lord Jesus Christ, that, though he was rich,
yet for your sakes he became poor, that ye through his poverty might be rich.
2 CORINTHIANS 8:9

I love to think about the fact that Jesus Christ is what God is. So many have a caricature idea of Jesus that does not fit into our Bibles.

Keep in mind that Jesus Christ is the second person of the Trinity, and as such He is everything the Father is and everything the Holy Spirit is. These three are absolutely equal in all things.

One of the aspects of the Trinity is that God never changes.

And the will of God never changes for moral creatures. God makes no exceptions; God is no respecter of persons. God means that moral creatures should always be like Him, always be holy, always pure, always true.

While God puts up with some things because we are still children and are struggling to grasp His eternal purposes for us, He is not excusing it. The pattern for our behavior is simply Jesus. If you want to know what God is like, read the story of Jesus. If you want to know what God expects out of you, get to know Jesus.

The full force of the Trinity in the fullness of the attributes of the Godhead is focused on making us like Jesus.

Thou didst leave Thy throne
And Thy kingly crown
When Thou camest to earth for me.
But in Bethlehem's home
Was there found no room
For Thy holy nativity.

EMILY E. S. ELLIOTT (1836–1897)

Our heavenly Father, I long to see the fullness of Jesus in me,
and I know Thy purpose is to complete this in my life.
May I walk today in that fullness. Amen.

And said unto him, Hearest thou what these say?
And Jesus saith unto them, Yea; have ye never read,
Out of the mouth of babes and sucklings thou hast perfected praise?
MATTHEW 21:16

A very interesting incident in the New Testament has to do with Jesus and babies. The disciples tried to keep them away because Jesus had more important work to do, or so they thought. Jesus changed their thinking about that, picked up a baby and put His hand on its head.

This incident shows how God feels about babies. I can understand how God can love babies. Who doesn't love a baby? God thought so much of babies that, when Jesus came into this world to be the Savior of the world, He came as a baby.

There are some things I do not understand about why God loves. I cannot for the life of me understand why God loves me so much. I think that is one of the deepest theological difficulties I have.

I am not trying to be humble; I am just stating a fact. I can understand why God loves babies, but I do not know why He loves me.

Jesus loved babies, picked them up and blessed them. The disciples believed that Jesus had more important work to do than pat a little baby on the head. We sometimes get so busy being thinkers and talking theology that we overlook the things that Jesus thought were important.

What Child is this, who, laid to rest, on Mary's lap is sleeping?
Whom angels greet with anthems sweet, while shepherds watch are keeping?
This, this is Christ the King, whom shepherds guard and angels sing;
Haste, haste to bring Him laud, the Babe, the Son of Mary.

WILLIAM CHATTERTON DIX (1837–1898)

Forgive me, Lord, when I am preoccupied with things that crowd out of my life those things that were important to You. May I today humble myself before Thee and learn to appreciate things as Thee appreciates them. Amen.

But Jesus said, Suffer little children, and forbid them not, to come unto me: for of such is the kingdom of heaven. And he laid his hands on them, and departed thence.
MATTHEW 19:14-15

In the city of Chicago was a Sunday School with mostly Italian children. One of the things they did in class was memorize verses of Scripture. Most of these children lived on the street. Their playpen was the sidewalk and their language was the language of the streets.

One little girl I was acquainted with was named Rosie. One Sunday she memorized the verse, "Suffer the little children to come unto me." The next day in school the teacher asked them to quote the passage they had learned in Sunday School the previous day. Rosie raised her hand, and the teacher said, "All right, Rosie, quote it for us."

She did not quite have the *King James Version* mastered at this point and said, "Let the little kids come to me, and don't ya tell them they can't, because they belongs by me." I think she knew that one. She at least got the concept of God's love.

The Lord loves the little children, and the harlot, and the publican and sinners of all varieties. He always did love and He still thinks the same concerning these people, and He offers them eternal life. God does not change His feelings toward people in spite of the fact that the vast majority reject Him.

> Little children, little children,
> Who love their Redeemer,
> Are the jewels, precious jewels,
> His loved and His own.
> WILLIAM O. CUSHING (1823–1902)

Dear Lord Jesus, who suffers the little children to come, I praise Thee that Thy love never changes. Thy unchanging love has dramatically changed me. Praise Thy wonderful name. Amen.

He sendeth forth his commandment upon earth: his word runneth very swiftly.
He giveth snow like wool: he scattereth the hoarfrost like ashes.
PSALM 147:15-16

We live in a world that changes all the time, and I am glad it does. I am glad the weather changes. If we hold out long enough, spring will come around and the birds will come back. They leave us when it gets cold and go down to Florida and South America and live there through the winter.

I always have felt just a little bit put out when the birds I love so much all leave me and go south. There are two kinds of birds: Those with feathers and what I call church birds. They go down south and do not return until the cold weather is gone and they can sit out on their front porch. Some of us, however, have to stick right through thick and thin, waiting for that change to come.

I like it when the weatherman says, "There'll be moderation today." "Moderation" is another word for "mutation"; it is going to change, it is going to warm up a bit. I like that, unless of course it's August, and I do not want to hear it then. Change makes our world what it is. That change would not be possible apart from the changeless nature and character of God.

All glory, laud, and honor
To Thee, Redeemer, King,
To whom the lips of children
Made sweet hosannas ring.
Thou art the King of Israel,
Thou David's royal Son,
Who in the Lord's name comest,
The King and blessed One.

THEODULPH OF ORLEANS (760–821)

O God, I praise Thee for Thy unchangeable nature. I praise Thee that in the middle of the worst winter, I can anticipate the coming spring and summer. Change is in Thy hands, and I praise Thee for it. Amen.

Now learn a parable of the fig tree; When his branch is yet tender,
and putteth forth leaves, ye know that summer is nigh: So likewise ye,
when ye shall see all these things, know that it is near, even at the doors.

MATTHEW 24:32-33

This is the season of change; and I say, let men change while God remains the same. I have seen eschatology change from a vivid eager expectation of Jesus to where we are now apologizing for the coming of Christ.

I have seen theology change in evangelical circles from certainty of the inspiration of Scriptures to uncertainty and an anemic apology. In evangelical circles, I have seen a change from believing that the church of Christ should separate from the world to a slow breaking down of that. It has come to a point where men are apologizing for our attitude toward the world and are trying to strike a common ground of understanding.

Obviously, we have forgotten what John said: "If any man love the world, the love of the Father is not in him" (1 John 2:15).

We often hear the phrase, "New days call for new ways." I think Solomon said it best when he said, "There is no new thing under the sun" (Eccles. 1:9).

I have seen all of these new changes; but what cheers my heart is that God has not changed. The Bible has not changed. God's truth has not changed. The blood of Jesus has not changed. God still has the solution to our problems. Thank God, that has not changed.

Holy Jesus, every day keep us in the narrow way;
And when earthly things are past, bring our ransomed souls at last
Where they need no star to guide, where no clouds Thy glory hide.

WILLIAM CHATTERTON DIX (1837-1898)

O Thou who art the Ancient of Days in whom there is no change nor
shadow of turning, I still believe the old ways, and that all things rest in
Thy hand, even my life today. Praise the name of Jesus. Amen.

The LORD by wisdom hath founded the earth;
by understanding hath he established the heavens.
PROVERBS 3:19

The wisdom of God is the preeminent theme in Scripture. From the Garden of Eden to the cradle in Bethlehem, God's wisdom was in play.

There was wisdom founding the earth, and understanding establishing the heavens, and discretion stretching out the world. The significance of all of this is that we begin with faith in God. We do not reason in order that we might believe; we reason because we already believe. If I have to reason myself into faith, then I can be reasoned back out of it again. Faith is an organ of knowledge; and what I believe I know is divinely revealed. When I know it by faith, then I can reason about it.

So we begin with faith in God. We do not offer proof that God is wise. If I were to try to prove that God is wise, the embittered soul would not believe it, no matter how perfectly convincing the prose I used. And the worshiping heart already knows that God is wise, and does not need to have it proved. The babe in Bethlehem's manger was the absolute epitome of God's wisdom, understanding and discretion. I believe it; therefore, I accept it.

> For lo, the days are hastening on,
> By prophet bards foretold;
> When with the ever circling years
> Comes round the age of gold.
> When peace shall over all the earth
> Its ancient splendors fling,
> And the whole world give back the song
> Which now the angels sing.
>
> EDMUND H. SEARS (1810–1876)

Father, we thank Thee for Thyself. We thank Thee for Thy character.
We thank Thee for Thy being. One God, one Majesty—
no God but Thee. Amen.

Glory to God in the highest, and on earth peace, good will toward men.
LUKE 2:14

We all are victims of time, obsessed with looking at our watch. If some would lose their watch, they would go into a panic. I am happy to report that there is One who contains time in His bosom. The Timeless One stepped out of eternity into time through the womb of the Virgin Mary.

At this point of the year, we celebrate so heartily that we often overlook the magnificent truth we are celebrating: that God, being who He is and all that He is, stepped from eternity into time to save the likes of me and you. I readily confess that I do not understand the virgin birth, but my understanding is not Lord in my life. Christ came into this world in a fashion that God created before the foundation of this world was established.

I know that Christ became a man; and because of that Incarnation, there is hope for us to break the chains of sin that have bound us for so many years. Christ has come into this world with me and you on His mind. I cannot shake that thought, especially during this time of the year.

Hark! the herald angels sing,
"Glory to the newborn King;
Peace on earth and mercy mild,
God and sinners reconciled!"
Joyful, all ye nations, rise,
Join the triumph of the skies;
With th'angelic hosts proclaim,
"Christ is born in Bethlehem."
Hark! the herald angels sing,
"Glory to the newborn King!"

CHARLES WESLEY (1707-1788)

*Our kind Father, we thank Thee that Thou hast not
left us in our sins, but hast brought Jesus Christ into our world as our Savior.
Blessed be the Savior who came into our world. Amen.*

And the angel answered and said unto her, The Holy Ghost shall come upon thee, and the power of the Highest shall overshadow thee: therefore also that holy thing which shall be born of thee shall be called the Son of God.

LUKE 1:35

The birth of our Lord in Bethlehem brought into our world the best that God could offer. The wonder of the Incarnation has puzzled men since that day. How can God, being who He is, be born of the Virgin Mary?

In Jesus Christ, God became man, not by the degradation of His Godhead, but by the lifting up of His manhood into God. Christ is divine and is God, and He was with the Father before the world came to be. When Jesus was born of the Virgin Mary, His deity did not become humanity. His deity was joined to His humanity because God is eternal and uncreated and can never become created. That which is not God cannot become God; and that which is God cannot become that which is not God.

God can come and dwell imminently within His creatures. The birth of Christ was the gateway for our new birth. Christ put on humanity in order that we can put on His deity and become the sons of God. That obscure little town of Bethlehem was the gateway into the new birth. Because He came as He did, I can come to Him and be received as His child.

O little town of Bethlehem,
How still we see thee lie!
Above thy deep and dreamless sleep
The silent stars go by.
Yet in thy dark streets shineth
The everlasting Light;
The hopes and fears of all the years
Are met in thee tonight.

PHILLIPS BROOKS (1835–1893)

I honor Thee, O God, for Thy provisions in Jesus Christ. He came into this world so that I might come into Thy world. Praise the name of Jesus. Amen.

And he went down with them, and came to Nazareth, and was subject unto them: but his mother kept all these sayings in her heart.
LUKE 2:51

As Protestants, I fear we unduly ignore the Virgin Mary. I certainly do not advocate worshiping her like some, but I do think we need to honor her for the simple fact that God honored her.

In thinking about Mary, I often wonder what was going through her mind as things developed from the Annunciation of the angel up to the birth of baby Jesus. What was going through her mind as she looked at that little baby that had just been born? That baby, who for nine months had been growing in her womb, of whom the angel said was the Son of God? The Scripture tells us that she kept these things in her heart.

Looking at Him as she was feeding Him, she whispered in her heart, "This is my Savior." Being a young woman, probably a teenager, she did not have all of the theological background to understand the significance of the Incarnation. All she had was the Word of the Lord.

As I celebrate this truth, I am mindful of those with all the theological background possible who do not understand the significance of the Incarnation—God in the flesh; those who do not know that He is our Savior.

Once in royal David's city
Stood a lowly cattle shed,
Where a mother laid her baby
In a manger for His bed;
Mary was that mother mild,
Jesus Christ, her little Child.

CECIL FRANCES ALEXANDER (1818–1895)

Now Father, I celebrate the coming of Thy dear Son, even our Lord and Savior Jesus Christ. May I this day reflect on the wondrous mystery of the Incarnation. Amen.

That I may shew forth all thy praise in the gates of the daughter of Zion:
I will rejoice in thy salvation.
PSALM 9:14

The great celebration of Christmas sets us up for the coming resurrection of Jesus. Without Christmas, there can be no resurrection; and without the resurrection, Christmas means nothing. This is something we can rest in for the rest of our life.

In his hymn, Philip Doddridge focuses on that wonderful truth. He talks about his "long-divided heart." I think I know what he meant. Division brings a certain sense of confusion; before I rested in Christ as my Savior, my heart was divided. The apostle Paul talked about this confusion in his own life and cried, "O wretched man that I am!" (Rom. 7:24)

All of our restlessness can be taken care of because of the Incarnation. St. Augustine said, "We are restless until we rest fully in Thee."

The coming of Christ in that manger in Bethlehem opened up the way for us to find our full rest in God. I can understand the theology of it all. I can believe what the Scripture says about it. However, until I experientially rest in the Christ of Bethlehem and Calvary, it does not mean anything at all.

Christmas is not a time merely to celebrate, but rather it is a time to embrace Christ and rest in Him for all the days of our life.

Now rest, my long-divided heart!
Fixed on this blissful center, rest;
Nor ever from my Lord depart,
With Him of every good possessed.

PHILIP DODDRIDGE (1702–1751)

O God, I am reminded of the blessed truth of the Incarnation.
As the Holy Spirit has opened up this truth to me, I have embraced it by faith
and now rest in the resurrected Christ. Hallelujah for the cross. Amen.

Which also said, Ye men of Galilee, why stand ye gazing up into heaven?
this same Jesus, which is taken up from you into heaven, shall so come in like
manner as ye have seen him go into heaven.
ACTS 1:11

We live in a rather turbulent world. Just when you think everything is calming down, something else stirs up and we are back where we started. "Change" is the watchword of our generation. Everybody speaks of change, and sometimes it goes from good to bad.

I think one thing that makes our times so troubling is the fact that things are changing. Nothing is more alarming than change because you don't know exactly what that change is going to be. Our politicians love to promise us change, but the change they have in mind does not usually agree with what we had in mind.

The thing that thrills my heart is that Jesus is always the same.

He is the same Jesus who raised the widow's son. He is the same Jesus who fed the multitudes when they were hungry. He is the same Jesus who calmed the raging sea that threatened the disciples.

Our hope is that someday our raptured eyes shall see this same Jesus. Oh what a blessed day when we shall see Him! I am looking forward to that. He may come before this year concludes, or the next year may be when this same Jesus comes for His own.

Come, sinners, to the living One, He's just the same Jesus
As when He raised the widow's son, the very same Jesus.
Come, feast upon the living Bread, He's just the same Jesus
As when the multitudes He fed, the very same Jesus.

ELIZA E. HEWITT (1851-1920)

Blessed Lord Jesus, I revel in the truth that Thou art the same, yesterday,
today and forever. I long to see this same Jesus. Amen and amen.

O LORD, how manifold are thy works!
in wisdom hast thou made them all: the earth is full of thy riches.
PSALM 104:24

In the beginning, God the Father Almighty, maker of heaven and earth, turned His mighty wisdom loose in the making of man. He said, "Let us make man in our own image" (Gen. 1:26). In His wisdom, He made a garden eastward in Eden and placed the man there, the most beautiful place imaginable because it was the result of the infinite wisdom of God. He spoke and creation leapt into existence.

George Washington Carver said that a weed was simply a plant or a flower out of place. Nothing was out of place in that magnificent Garden of Eden. Everything was in place; everything had purpose and everything was fulfilling that purpose.

Then God said to the man, "I'll make you a help meet" (Gen. 2:18). He put the man to sleep, took a rib from him, made a woman and presented her to Adam. Adam called her Eve.

The Garden of Eden was the most beautiful of all gardens and most lovely of all worlds, populated by the most radiant of all creatures, made in the image of God. That was a result of God's wisdom. The wisdom that did all of that is now available to us through the Lord Jesus Christ.

Be Thou my Vision, O Lord of my heart;
Naught be all else to me, save that Thou art;
Thou my best thought, by day or by night,
Waking or sleeping, Thy presence my light.

IRISH HYMN C. EIGHTH CENTURY;
TRANS.MARY E. BYRNE (1880–1931);
VERSIFIED BY ELEANOR HULL (1860–1935)

Father Almighty, maker of heaven and earth, Thy wisdom has resulted in everything created. Thy infinite wisdom is now my portion of the Lord Jesus Christ. May this day be lived by that wisdom from on High. Amen.

*Daniel answered and said, Blessed be the name of God for ever and ever:
for wisdom and might are his: And he changeth the times and the seasons:
he removeth kings, and setteth up kings: he giveth wisdom unto the wise,
and knowledge to them that know understanding.*

DANIEL 2:20-21

All through creation, we can see the wisdom of God in planning His world
and His creation and His redemption. God being good has plans for the
highest good, for the highest number and for the longest time.

This is the time of the year for religious opportunists. I hate that
word. These opportunists plague the church of our day. They are out for
what they can get now. They are not above using a holiday to further their
opportunistic activities. These opportunists have a plan that includes
their good right now. They are not thinking about next year or eternity.
They only think about the next time they have to send in the report to
show how important they are now.

Winding this year down makes me pause to think and in my thinking
I thank God that in His wisdom He has my best in mind for the longest
period of time. What God is doing in my life right now cannot be defined
by the word "now." I have lived long enough to realize that God has all of
my tomorrows in mind when He is opening or closing a door now, today.

When God plans to bless a man, He breathes into that man eternity
and immortality and endlessness.

Wherever He may guide me, no want shall turn me back;
My Shepherd is beside me, and nothing can I lack.
His wisdom ever waketh; His sight is never dim.
He knows the way He taketh, and I will walk with Him.

ANNA L. WARING (1823-1910)

*O God, I stand between time and eternity. The only thing linking
these two in my life is Thee. Thou hast my best interests in mind for the
longest period of time. I rejoice in this truth. Amen and amen.*

And we know that all things work together for good to them that love God,
to them who are the called according to his purpose.
ROMANS 8:28

Of all the providential dealings of God toward me throughout the year, I must take my stand and testify that God's way is right. When things seem to go wrong with me, instead of believing they are going wrong, I stand upon the authority of God's Word.

I decided long ago that instead of trusting my way, I will gladly trust blindly in the wisdom of God. If I trust blindly in God's wisdom, He will lead me by a way I know not. He will guide in paths where I have not been before. He will make darkness light before me and make crooked things straight, and will lead me through into His marvelous light.

God will lead me into a rich place and make me rich with treasures that can never die. If I want my own way, God will let me go my way. Many Christians do just that. They insist on their plans and their ambitions and imperil everything because they lack the wisdom to know how to do it.

God's way is the best way, because it is backed up by the infinite wisdom of God. Gladly will I blindly trust God's way instead of my own.

O to be like Thee!
Blessed Redeemer,
This is my constant
Longing and prayer;
Gladly I'll forfeit
All of earth's treasures,
Jesus, Thy perfect
Likeness to wear.

THOMAS O. CHISHOLM (1866–1960)

Father, I have tried my way and gotten nowhere.
I pray that I may be willing to turn my back on my way and go Thy way,
and be like Jesus. This I pray in Jesus' name. Amen.